DEADPOOL #13 70TH ANNIVERSARY FRAME VARIANT
y Stephen Segovia

Some jobs are just too tough for your average fast-talkin' high-tech gun-for-hire. Sometimes...to get the job done right...you need someone crazier than a sack'a ferrets. You need Wade Wilson. The Crimson Comedian. The Regeneratin' Degenerate. The Merc with a Mouth...

# DEADPOOL

Norman Osborn swindled Deadpool out of a ton of cash. When Deadpool tried to collect, Norman sent his covert strike force, the Thunderbolts after him. After Deadpool wiped the floor with the whole team, Norman sent the Dark Avenger Hawkeye (really the assassin Bullseye in disguise) to take Deadpool out. He failed. And rather than return to his boss with the news that he was defeated...and rather than, you know, get killed with a chainsaw, Bullseye chose to pay Deadpool the money that Norman owed him.

But none of that really matters. What matters is that Wade's just gotten paid a lot of money. And I mean STUPID money.

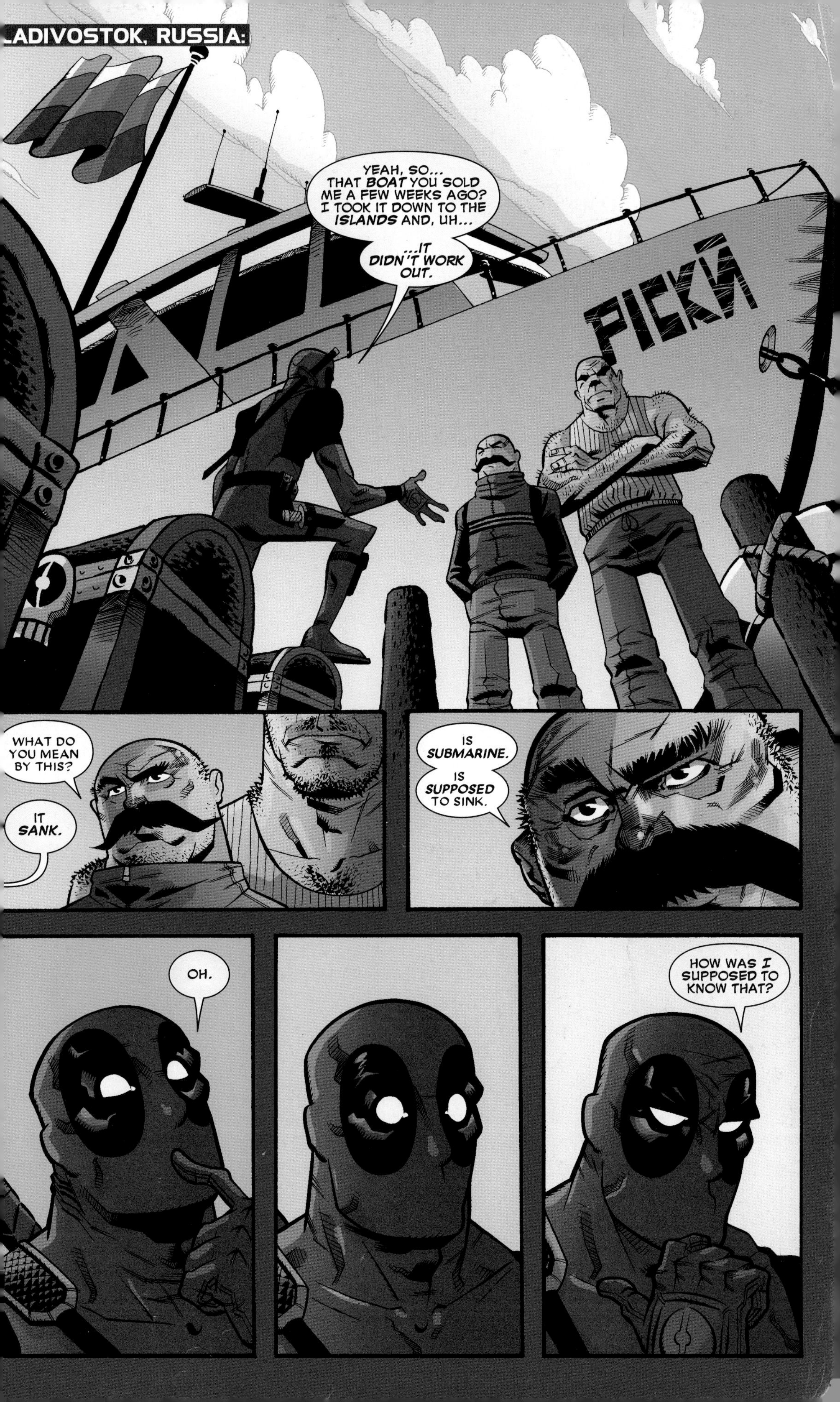
LADIVOSTOK, RUSSIA:
YEAH, SO... THAT BOAT YOU SOLD ME A FEW WEEKS AGO? I TOOK IT DOWN TO THE ISLANDS AND, UH...
...IT DIDN'T WORK OUT.
PICKИ
WHAT DO YOU MEAN BY THIS?
IT SANK.
IS SUBMARINE.
IS SUPPOSED TO SINK.
OH.
HOW WAS I SUPPOSED TO KNOW THAT?

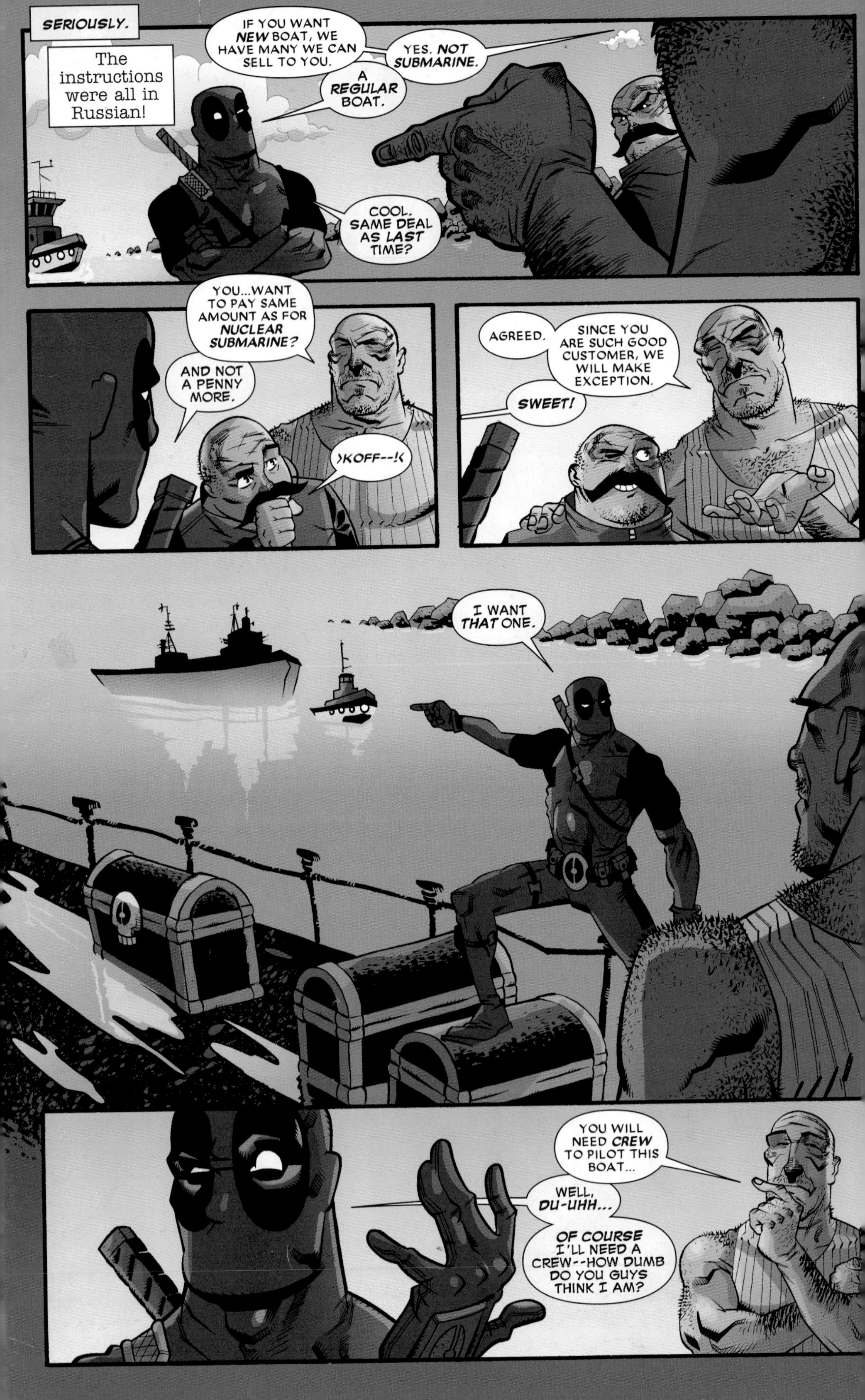
SERIOUSLY.
The instructions were all in Russian!
IF YOU WANT NEW BOAT, WE HAVE MANY WE CAN SELL TO YOU.
YES. NOT SUBMARINE.
A REGULAR BOAT.
COOL. SAME DEAL AS LAST TIME?
YOU...WANT TO PAY SAME AMOUNT AS FOR NUCLEAR SUBMARINE?
AND NOT A PENNY MORE.
>KOFF--!<
AGREED.
SINCE YOU ARE SUCH GOOD CUSTOMER, WE WILL MAKE EXCEPTION.
SWEET!
I WANT THAT ONE.
YOU WILL NEED CREW TO PILOT THIS BOAT...
WELL, DU-UHH...
OF COURSE I'LL NEED A CREW--HOW DUMB DO YOU GUYS THINK I AM?

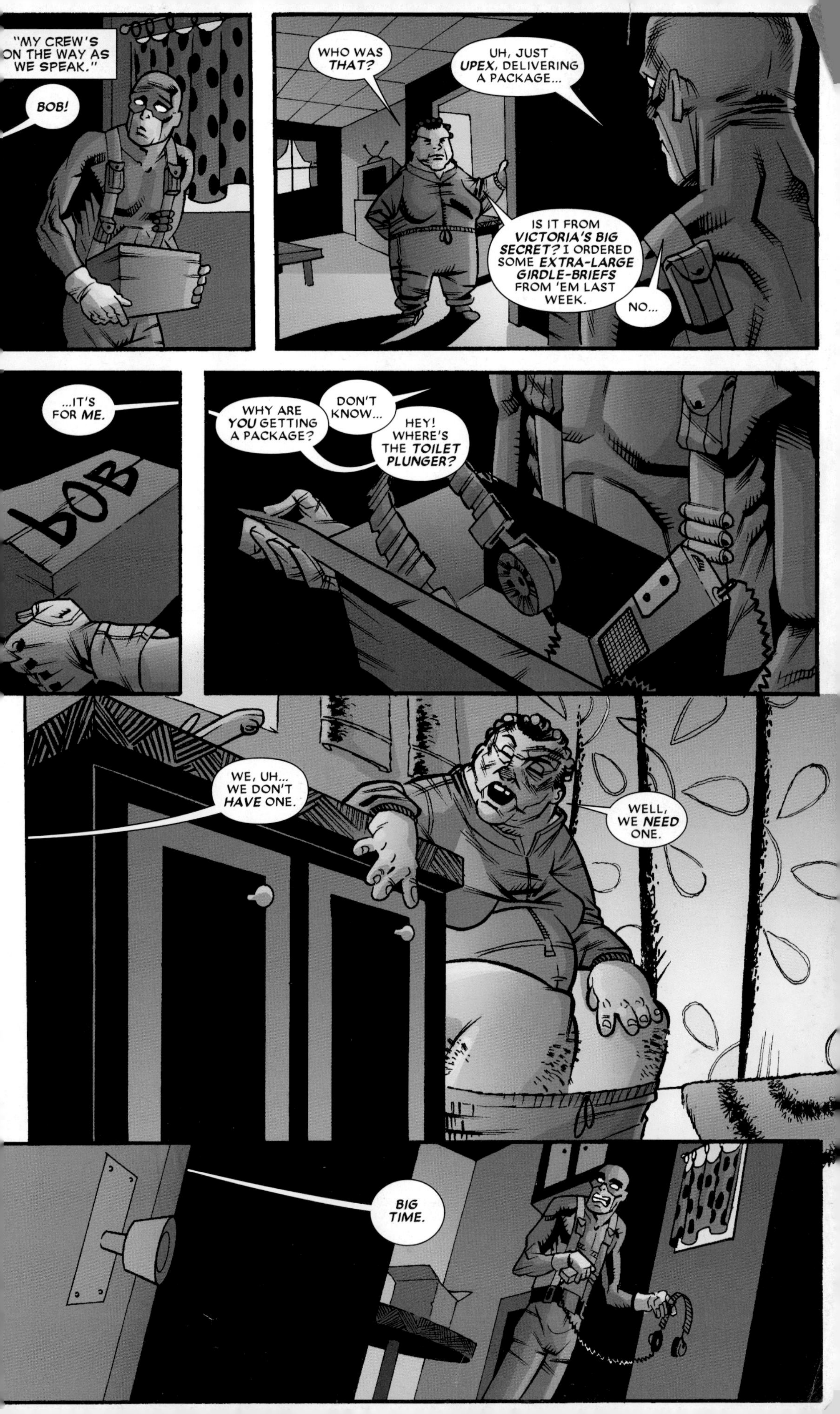
"MY CREW'S ON THE WAY AS WE SPEAK."
BOB!
WHO WAS *THAT?*
UH, JUST *UPEX*, DELIVERING A PACKAGE...
IS IT FROM *VICTORIA'S BIG SECRET?* I ORDERED SOME *EXTRA-LARGE GIRDLE-BRIEFS* FROM 'EM LAST WEEK.
NO...
...IT'S FOR *ME.*
BOB
WHY ARE *YOU* GETTING A PACKAGE?
DON'T KNOW...
HEY! WHERE'S THE *TOILET PLUNGER?*
WE, UH... WE DON'T *HAVE* ONE.
WELL, WE *NEED* ONE.
*BIG TIME.*

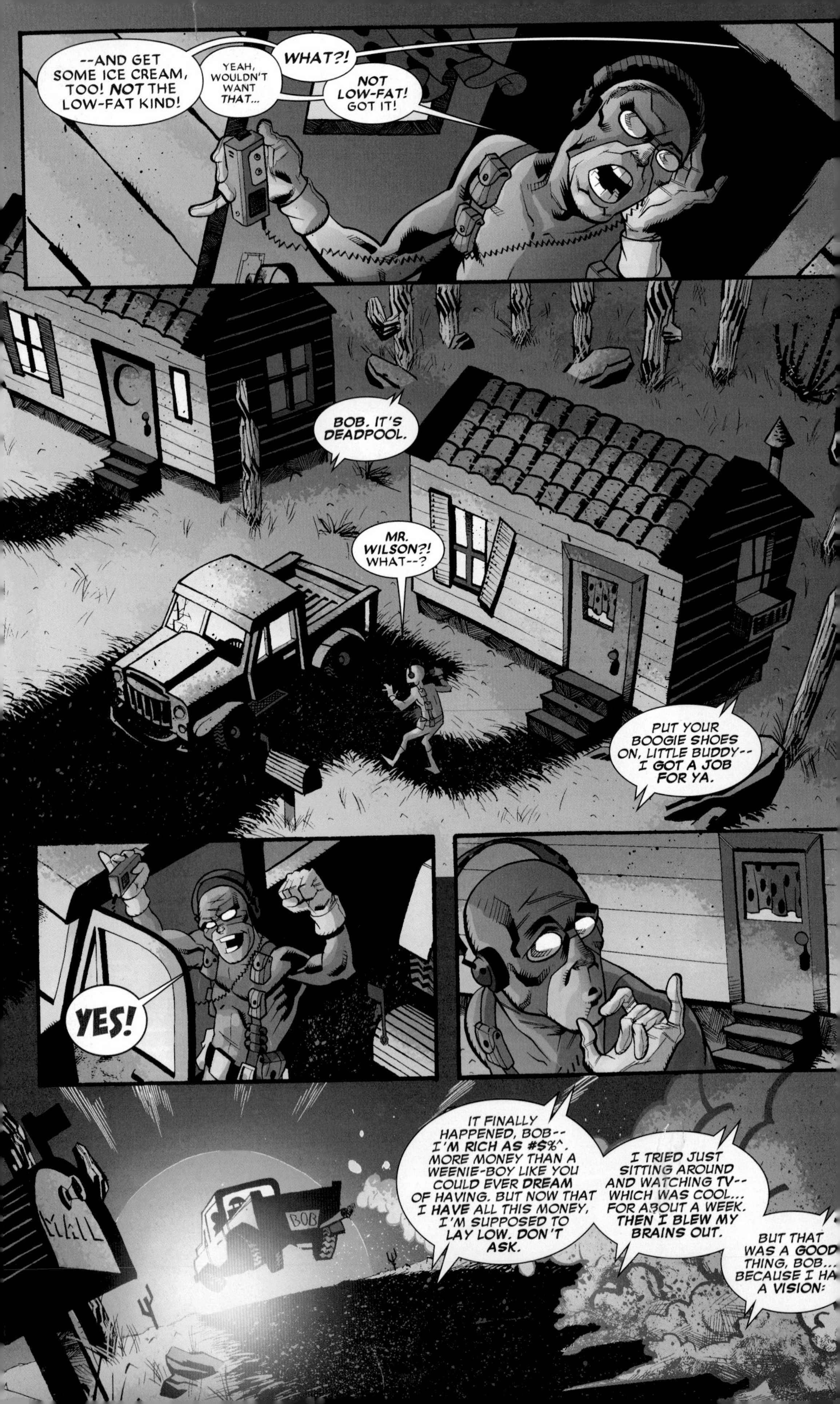
--AND GET SOME ICE CREAM, TOO! NOT THE LOW-FAT KIND!
YEAH, WOULDN'T WANT THAT...
WHAT?!
NOT LOW-FAT! GOT IT!
BOB. IT'S DEADPOOL.
MR. WILSON?! WHAT--?
PUT YOUR BOOGIE SHOES ON, LITTLE BUDDY-- I GOT A JOB FOR YA.
YES!
MAIL
BOB
IT FINALLY HAPPENED, BOB-- I'M RICH AS #$%^. MORE MONEY THAN A WEENIE-BOY LIKE YOU COULD EVER DREAM OF HAVING. BUT NOW THAT I HAVE ALL THIS MONEY, I'M SUPPOSED TO LAY LOW. DON'T ASK.
I TRIED JUST SITTING AROUND AND WATCHING TV-- WHICH WAS COOL... FOR ABOUT A WEEK. THEN I BLEW MY BRAINS OUT.
BUT THAT WAS A GOOD THING, BOB... BECAUSE I HA A VISION:

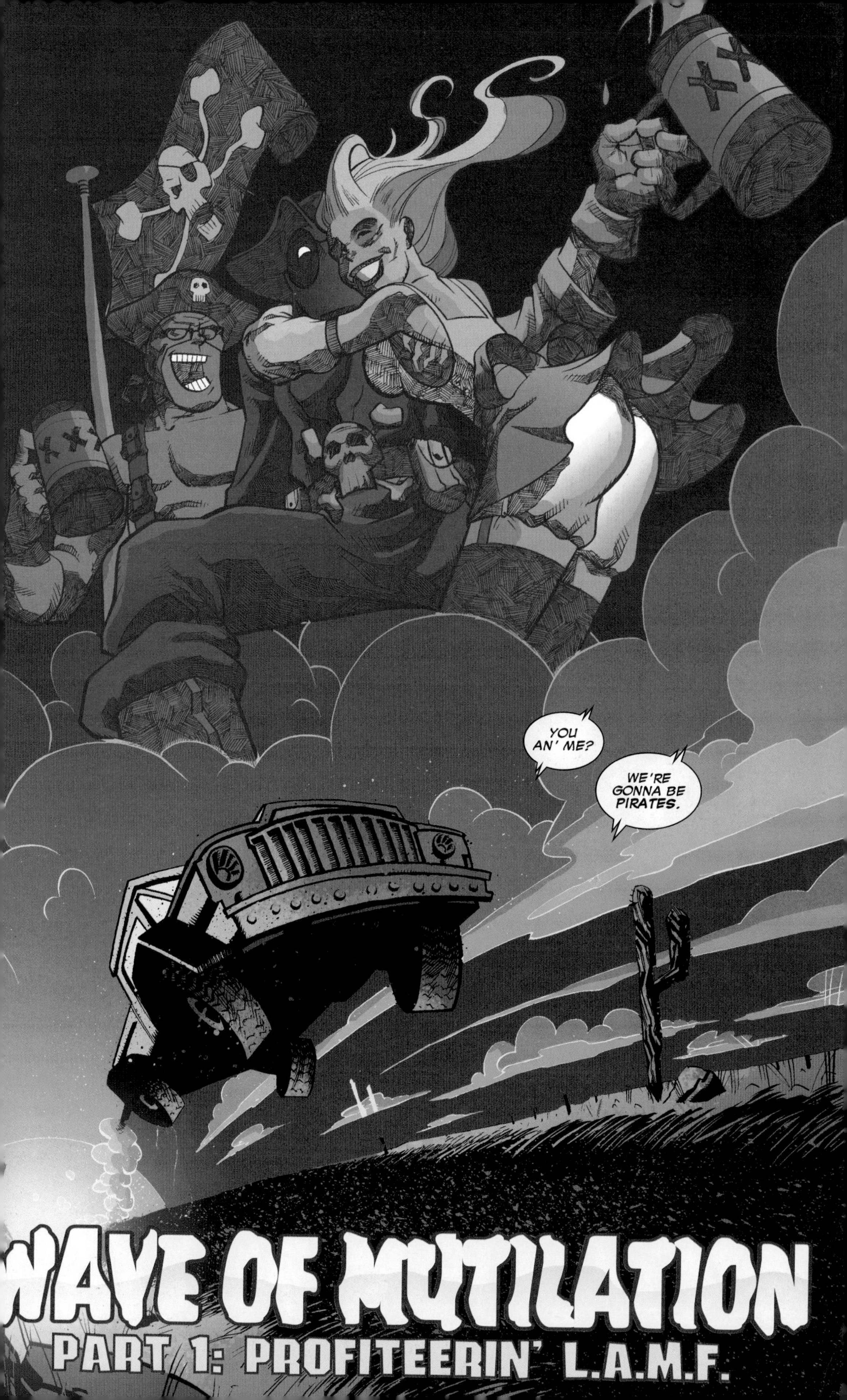
YOU AN' ME?
WE'RE GONNA BE PIRATES.
WAVE OF MUTILATION
PART 1: PROFITEERIN' L.A.M.F.

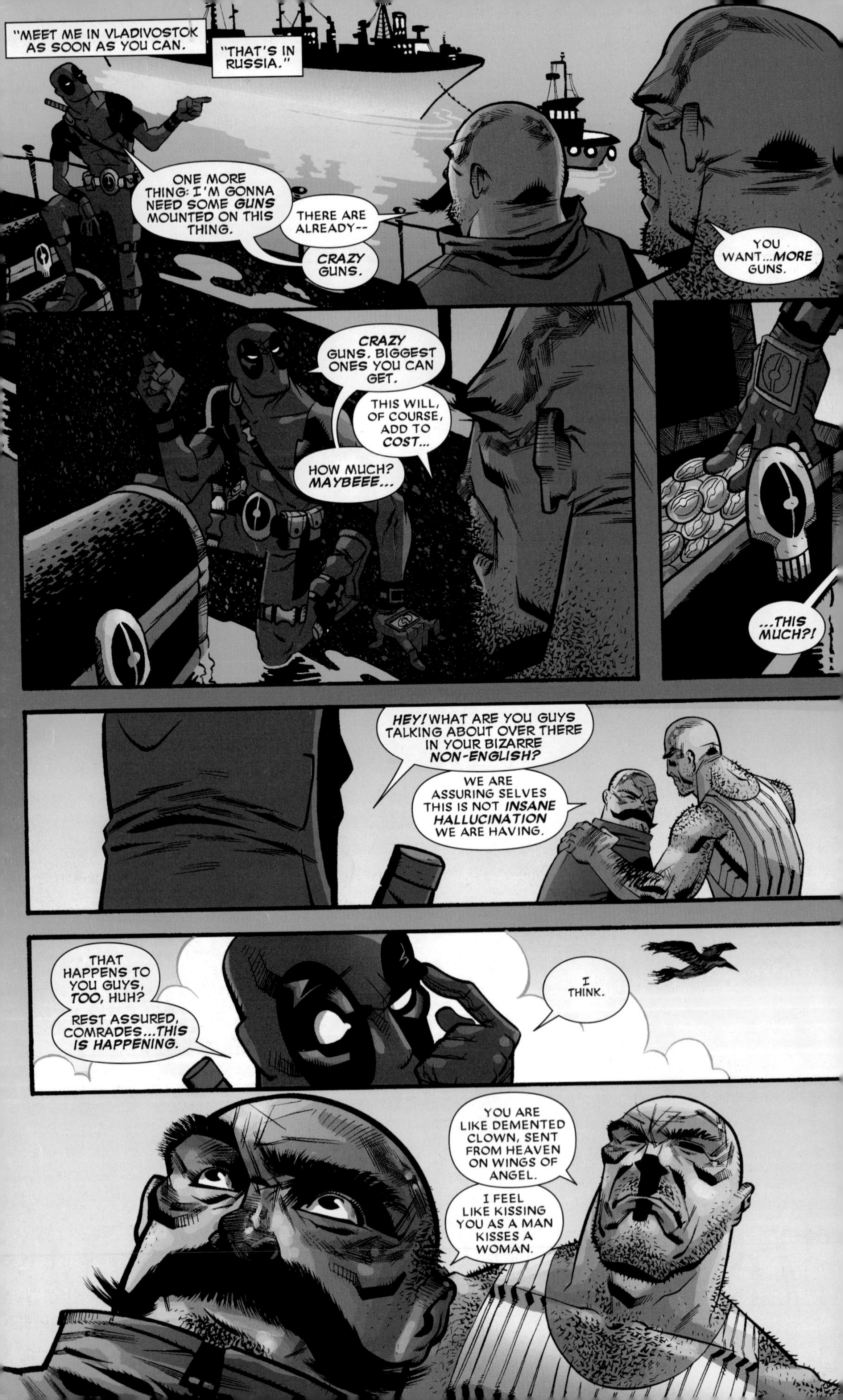
"MEET ME IN VLADIVOSTOK AS SOON AS YOU CAN.
"THAT'S IN RUSSIA."
ONE MORE THING: I'M GONNA NEED SOME GUNS MOUNTED ON THIS THING.
THERE ARE ALREADY--
CRAZY GUNS.
YOU WANT...MORE GUNS.
CRAZY GUNS. BIGGEST ONES YOU CAN GET.
THIS WILL, OF COURSE, ADD TO COST...
HOW MUCH? MAYBEEE...
...THIS MUCH?!
HEY! WHAT ARE YOU GUYS TALKING ABOUT OVER THERE IN YOUR BIZARRE NON-ENGLISH?
WE ARE ASSURING SELVES THIS IS NOT INSANE HALLUCINATION WE ARE HAVING.
THAT HAPPENS TO YOU GUYS, TOO, HUH?
REST ASSURED, COMRADES...THIS IS HAPPENING.
I THINK.
YOU ARE LIKE DEMENTED CLOWN, SENT FROM HEAVEN ON WINGS OF ANGEL.
I FEEL LIKE KISSING YOU AS A MAN KISSES A WOMAN.

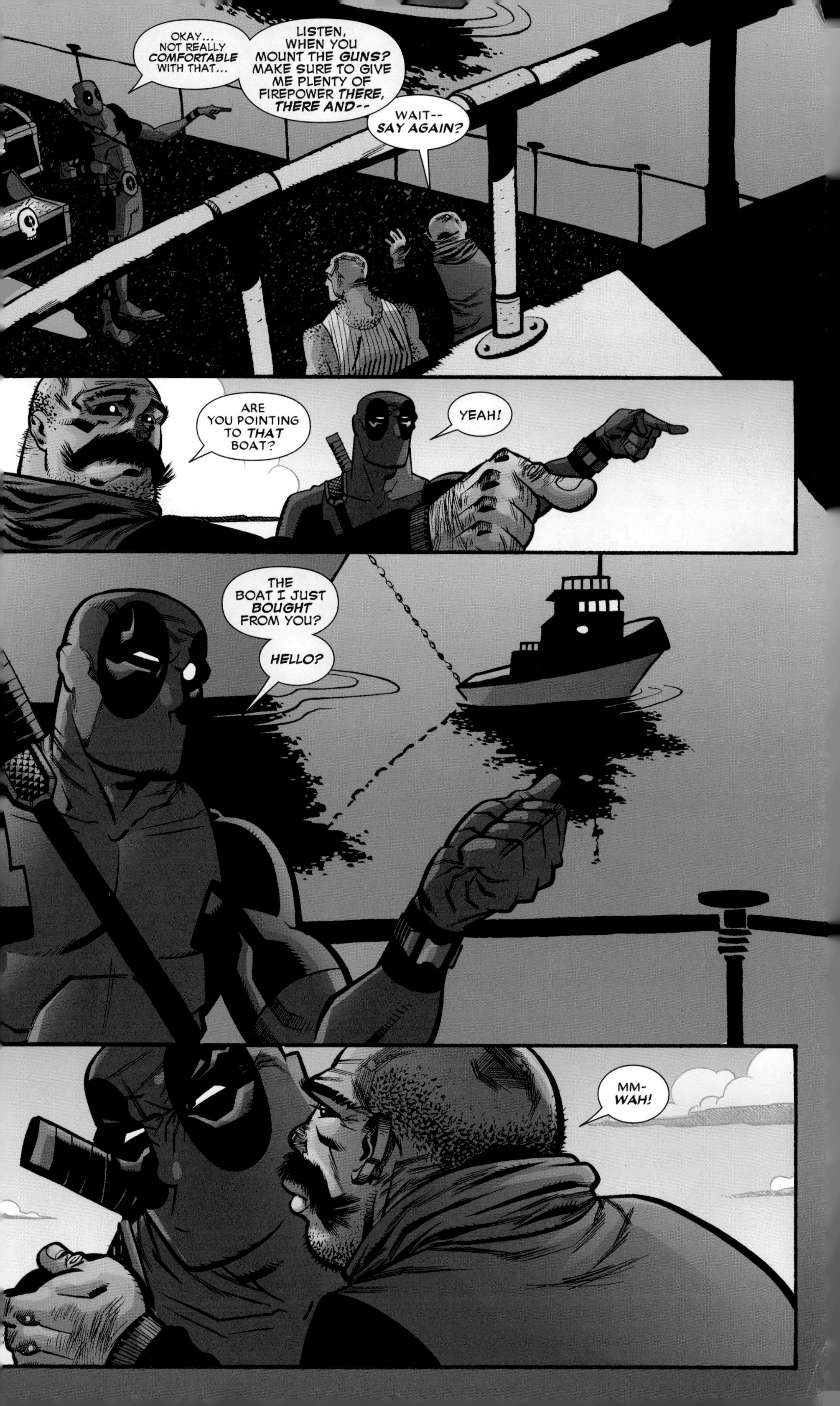
OKAY... NOT REALLY COMFORTABLE WITH THAT...
LISTEN, WHEN YOU MOUNT THE GUNS? MAKE SURE TO GIVE ME PLENTY OF FIREPOWER THERE, THERE AND--
WAIT-- SAY AGAIN?
ARE YOU POINTING TO THAT BOAT?
YEAH!
THE BOAT I JUST BOUGHT FROM YOU?
HELLO?
MM-WAH!

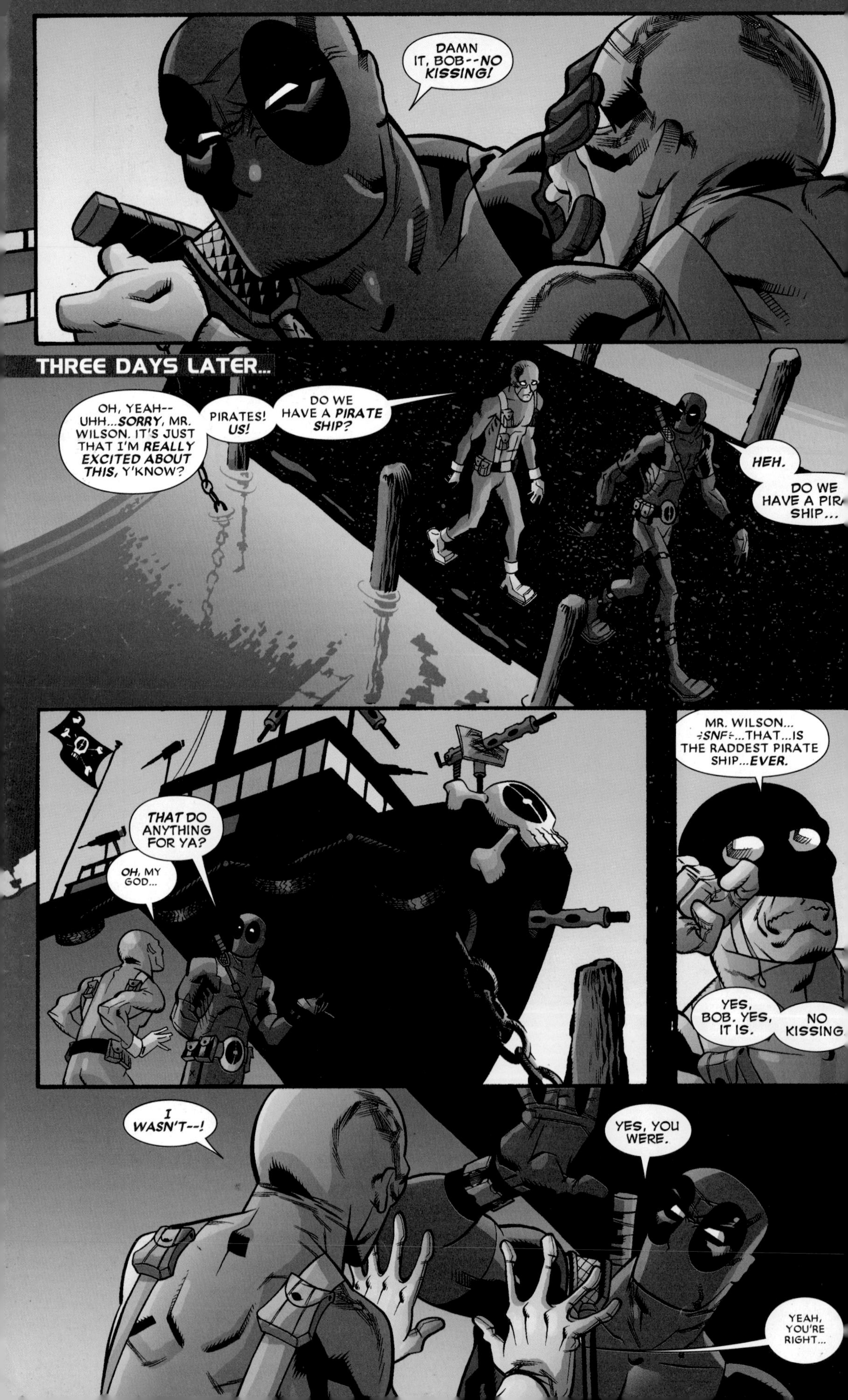
DAMN IT, BOB--NO KISSING!
THREE DAYS LATER...
DO WE HAVE A PIRATE SHIP?
PIRATES! US!
OH, YEAH-- UHH...SORRY, MR. WILSON. IT'S JUST THAT I'M REALLY EXCITED ABOUT THIS, Y'KNOW?
HEH.
DO WE HAVE A PIR SHIP...
THAT DO ANYTHING FOR YA?
OH, MY GOD...
MR. WILSON... ≠SNF≠...THAT...IS THE RADDEST PIRATE SHIP...EVER.
YES, BOB. YES, IT IS.
NO KISSING
I WASN'T--!
YES, YOU WERE.
YEAH, YOU'RE RIGHT...

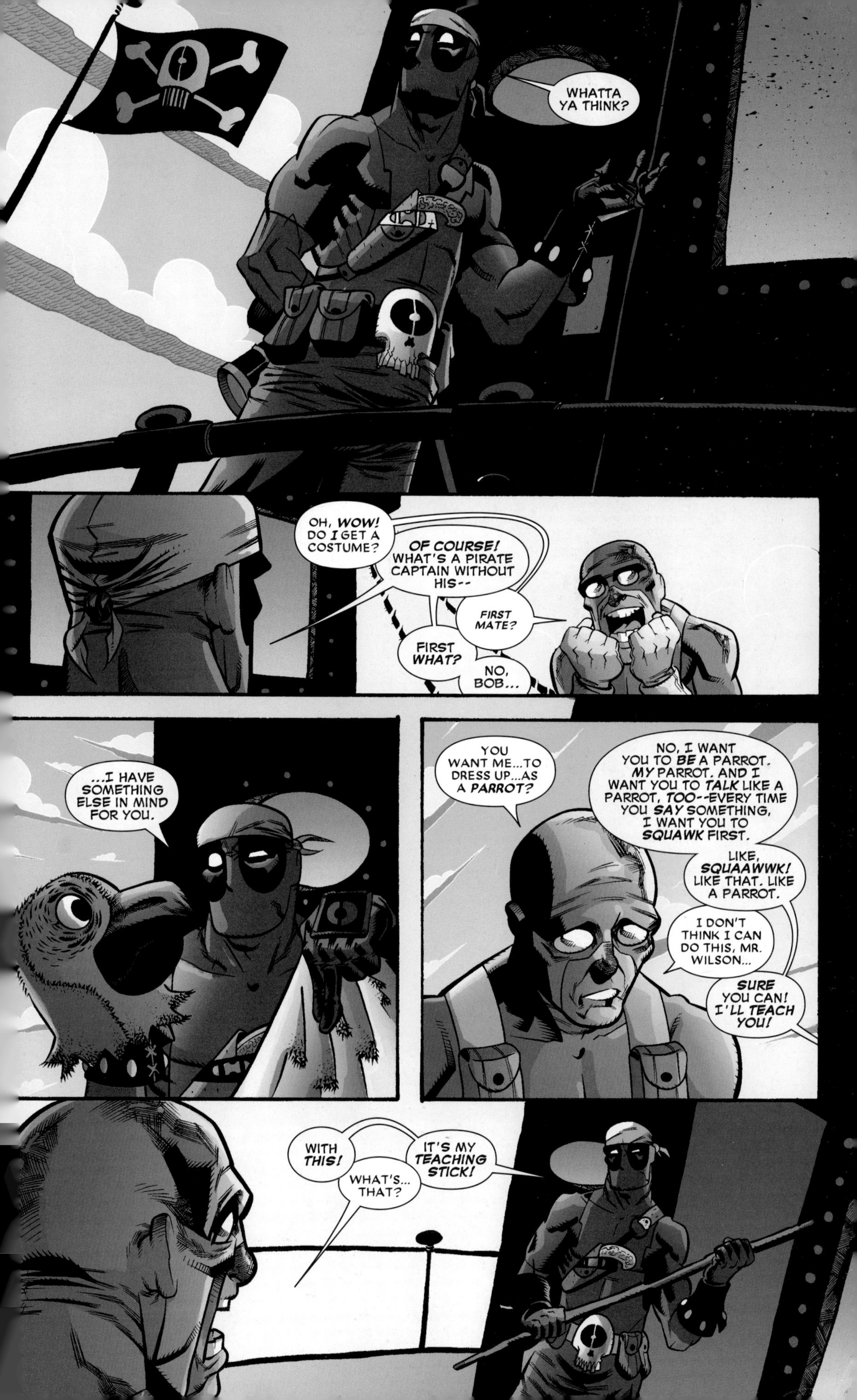
WHATTA YA THINK?
OH, WOW! DO I GET A COSTUME?
OF COURSE! WHAT'S A PIRATE CAPTAIN WITHOUT HIS--
FIRST MATE?
FIRST WHAT?
NO, BOB...
...I HAVE SOMETHING ELSE IN MIND FOR YOU.
YOU WANT ME...TO DRESS UP...AS A PARROT?
NO, I WANT YOU TO BE A PARROT. MY PARROT. AND I WANT YOU TO TALK LIKE A PARROT, TOO--EVERY TIME YOU SAY SOMETHING, I WANT YOU TO SQUAWK FIRST.
LIKE, SQUAAWWK! LIKE THAT. LIKE A PARROT.
I DON'T THINK I CAN DO THIS, MR. WILSON...
SURE YOU CAN! I'LL TEACH YOU!
WITH THIS!
WHAT'S... THAT?
IT'S MY TEACHING STICK!

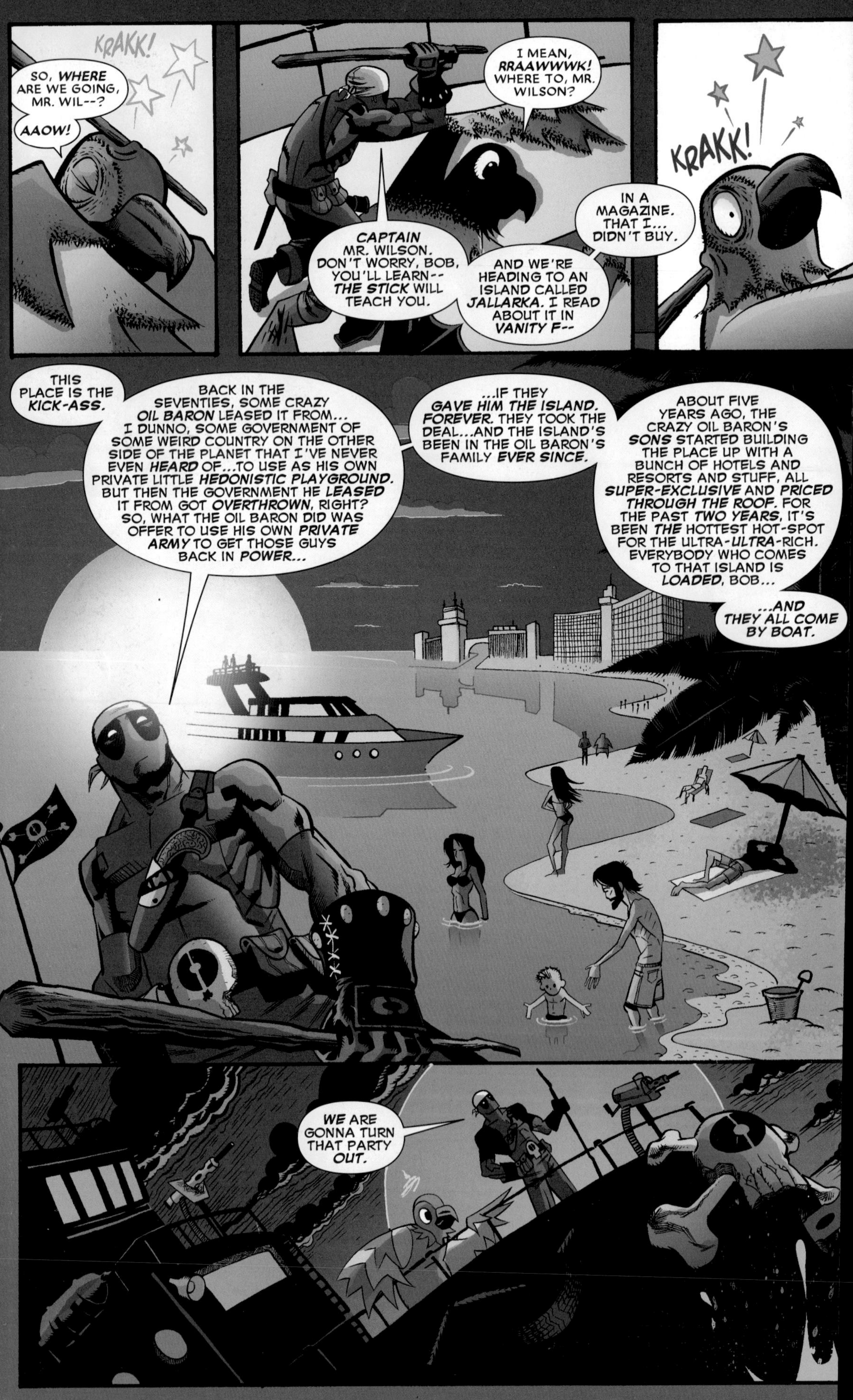
KRAKK!
SO, WHERE ARE WE GOING, MR. WIL--?
AAOW!
I MEAN, RRAAWWWK! WHERE TO, MR. WILSON?
CAPTAIN MR. WILSON. DON'T WORRY, BOB, YOU'LL LEARN-- THE STICK WILL TEACH YOU.
AND WE'RE HEADING TO AN ISLAND CALLED JALLARKA. I READ ABOUT IT IN VANITY F--
KRAKK!
IN A MAGAZINE. THAT I... DIDN'T BUY.
THIS PLACE IS THE KICK-ASS.
BACK IN THE SEVENTIES, SOME CRAZY OIL BARON LEASED IT FROM... I DUNNO, SOME GOVERNMENT OF SOME WEIRD COUNTRY ON THE OTHER SIDE OF THE PLANET THAT I'VE NEVER EVEN HEARD OF...TO USE AS HIS OWN PRIVATE LITTLE HEDONISTIC PLAYGROUND. BUT THEN THE GOVERNMENT HE LEASED IT FROM GOT OVERTHROWN, RIGHT? SO, WHAT THE OIL BARON DID WAS OFFER TO USE HIS OWN PRIVATE ARMY TO GET THOSE GUYS BACK IN POWER...
...IF THEY GAVE HIM THE ISLAND. FOREVER. THEY TOOK THE DEAL...AND THE ISLAND'S BEEN IN THE OIL BARON'S FAMILY EVER SINCE.
ABOUT FIVE YEARS AGO, THE CRAZY OIL BARON'S SONS STARTED BUILDING THE PLACE UP WITH A BUNCH OF HOTELS AND RESORTS AND STUFF, ALL SUPER-EXCLUSIVE AND PRICED THROUGH THE ROOF. FOR THE PAST TWO YEARS, IT'S BEEN THE HOTTEST HOT-SPOT FOR THE ULTRA-ULTRA-RICH. EVERYBODY WHO COMES TO THAT ISLAND IS LOADED, BOB...
...AND THEY ALL COME BY BOAT.
WE ARE GONNA TURN THAT PARTY OUT.

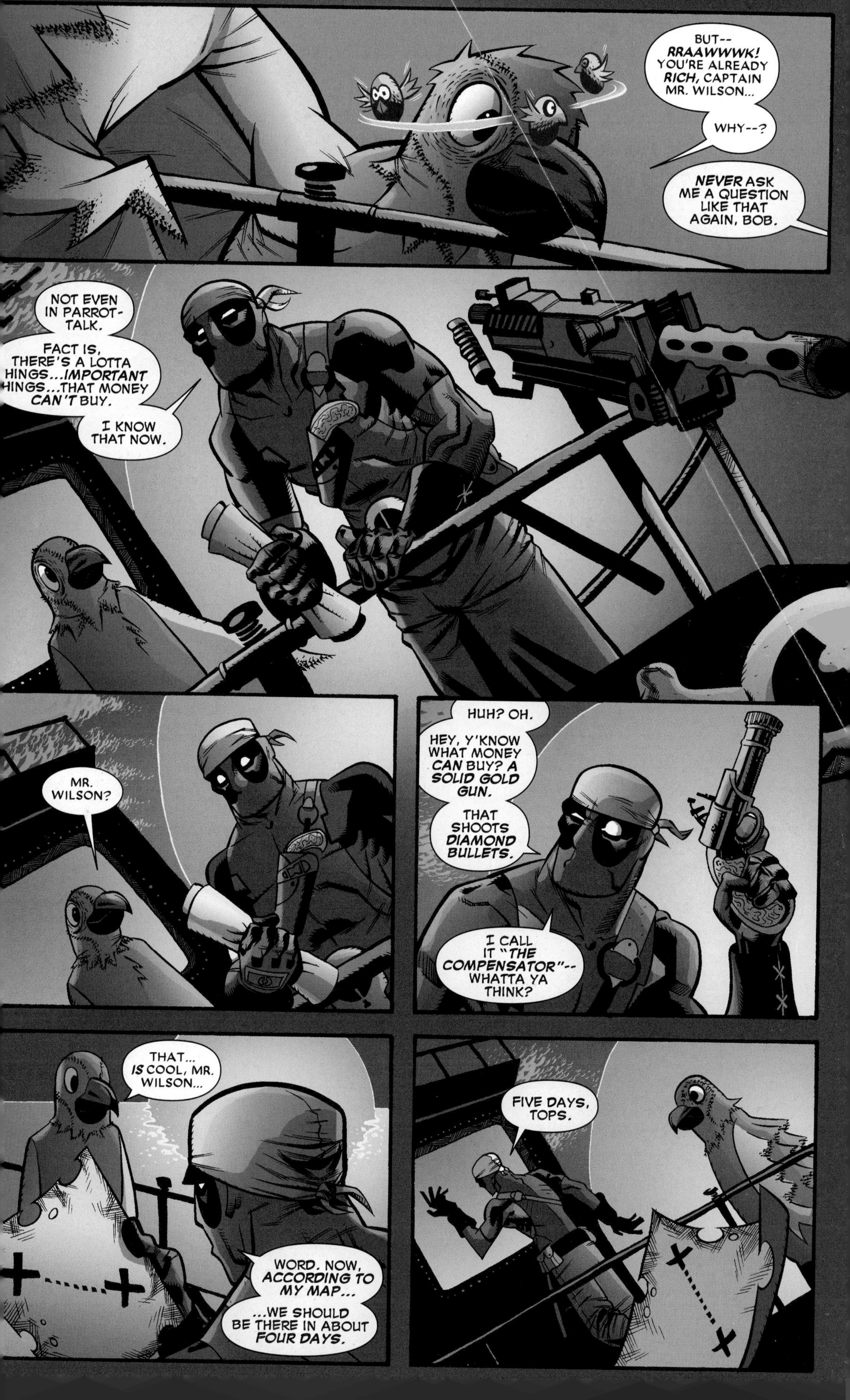
BUT-- RRAAWWWK! YOU'RE ALREADY RICH, CAPTAIN MR. WILSON...
WHY--?
NEVER ASK ME A QUESTION LIKE THAT AGAIN, BOB.
NOT EVEN IN PARROT-TALK.
FACT IS, THERE'S A LOTTA HINGS...IMPORTANT HINGS...THAT MONEY CAN'T BUY.
I KNOW THAT NOW.
MR. WILSON?
HUH? OH.
HEY, Y'KNOW WHAT MONEY CAN BUY? A SOLID GOLD GUN.
THAT SHOOTS DIAMOND BULLETS.
I CALL IT "THE COMPENSATOR"-- WHATTA YA THINK?
THAT... IS COOL, MR. WILSON...
WORD. NOW, ACCORDING TO MY MAP...
...WE SHOULD BE THERE IN ABOUT FOUR DAYS.
FIVE DAYS, TOPS.

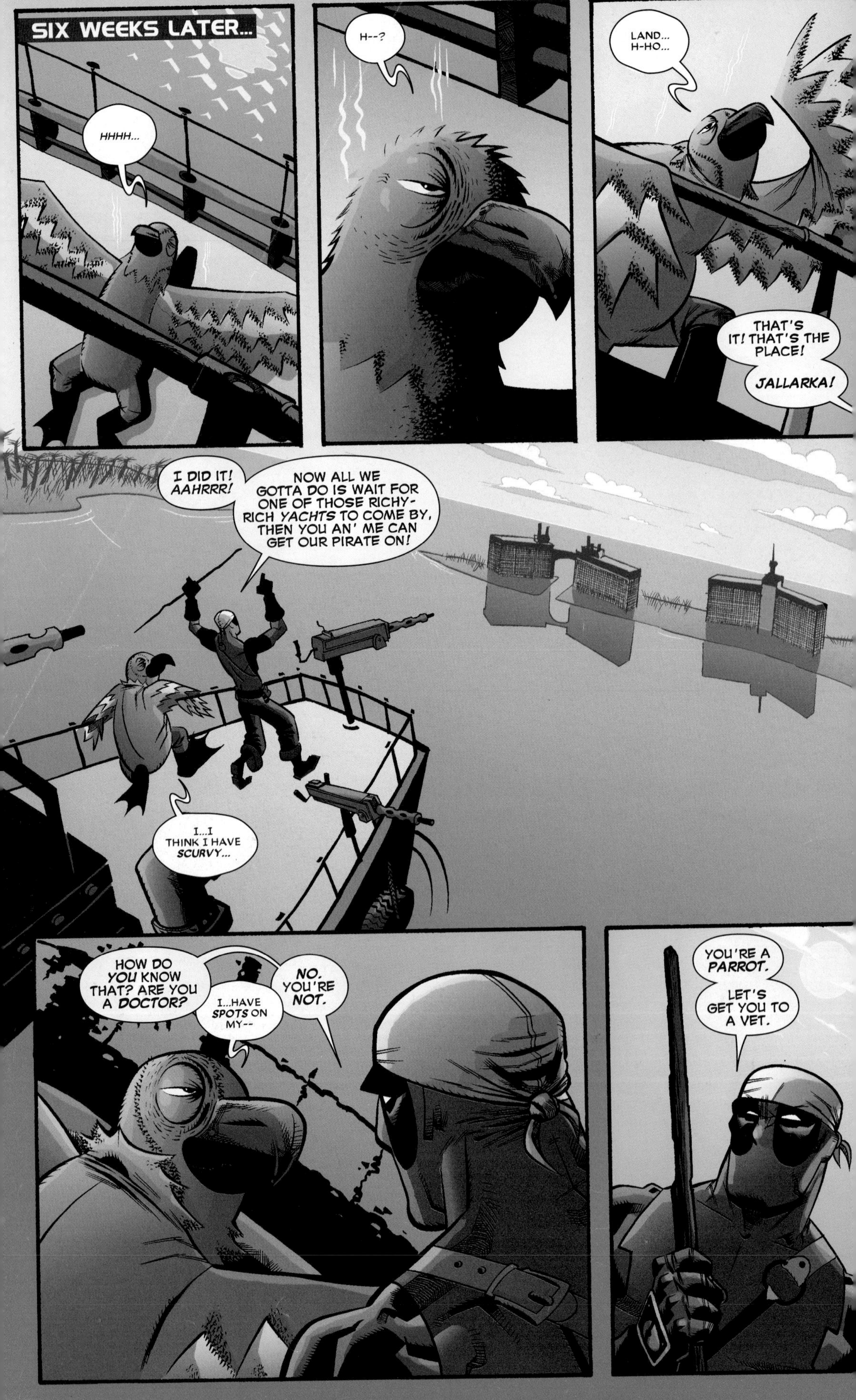
SIX WEEKS LATER...
HHHH...
H--?
LAND... H-HO...
THAT'S IT! THAT'S THE PLACE!
JALLARKA!
I DID IT! AAHRRR!
NOW ALL WE GOTTA DO IS WAIT FOR ONE OF THOSE RICHY-RICH YACHTS TO COME BY, THEN YOU AN' ME CAN GET OUR PIRATE ON!
I...I THINK I HAVE SCURVY...
HOW DO YOU KNOW THAT? ARE YOU A DOCTOR?
I...HAVE SPOTS ON MY--
NO. YOU'RE NOT.
YOU'RE A PARROT.
LET'S GET YOU TO A VET.

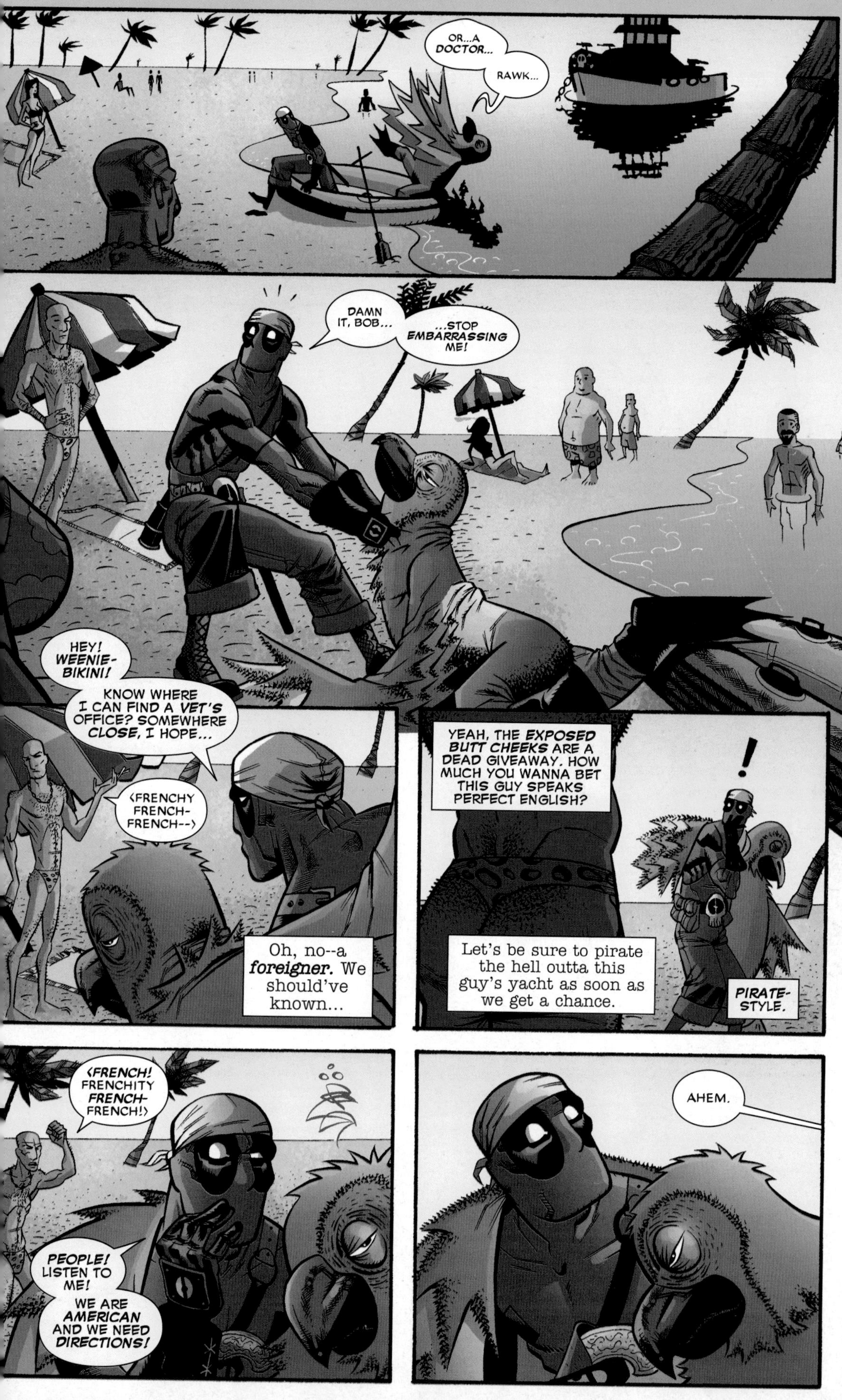

OR...A DOCTOR...
RAWK...
DAMN IT, BOB...
...STOP EMBARRASSING ME!
HEY! WEENIE-BIKINI!
KNOW WHERE I CAN FIND A VET'S OFFICE? SOMEWHERE CLOSE, I HOPE...
‹FRENCHY FRENCH-FRENCH--›
Oh, no--a foreigner. We should've known...
YEAH, THE EXPOSED BUTT CHEEKS ARE A DEAD GIVEAWAY. HOW MUCH YOU WANNA BET THIS GUY SPEAKS PERFECT ENGLISH?
!
Let's be sure to pirate the hell outta this guy's yacht as soon as we get a chance.
PIRATE-STYLE.
‹FRENCH! FRENCHITY FRENCH-FRENCH!›
PEOPLE! LISTEN TO ME!
WE ARE AMERICAN AND WE NEED DIRECTIONS!
AHEM.

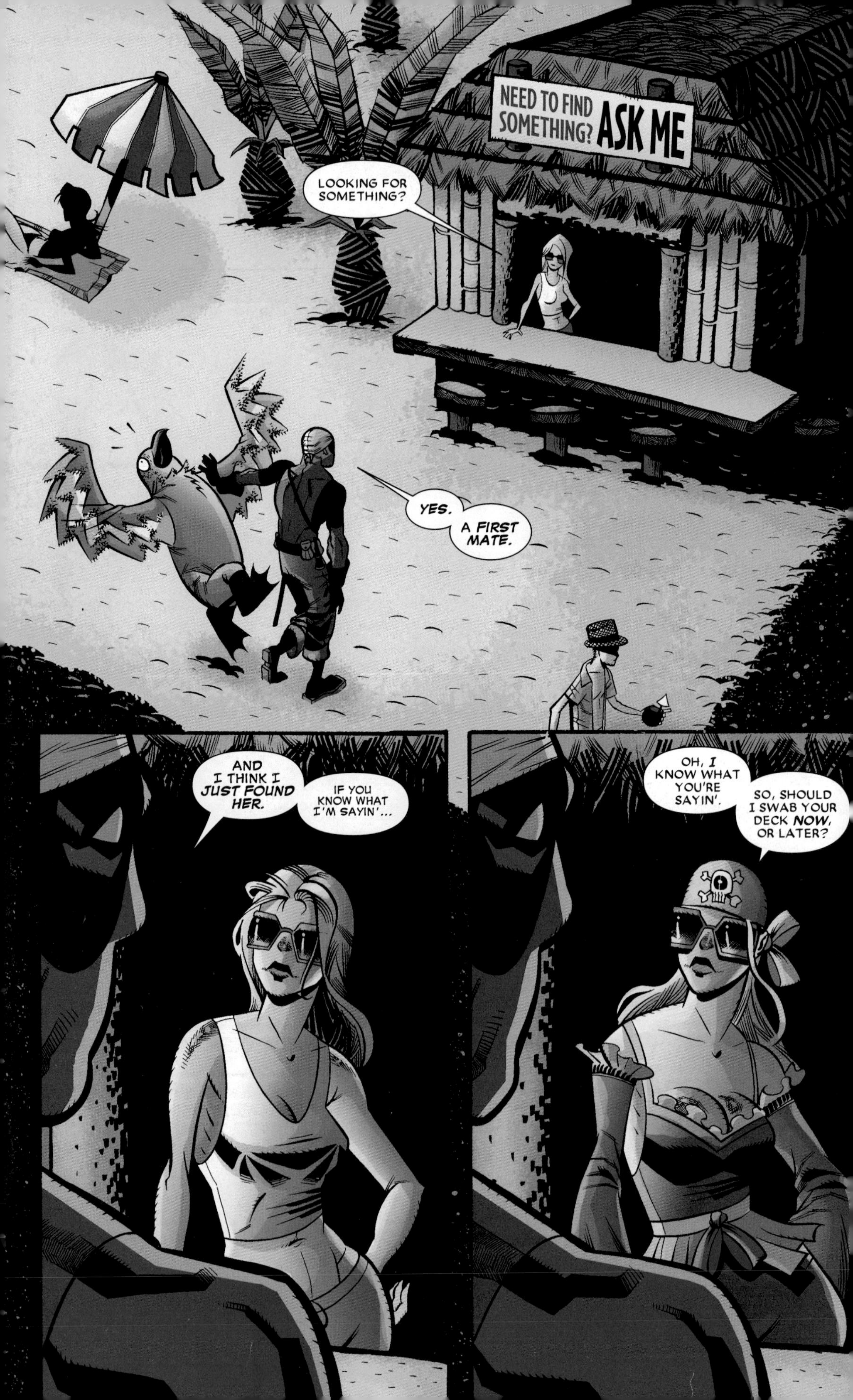
NEED TO FIND SOMETHING? ASK ME
LOOKING FOR SOMETHING?
YES.
A FIRST MATE.
AND I THINK I JUST FOUND HER.
IF YOU KNOW WHAT I'M SAYIN'...
OH, I KNOW WHAT YOU'RE SAYIN'.
SO, SHOULD I SWAB YOUR DECK NOW, OR LATER?

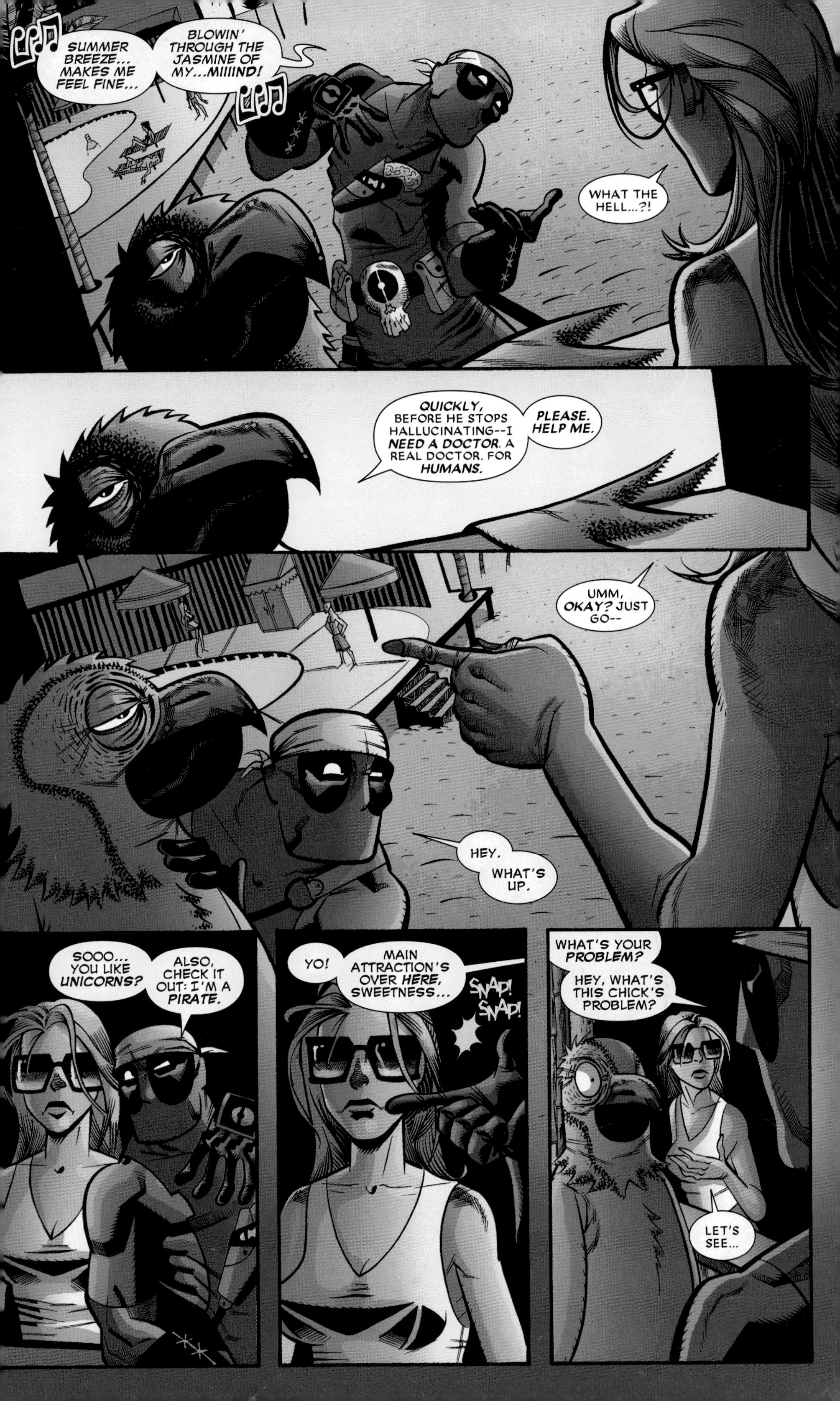
SUMMER BREEZE... MAKES ME FEEL FINE...
BLOWIN' THROUGH THE JASMINE OF MY...MIIIIND!
WHAT THE HELL...?!
QUICKLY, BEFORE HE STOPS HALLUCINATING--I NEED A DOCTOR. A REAL DOCTOR. FOR HUMANS.
PLEASE. HELP ME.
UMM, OKAY? JUST GO--
HEY. WHAT'S UP.
SOOO... YOU LIKE UNICORNS?
ALSO, CHECK IT OUT: I'M A PIRATE.
YO!
MAIN ATTRACTION'S OVER HERE, SWEETNESS...
SNAP! SNAP!
WHAT'S YOUR PROBLEM?
HEY, WHAT'S THIS CHICK'S PROBLEM?
LET'S SEE...

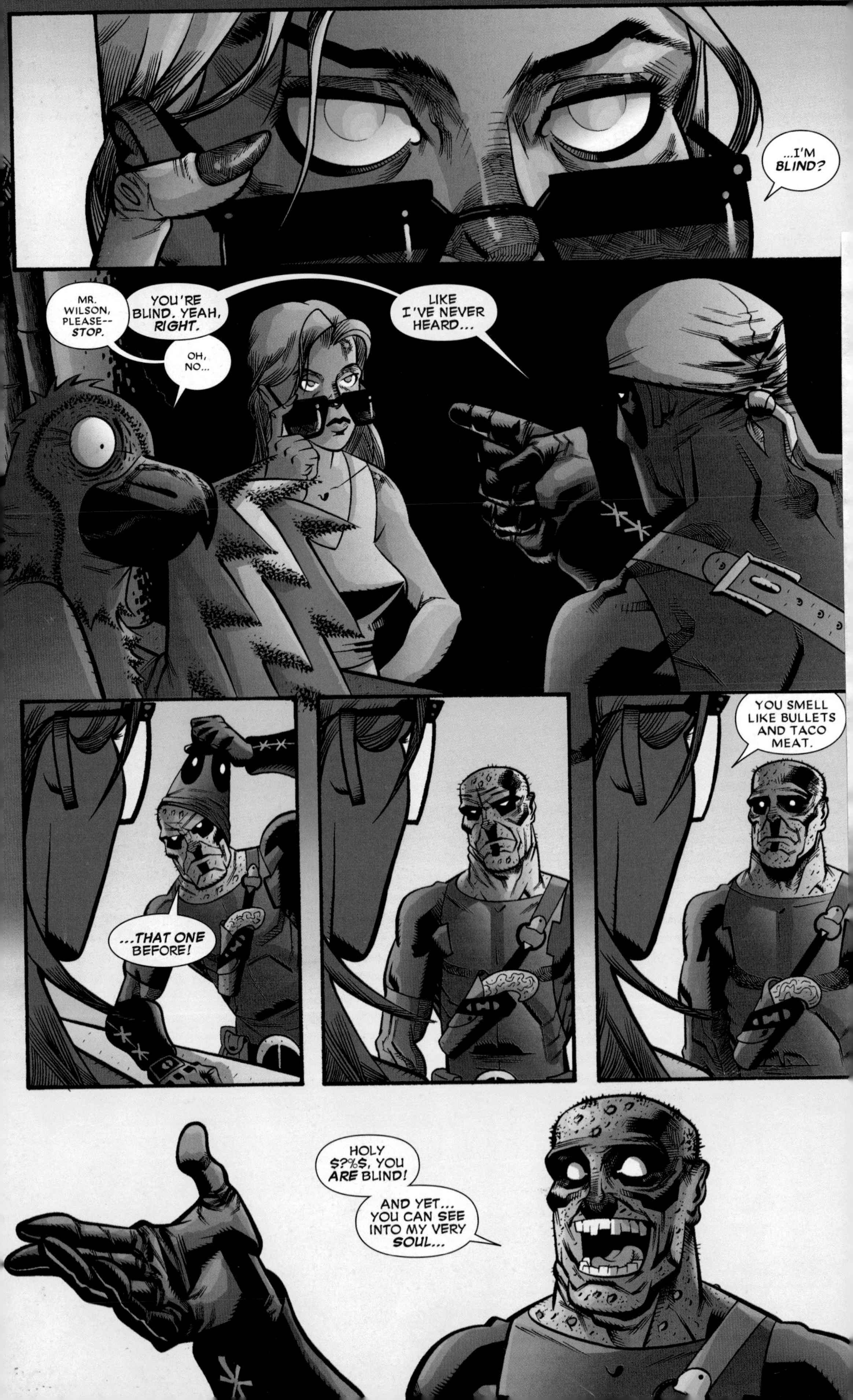
...I'M BLIND?
MR. WILSON, PLEASE-- STOP.
YOU'RE BLIND. YEAH, RIGHT.
LIKE I'VE NEVER HEARD...
OH, NO...
...THAT ONE BEFORE!
YOU SMELL LIKE BULLETS AND TACO MEAT.
HOLY $?%$, YOU ARE BLIND!
AND YET... YOU CAN SEE INTO MY VERY SOUL...

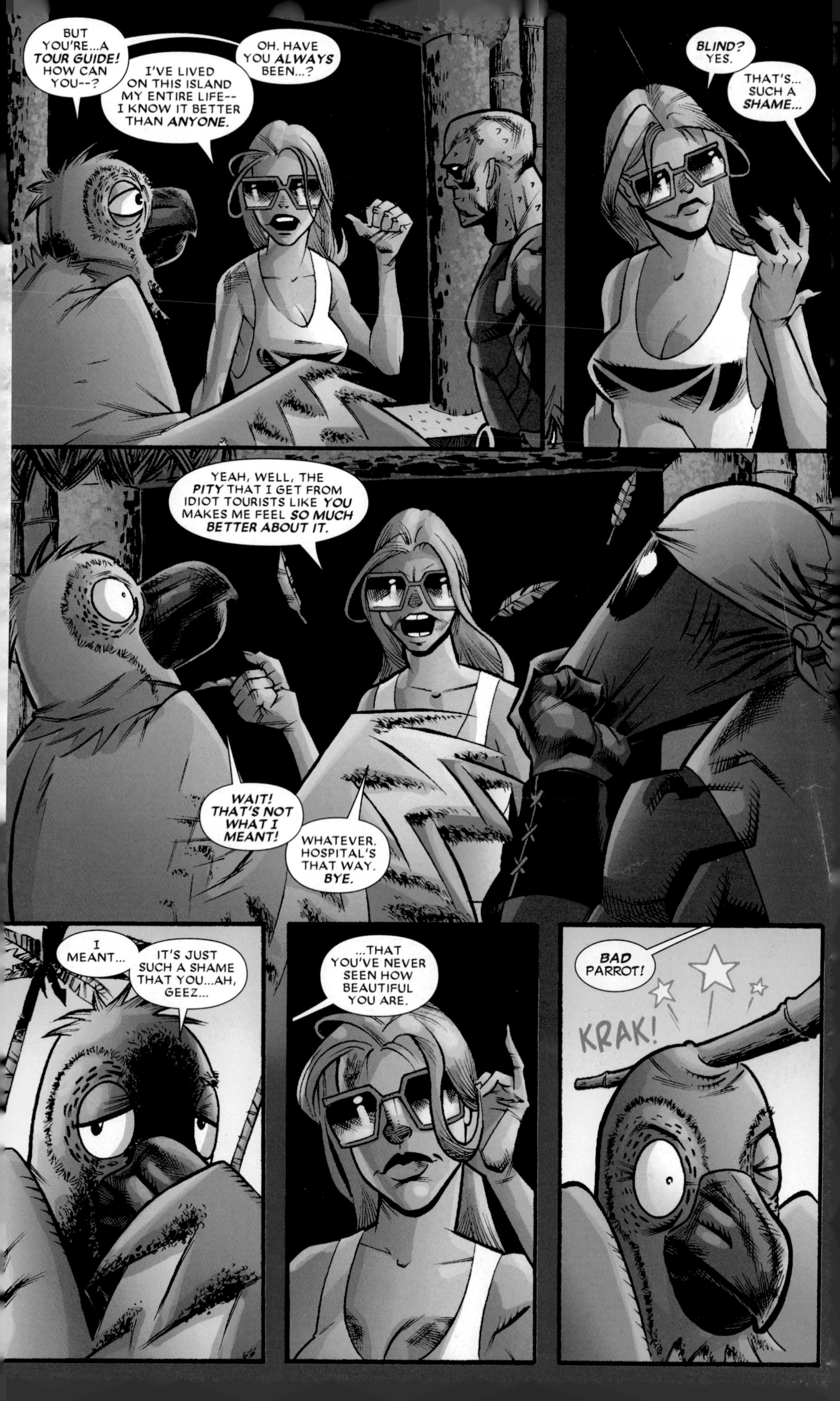

BUT YOU'RE...A TOUR GUIDE! HOW CAN YOU--?
I'VE LIVED ON THIS ISLAND MY ENTIRE LIFE-- I KNOW IT BETTER THAN ANYONE.
OH. HAVE YOU ALWAYS BEEN...?
BLIND? YES.
THAT'S... SUCH A SHAME...
YEAH, WELL, THE PITY THAT I GET FROM IDIOT TOURISTS LIKE YOU MAKES ME FEEL SO MUCH BETTER ABOUT IT.
WAIT! THAT'S NOT WHAT I MEANT!
WHATEVER. HOSPITAL'S THAT WAY. BYE.
I MEANT...
IT'S JUST SUCH A SHAME THAT YOU...AH, GEEZ...
...THAT YOU'VE NEVER SEEN HOW BEAUTIFUL YOU ARE.
BAD PARROT!
KRAK!

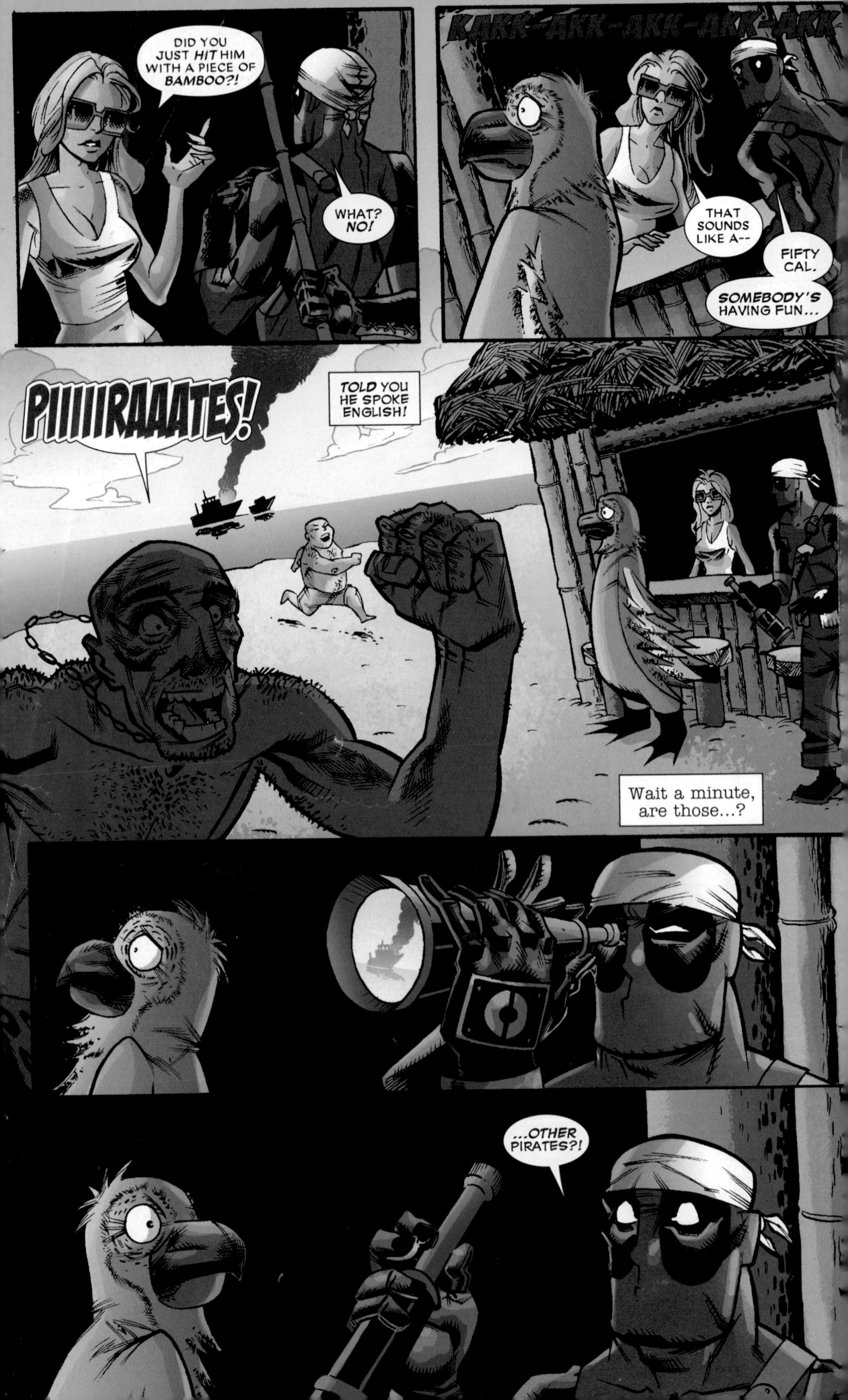
DID YOU JUST HIT HIM WITH A PIECE OF BAMBOO?!
WHAT? NO!
KAKK-AKK-AKK-AKK-AKK
THAT SOUNDS LIKE A--
FIFTY CAL.
SOMEBODY'S HAVING FUN...
PIIIIRAAAATES!
TOLD YOU HE SPOKE ENGLISH!
Wait a minute, are those...?
...OTHER PIRATES?!

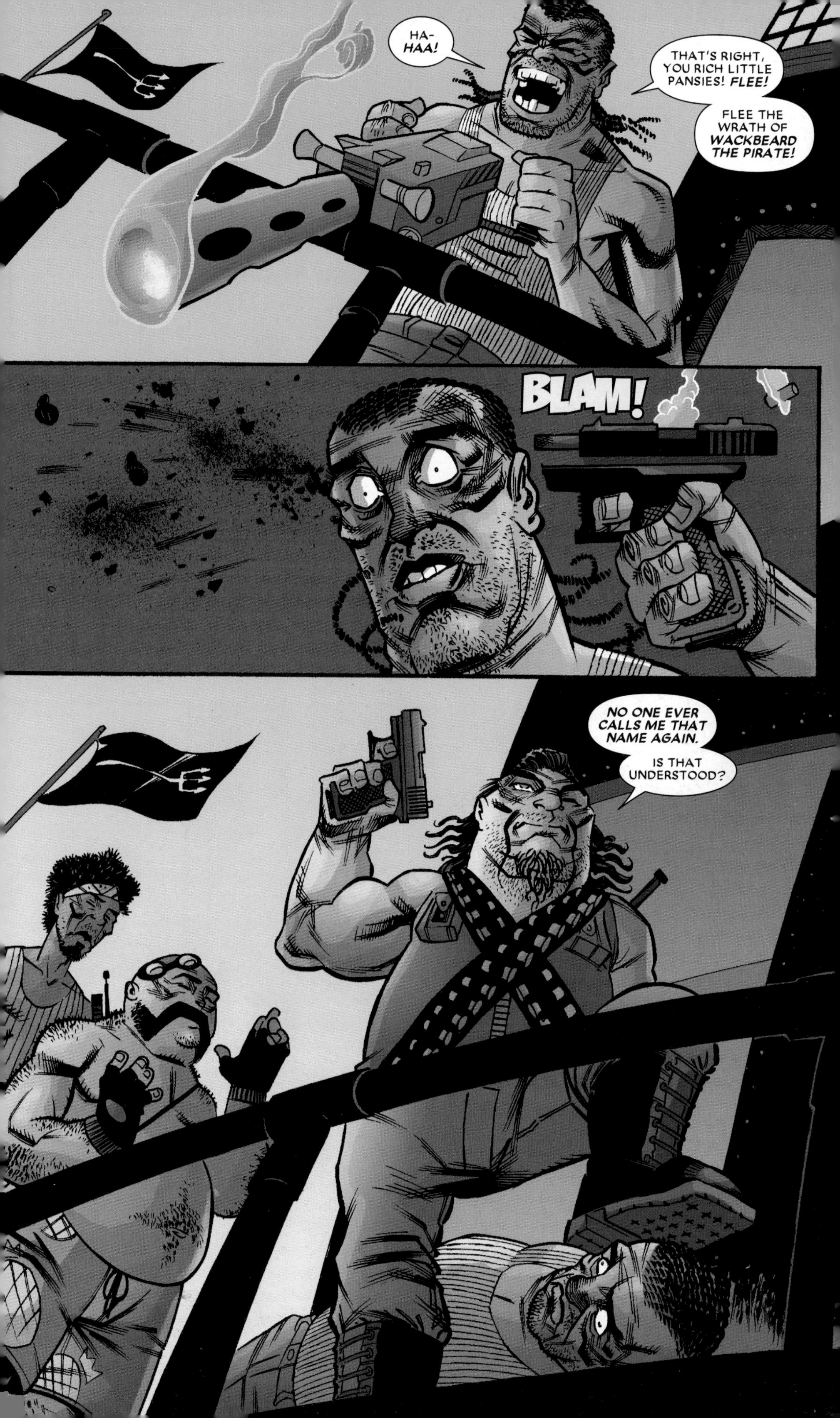
HA-
HAA!
THAT'S RIGHT, YOU RICH LITTLE PANSIES! FLEE!
FLEE THE WRATH OF WACKBEARD THE PIRATE!
BLAM!
NO ONE EVER CALLS ME THAT NAME AGAIN.
IS THAT UNDERSTOOD?

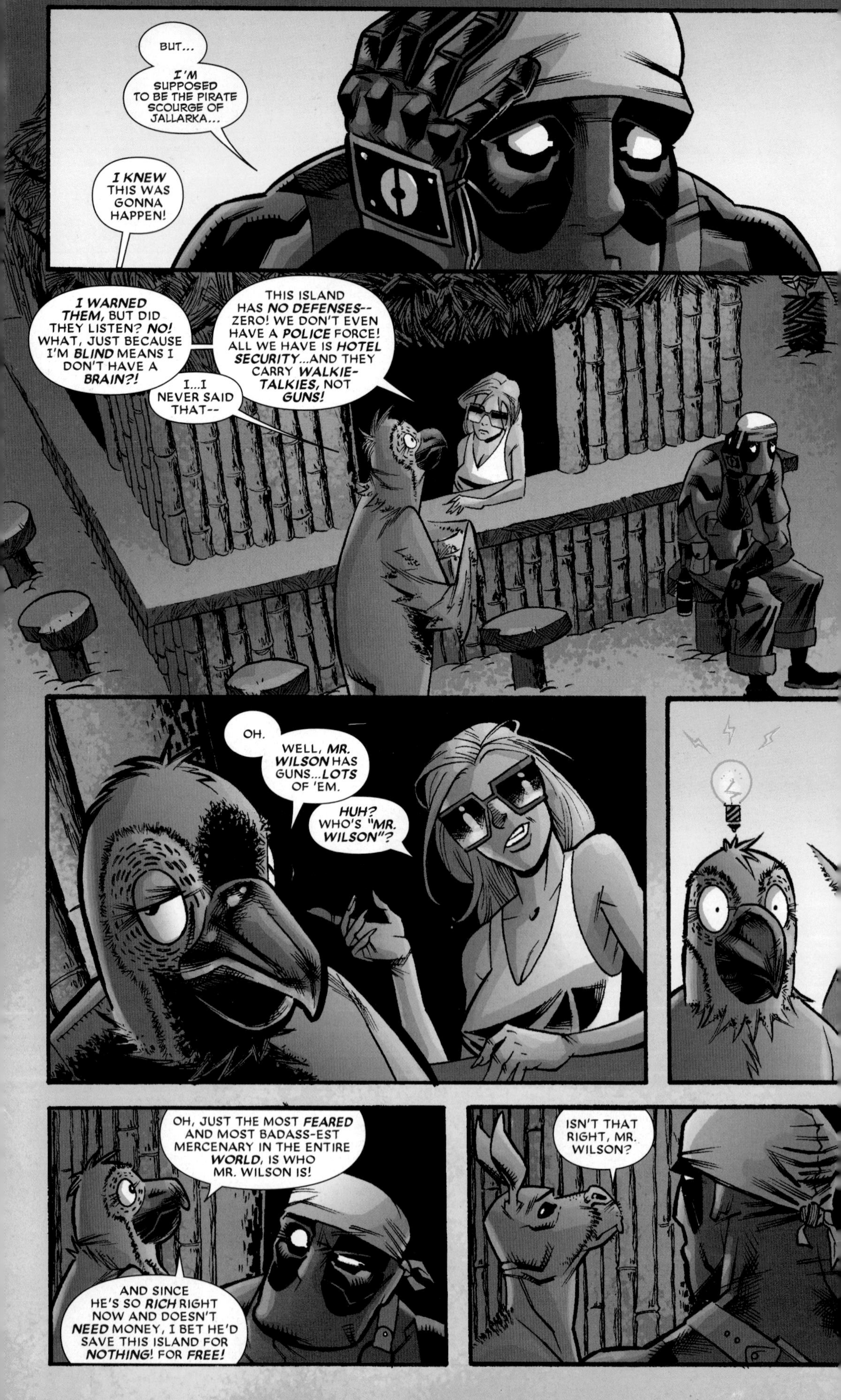
BUT...
I'M SUPPOSED TO BE THE PIRATE SCOURGE OF JALLARKA...
I KNEW THIS WAS GONNA HAPPEN!
I WARNED THEM, BUT DID THEY LISTEN? NO! WHAT, JUST BECAUSE I'M BLIND MEANS I DON'T HAVE A BRAIN?!
THIS ISLAND HAS NO DEFENSES--ZERO! WE DON'T EVEN HAVE A POLICE FORCE! ALL WE HAVE IS HOTEL SECURITY...AND THEY CARRY WALKIE-TALKIES, NOT GUNS!
I...I NEVER SAID THAT--
OH.
WELL, MR. WILSON HAS GUNS...LOTS OF 'EM.
HUH? WHO'S "MR. WILSON"?
OH, JUST THE MOST FEARED AND MOST BADASS-EST MERCENARY IN THE ENTIRE WORLD, IS WHO MR. WILSON IS!
AND SINCE HE'S SO RICH RIGHT NOW AND DOESN'T NEED MONEY, I BET HE'D SAVE THIS ISLAND FOR NOTHING! FOR FREE!
ISN'T THAT RIGHT, MR. WILSON?

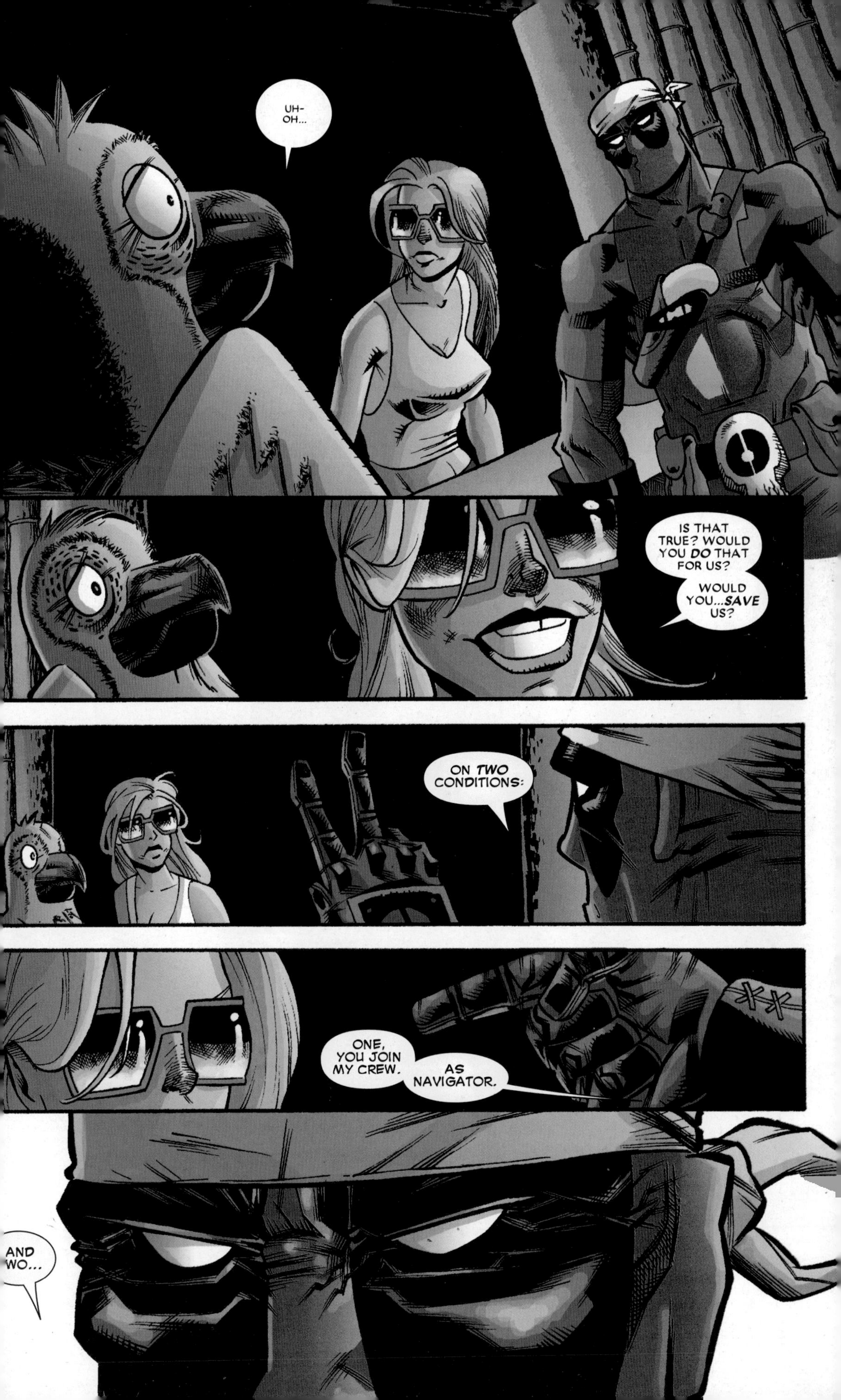
UH-
OH...
IS THAT TRUE? WOULD YOU DO THAT FOR US?
WOULD YOU...SAVE US?
ON TWO CONDITIONS:
ONE, YOU JOIN MY CREW.
AS NAVIGATOR.
AND WO...

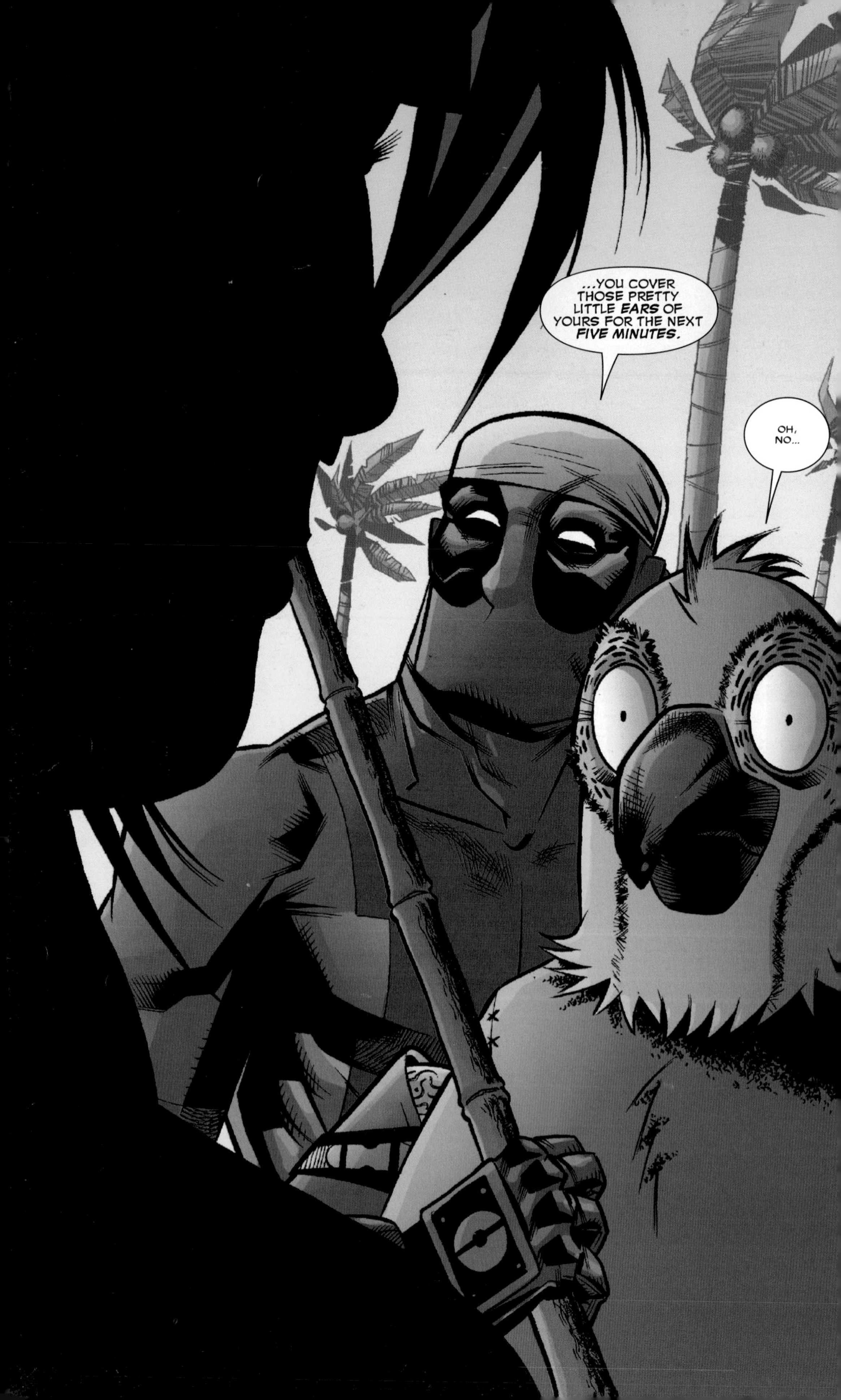

...YOU COVER THOSE PRETTY LITTLE *EARS* OF YOURS FOR THE NEXT *FIVE MINUTES.*
OH, NO...

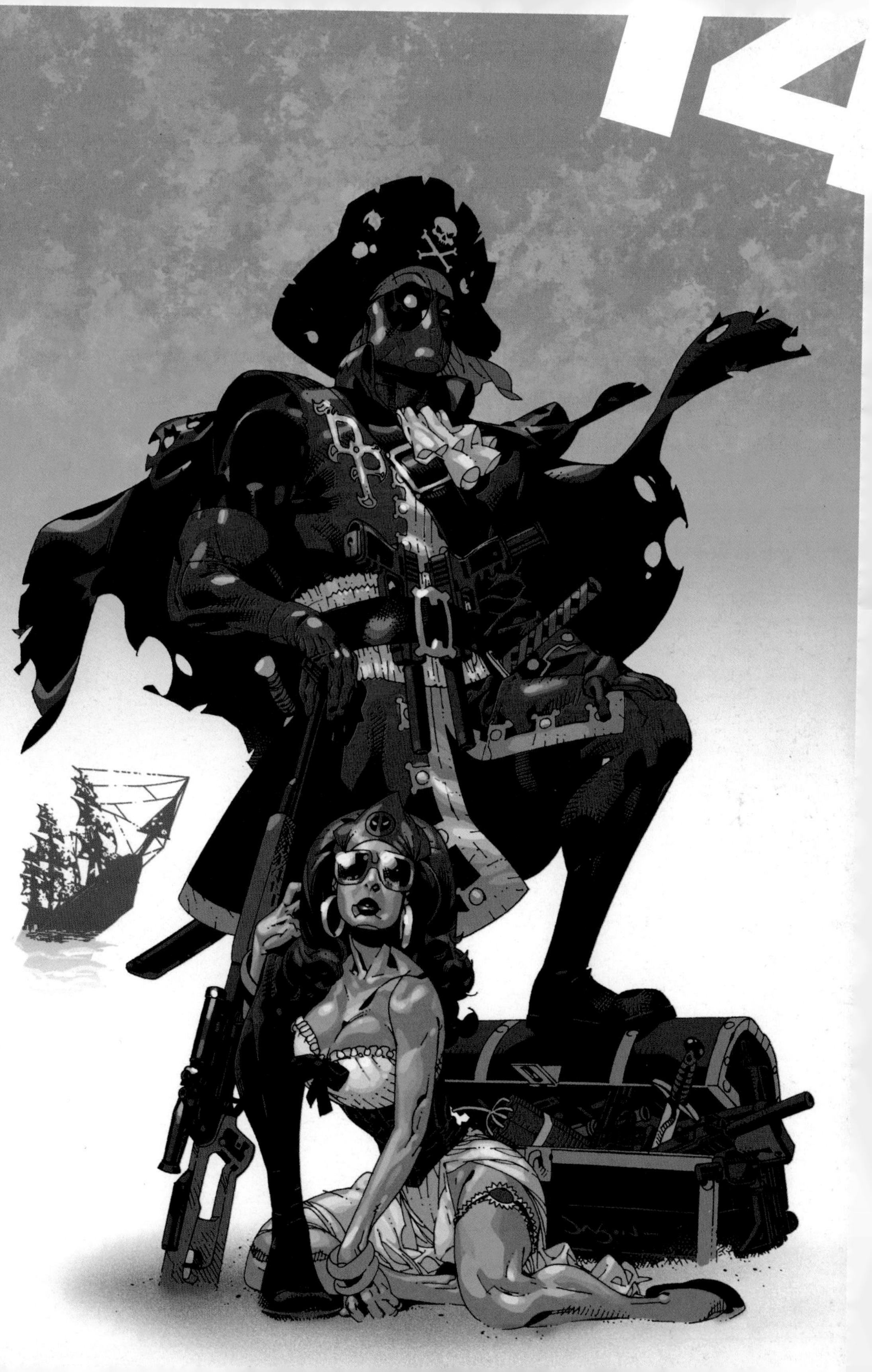
14

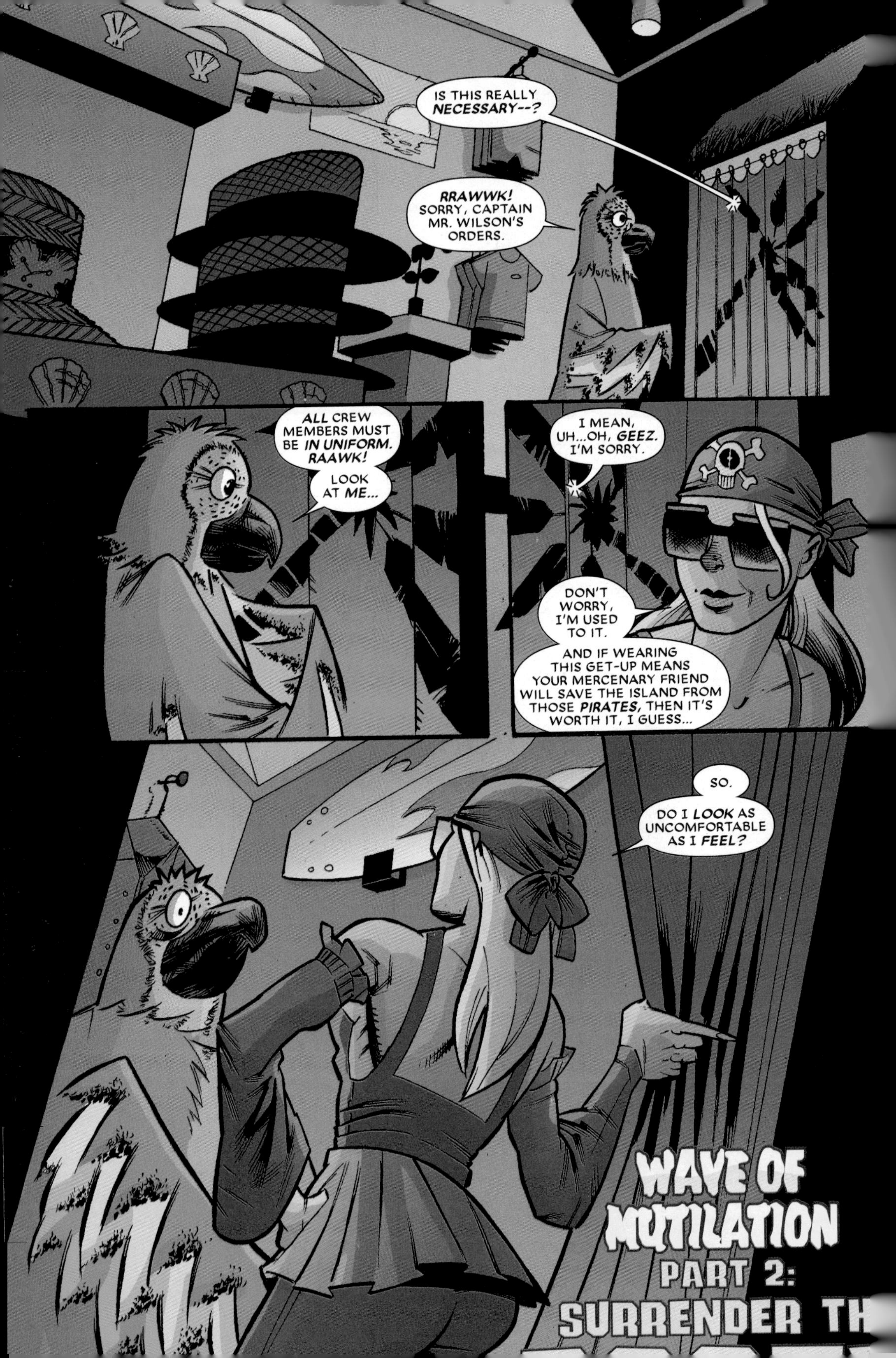
IS THIS REALLY NECESSARY--?
RRAWWK! SORRY, CAPTAIN MR. WILSON'S ORDERS.
ALL CREW MEMBERS MUST BE IN UNIFORM. RAAWK!
LOOK AT ME...
I MEAN, UH...OH, GEEZ. I'M SORRY.
DON'T WORRY, I'M USED TO IT.
AND IF WEARING THIS GET-UP MEANS YOUR MERCENARY FRIEND WILL SAVE THE ISLAND FROM THOSE PIRATES, THEN IT'S WORTH IT, I GUESS...
SO.
DO I LOOK AS UNCOMFORTABLE AS I FEEL?
WAVE OF MUTILATION
PART 2:
SURRENDER TH

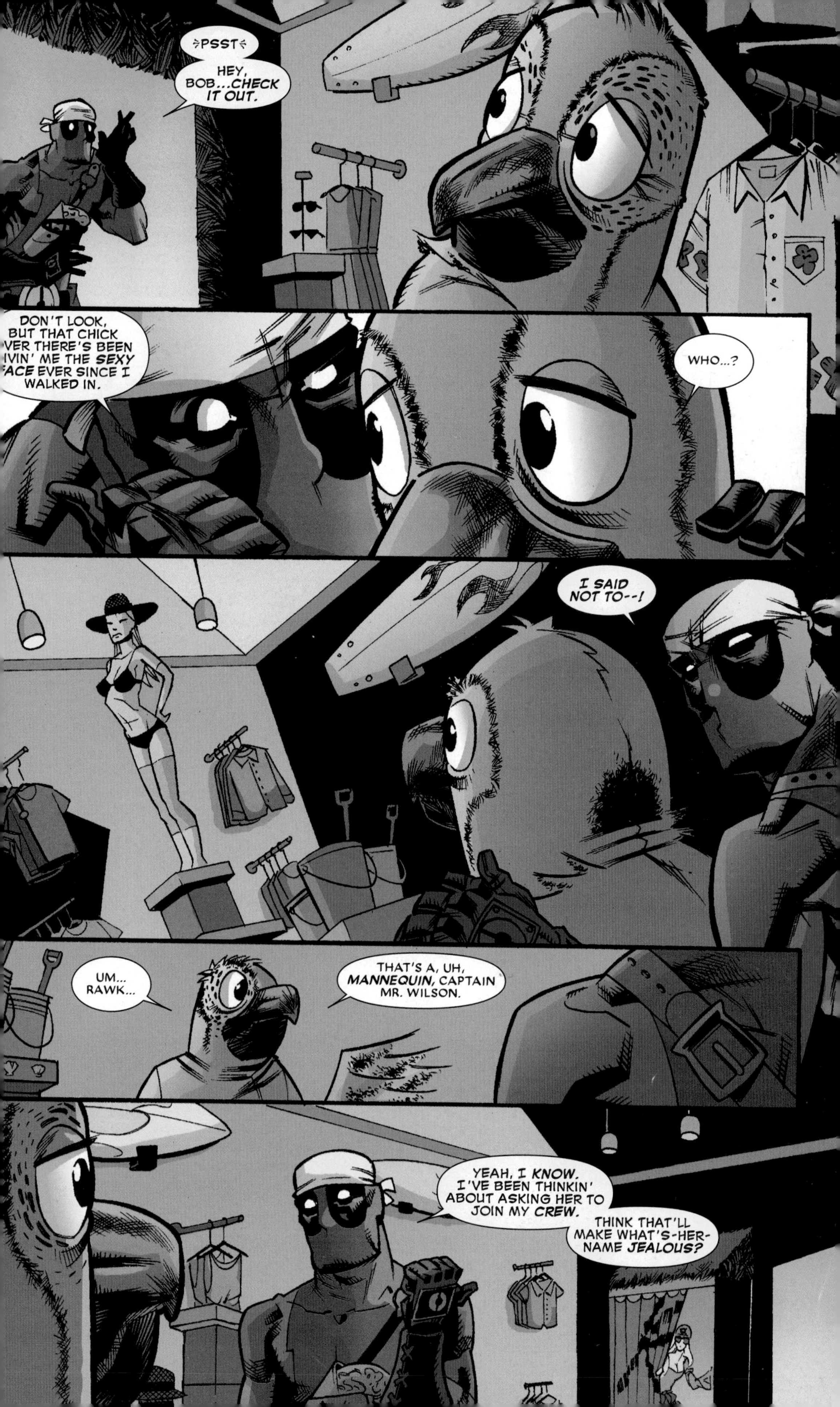

PSST
HEY, BOB...CHECK IT OUT.
DON'T LOOK, BUT THAT CHICK OVER THERE'S BEEN GIVIN' ME THE SEXY FACE EVER SINCE I WALKED IN.
WHO...?
I SAID NOT TO--!
UM... RAWK...
THAT'S A, UH, MANNEQUIN, CAPTAIN MR. WILSON.
YEAH, I KNOW. I'VE BEEN THINKIN' ABOUT ASKING HER TO JOIN MY CREW.
THINK THAT'LL MAKE WHAT'S-HER-NAME JEALOUS?

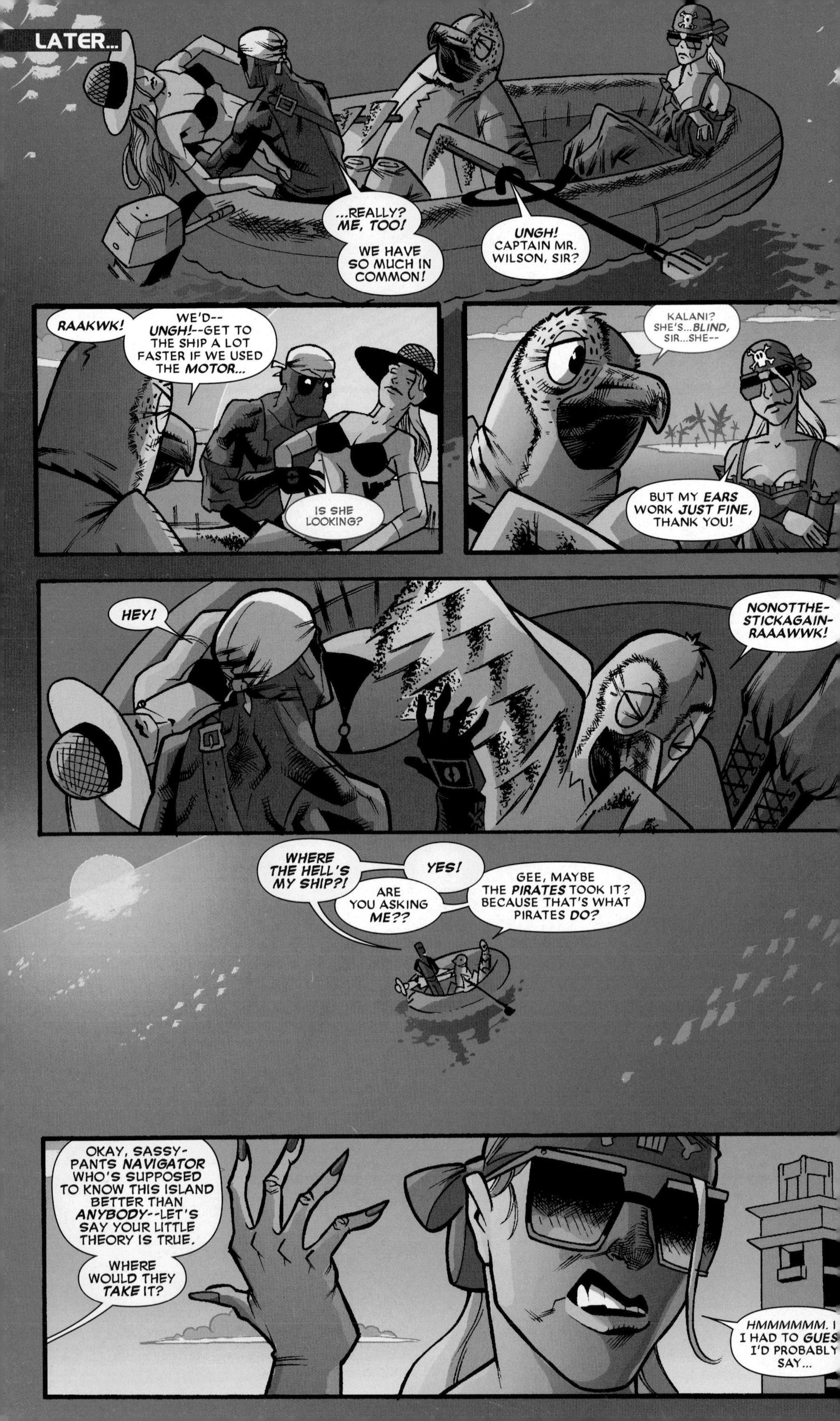
LATER...
...REALLY? ME, TOO!
WE HAVE SO MUCH IN COMMON!
UNGH! CAPTAIN MR. WILSON, SIR?
RAAKWK!
WE'D--UNGH!--GET TO THE SHIP A LOT FASTER IF WE USED THE MOTOR...
IS SHE LOOKING?
KALANI? SHE'S...BLIND, SIR...SHE--
BUT MY EARS WORK JUST FINE, THANK YOU!
HEY!
NONOTTHE-STICKAGAIN-RAAAWWK!
WHERE THE HELL'S MY SHIP?!
YES!
ARE YOU ASKING ME??
GEE, MAYBE THE PIRATES TOOK IT? BECAUSE THAT'S WHAT PIRATES DO?
OKAY, SASSY-PANTS NAVIGATOR WHO'S SUPPOSED TO KNOW THIS ISLAND BETTER THAN ANYBODY--LET'S SAY YOUR LITTLE THEORY IS TRUE.
WHERE WOULD THEY TAKE IT?
HMMMMMM. I I HAD TO GUES I'D PROBABLY SAY...

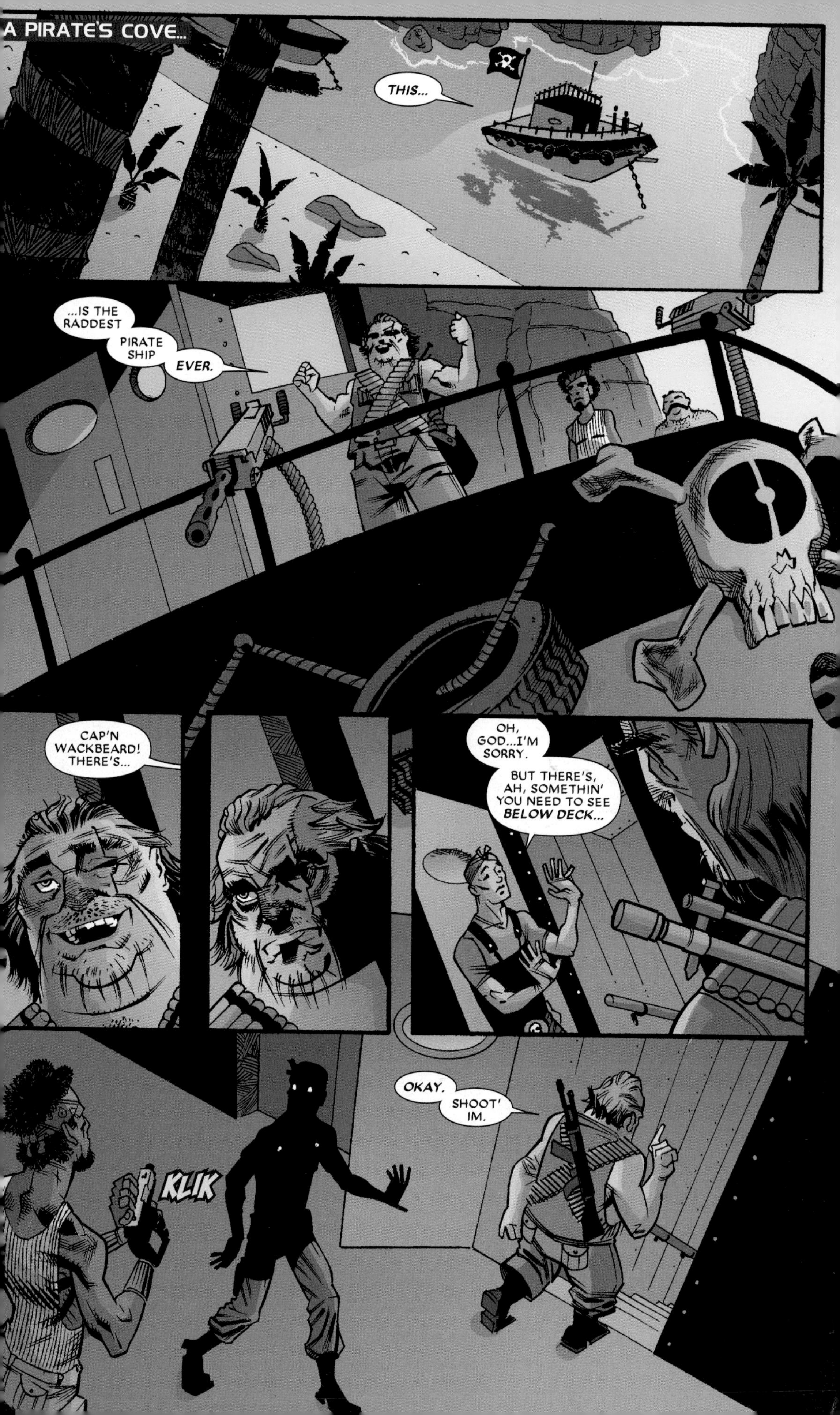
A PIRATE'S COVE...
THIS...
...IS THE RADDEST PIRATE SHIP EVER.
CAP'N WACKBEARD! THERE'S...
OH, GOD...I'M SORRY.
BUT THERE'S, AH, SOMETHIN' YOU NEED TO SEE BELOW DECK...
OKAY.
SHOOT' IM.
KLIK

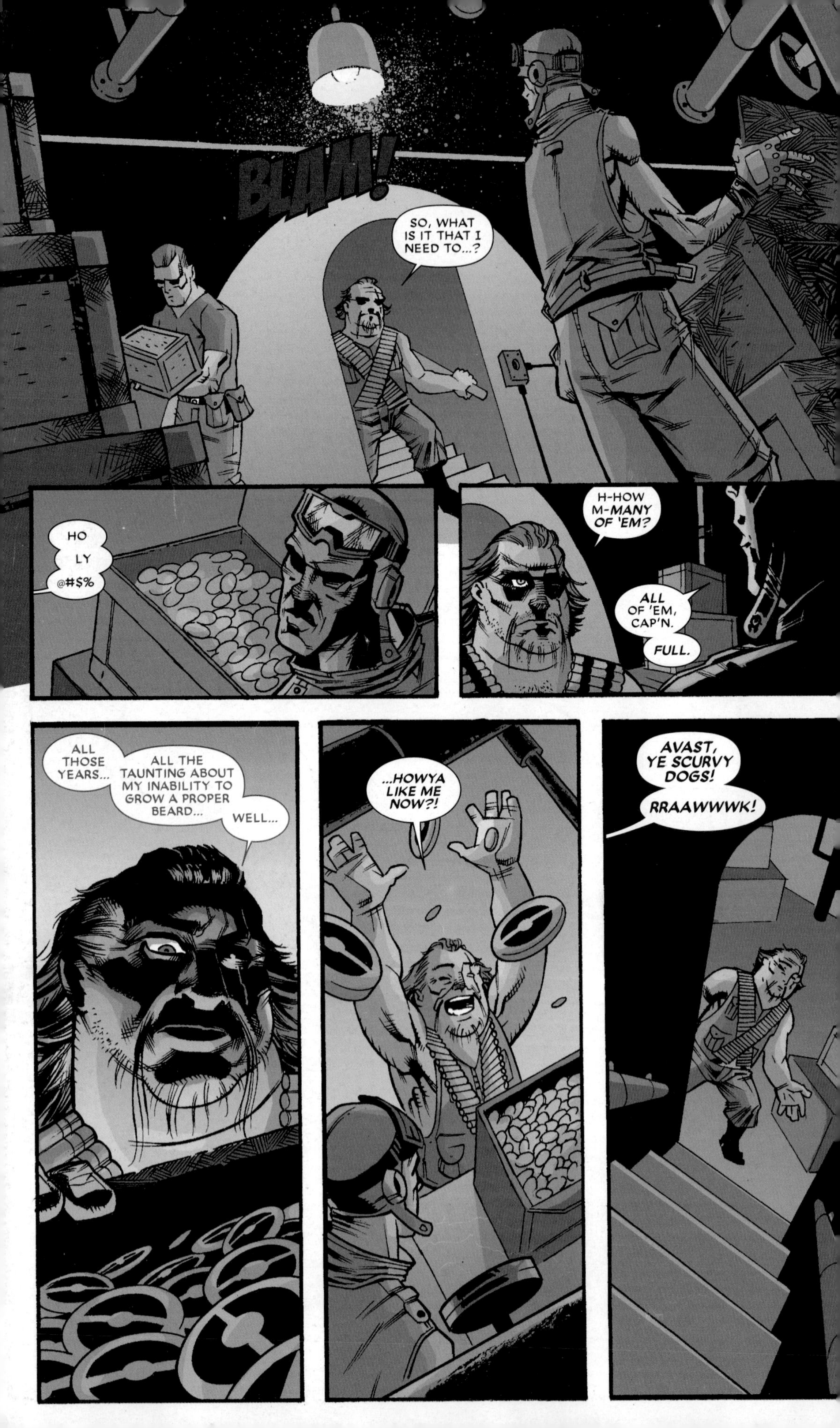
BLAM!
SO, WHAT IS IT THAT I NEED TO...?
HO
LY
@#$%
H-HOW M-MANY OF 'EM?
ALL OF 'EM, CAP'N.
FULL.
ALL THOSE YEARS...
ALL THE TAUNTING ABOUT MY INABILITY TO GROW A PROPER BEARD...
WELL...
...HOWYA LIKE ME NOW?!
AVAST, YE SCURVY DOGS!
RRAAWWWK!

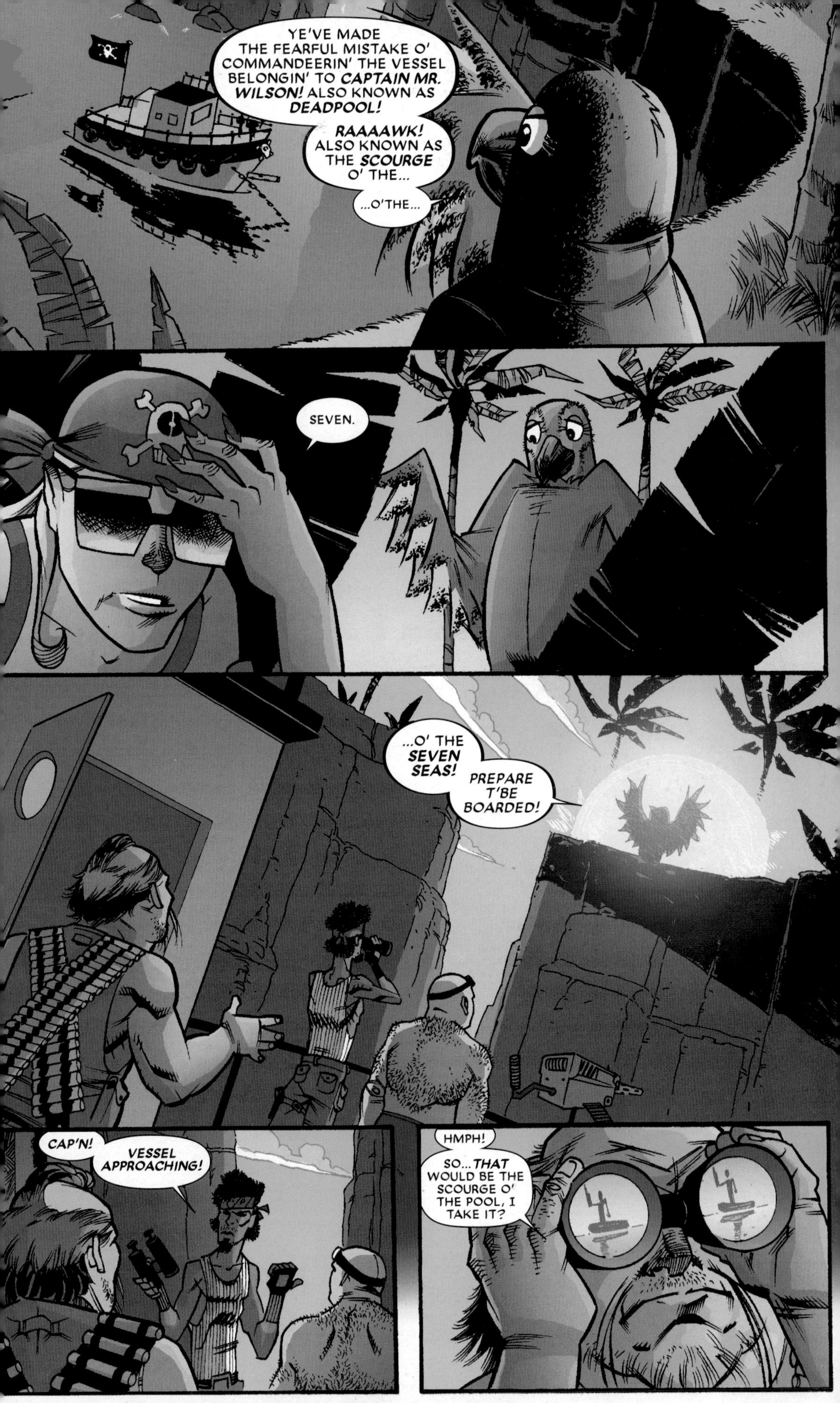
YE'VE MADE THE FEARFUL MISTAKE O' COMMANDEERIN' THE VESSEL BELONGIN' TO CAPTAIN MR. WILSON! ALSO KNOWN AS DEADPOOL!
RAAAAWK! ALSO KNOWN AS THE SCOURGE O' THE...
...O'THE...
SEVEN.
...O' THE SEVEN SEAS!
PREPARE T'BE BOARDED!
CAP'N!
VESSEL APPROACHING!
HMPH!
SO...THAT WOULD BE THE SCOURGE O' THE POOL, I TAKE IT?

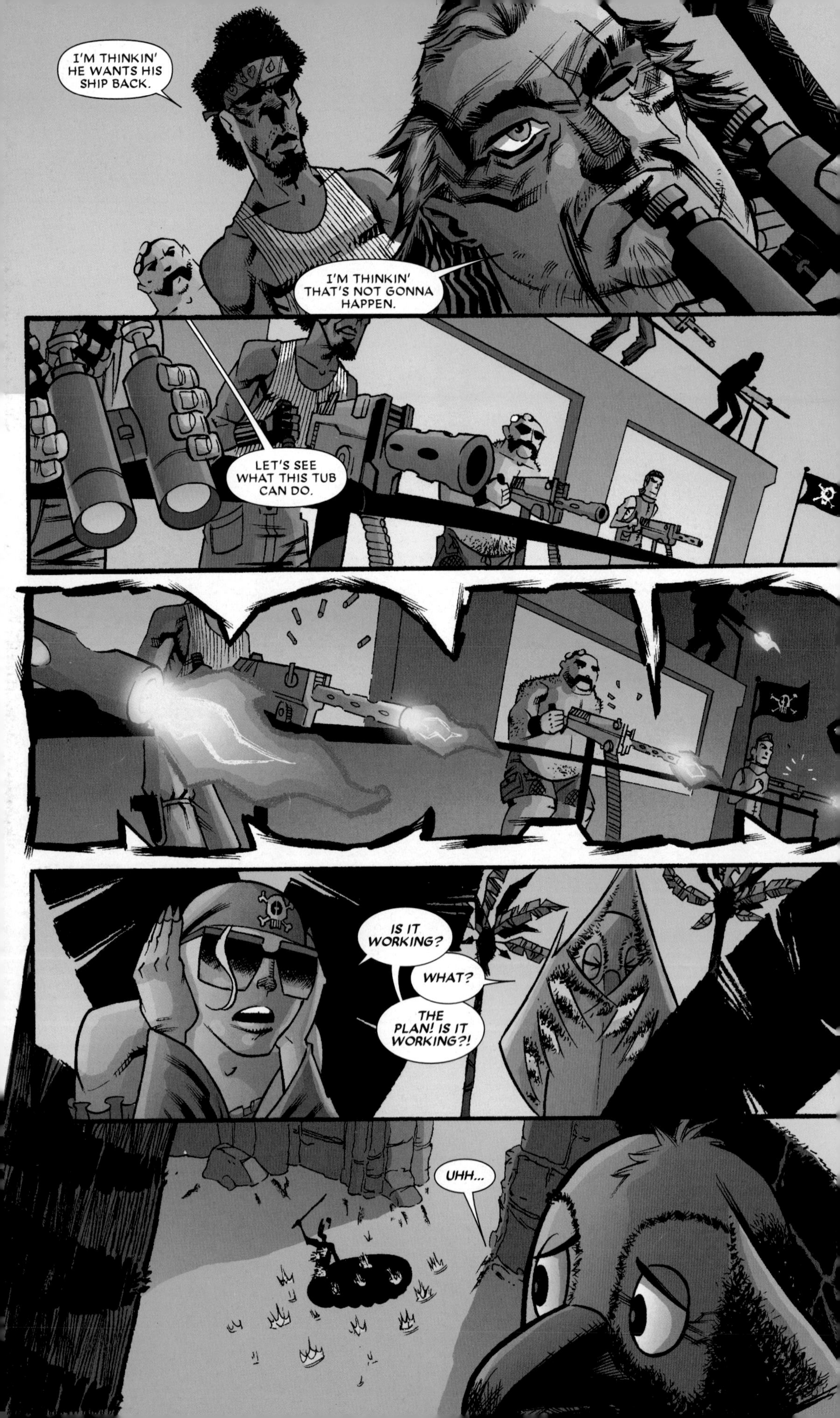
I'M THINKIN' HE WANTS HIS SHIP BACK.
I'M THINKIN' THAT'S NOT GONNA HAPPEN.
LET'S SEE WHAT THIS TUB CAN DO.
IS IT WORKING?
WHAT?
THE PLAN! IS IT WORKING?!
UHH...

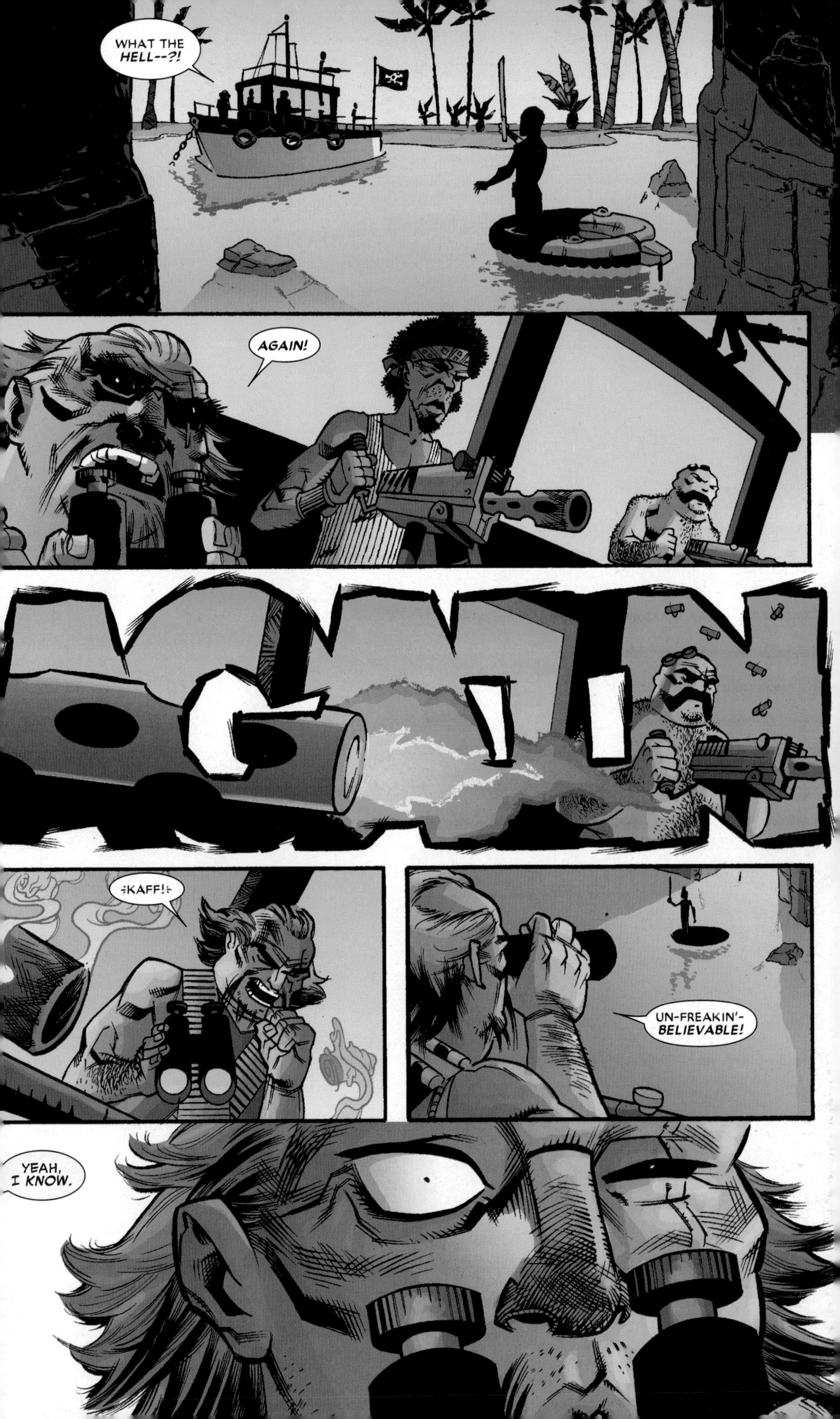
WHAT THE HELL--?!
AGAIN!
=KAFF!=
UN-FREAKIN'-BELIEVABLE!
YEAH, I KNOW.

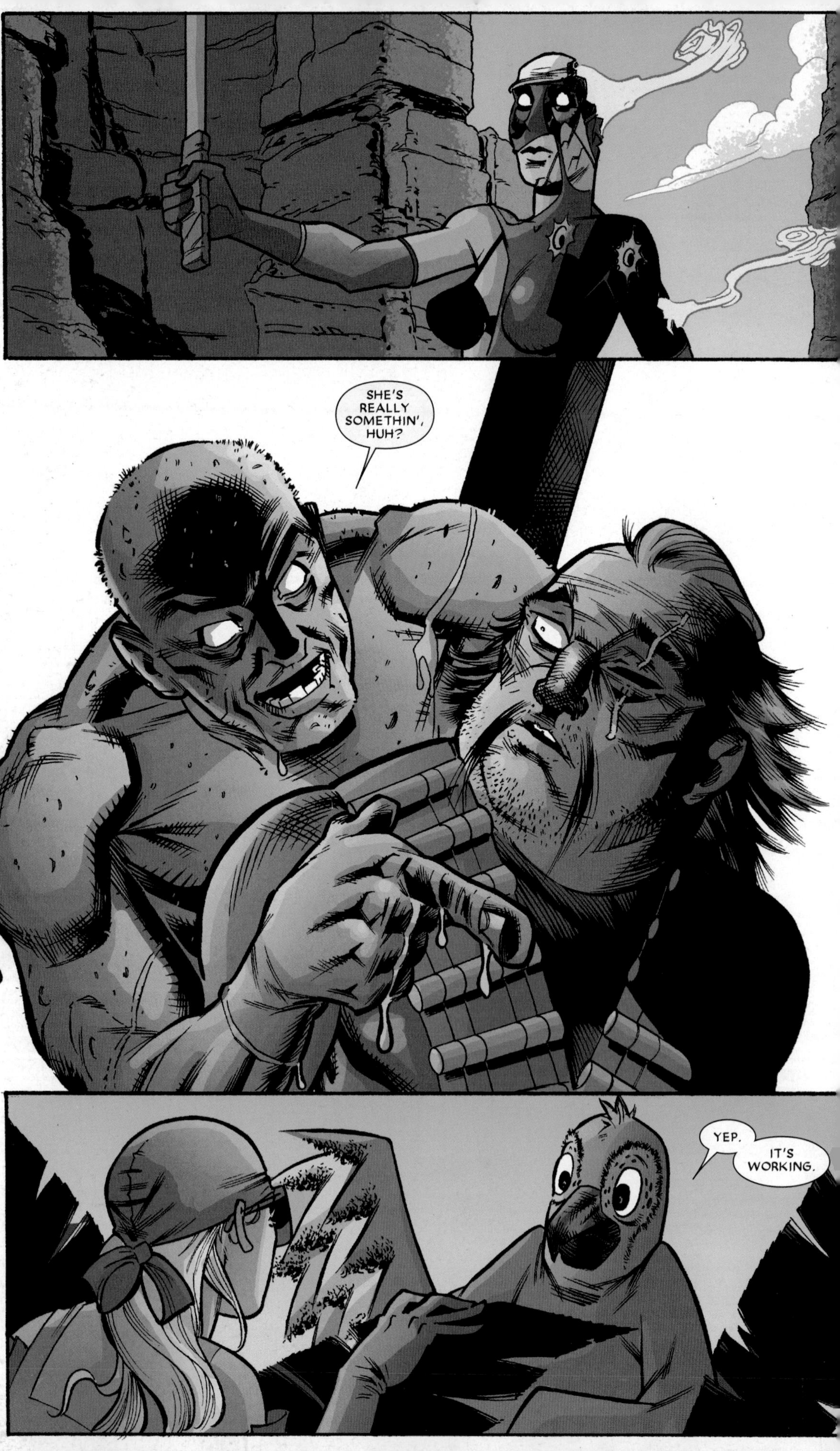
SHE'S REALLY SOMETHIN', HUH?
YEP.
IT'S WORKING.

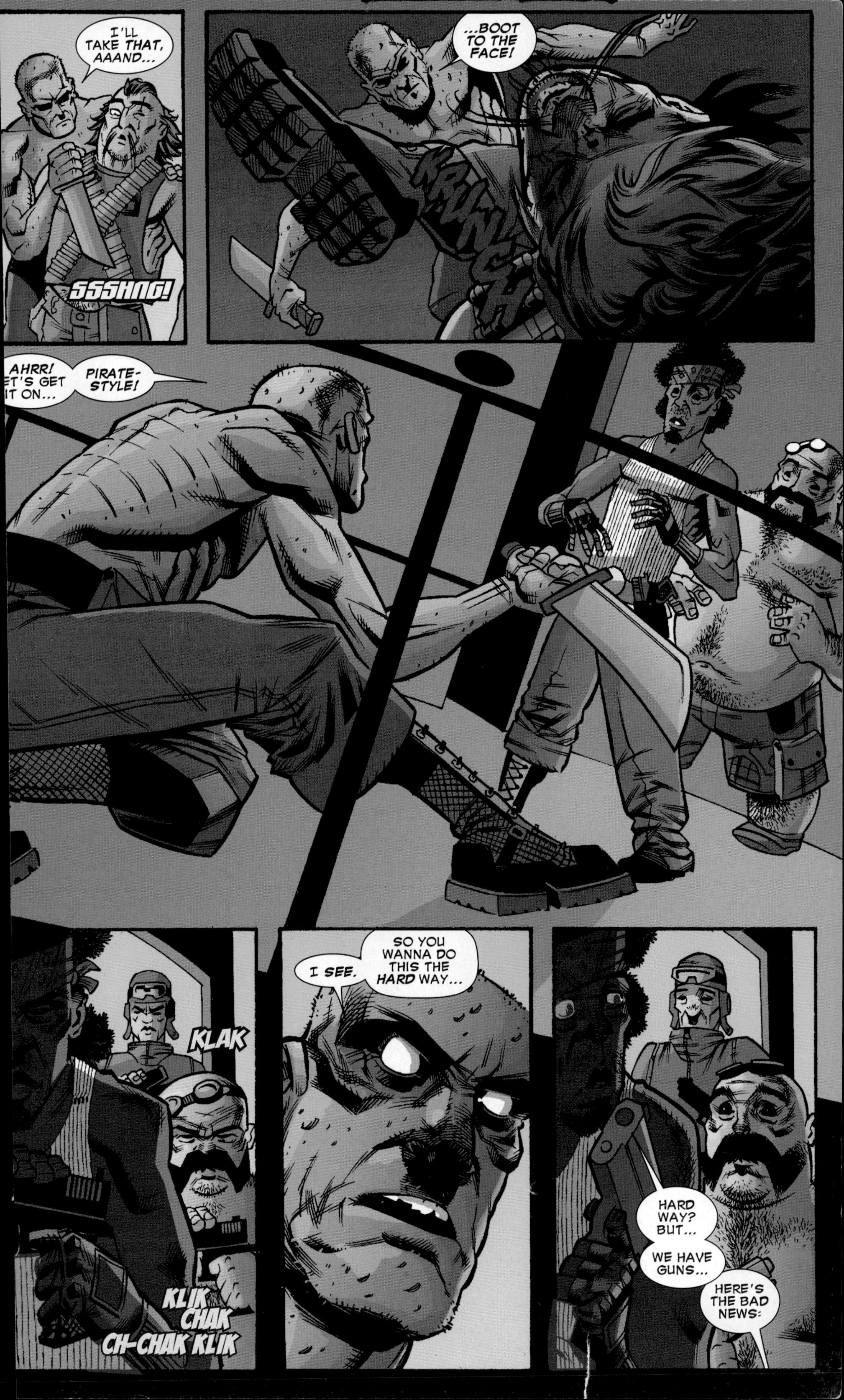

I'LL TAKE THAT, AAAND...
SSSHNG!
...BOOT TO THE FACE!
KRUNCH
AHRR! LET'S GET IT ON...
PIRATE-STYLE!
KLAK
KLIK
CHAK
CH-CHAK KLIK
I SEE.
SO YOU WANNA DO THIS THE HARD WAY...
HARD WAY? BUT...
WE HAVE GUNS...
HERE'S THE BAD NEWS:

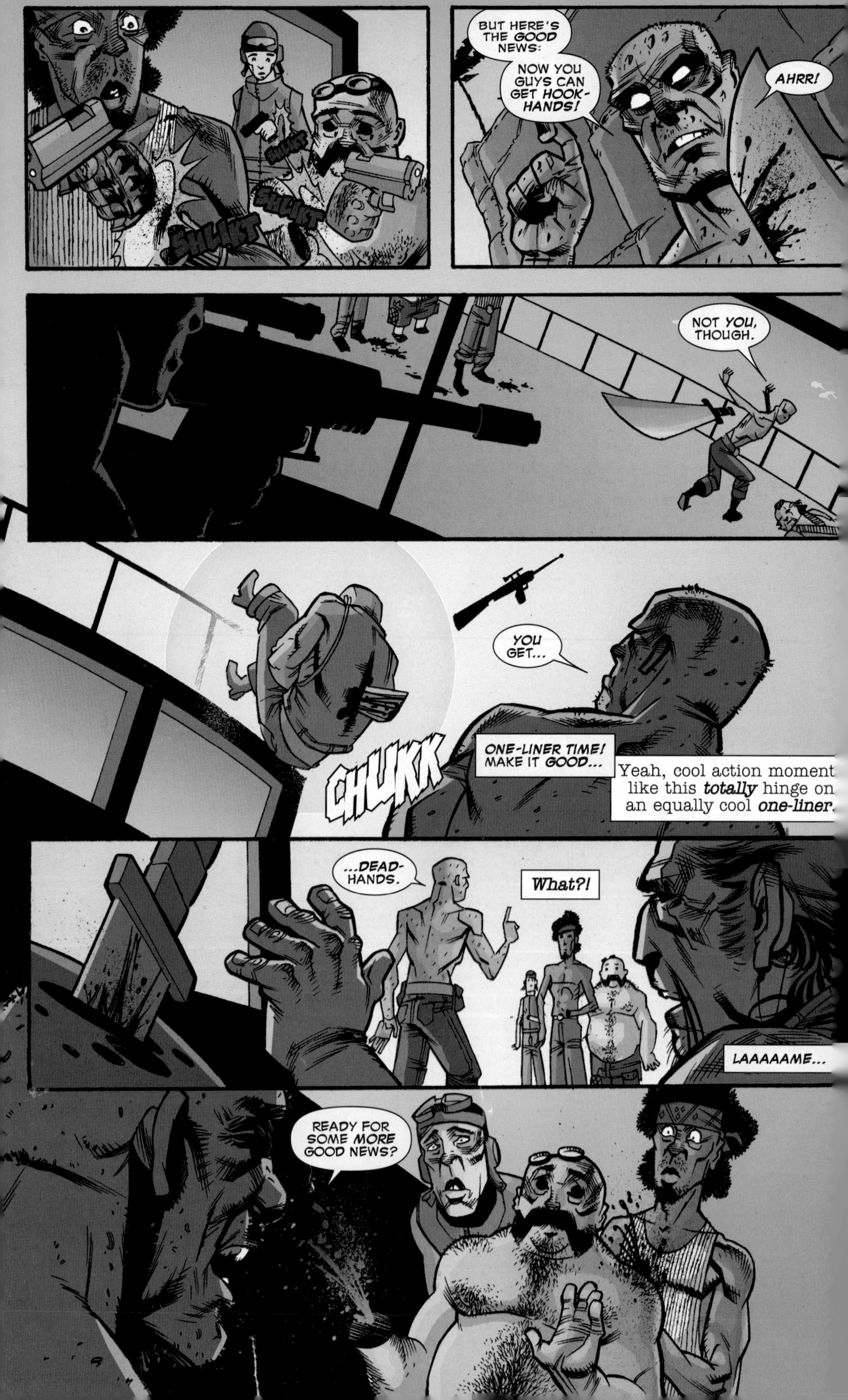

SHUKT
SHUKT
SHUKT
SHUKT
BUT HERE'S THE *GOOD* NEWS:
NOW YOU GUYS CAN GET *HOOK-HANDS!*
*AHRR!*
NOT *YOU,* THOUGH.
*YOU GET...*
CHUKK
*ONE-LINER TIME! MAKE IT GOOD...*
Yeah, cool action moment like this ***totally*** hinge on an equally cool ***one-liner.***
*...DEAD-HANDS.*
*What?!*
*LAAAAAME...*
READY FOR SOME *MORE* GOOD NEWS?

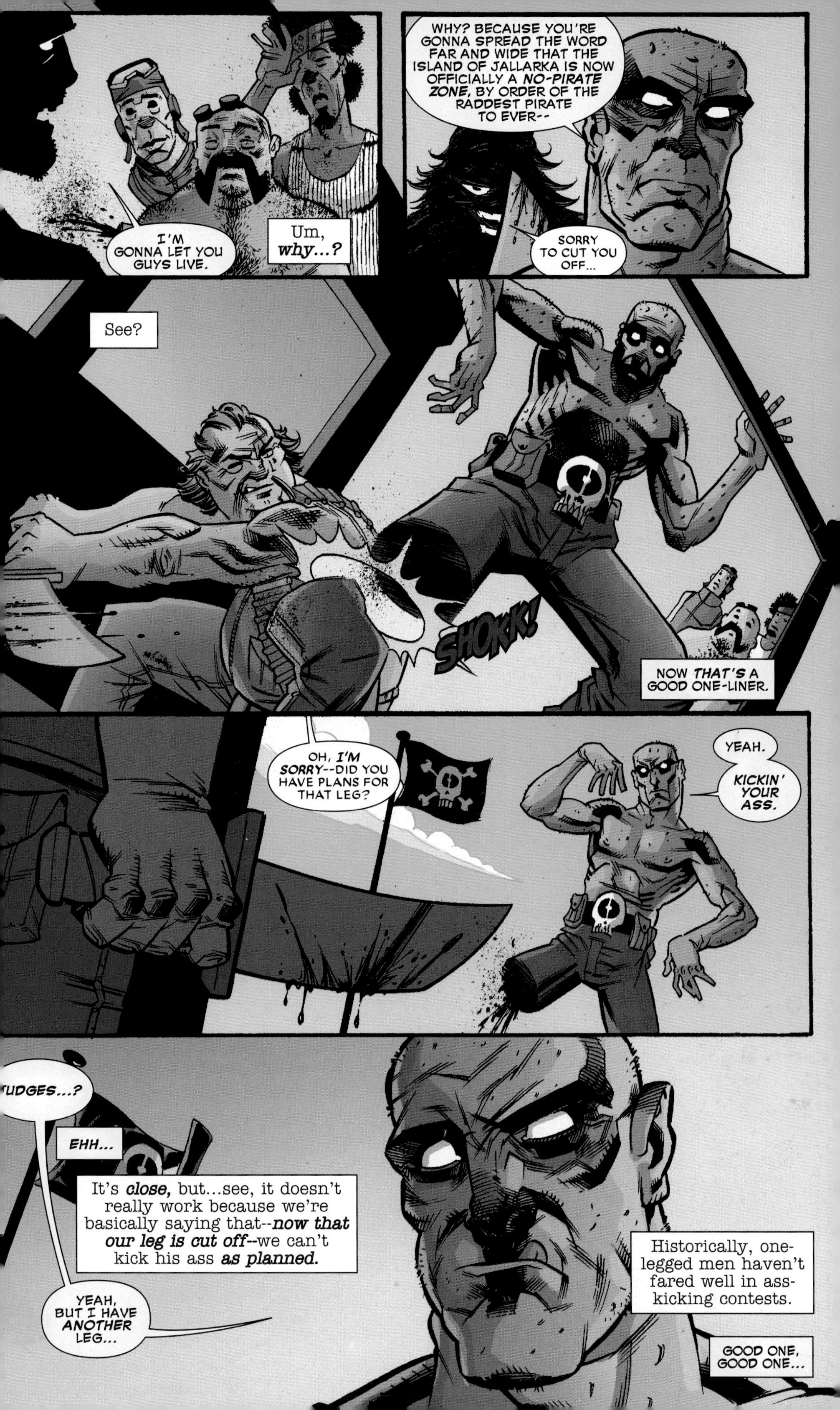

I'M GONNA LET YOU GUYS LIVE.
Um, why...?
WHY? BECAUSE YOU'RE GONNA SPREAD THE WORD FAR AND WIDE THAT THE ISLAND OF JALLARKA IS NOW OFFICIALLY A NO-PIRATE ZONE, BY ORDER OF THE RADDEST PIRATE TO EVER--
SORRY TO CUT YOU OFF...
See?
SHOKK!
NOW THAT'S A GOOD ONE-LINER.
OH, I'M SORRY--DID YOU HAVE PLANS FOR THAT LEG?
YEAH.
KICKIN' YOUR ASS.
UDGES...?
EHH...
It's close, but...see, it doesn't really work because we're basically saying that--now that our leg is cut off--we can't kick his ass as planned.
YEAH, BUT I HAVE ANOTHER LEG...
Historically, one-legged men haven't fared well in ass-kicking contests.
GOOD ONE, GOOD ONE...

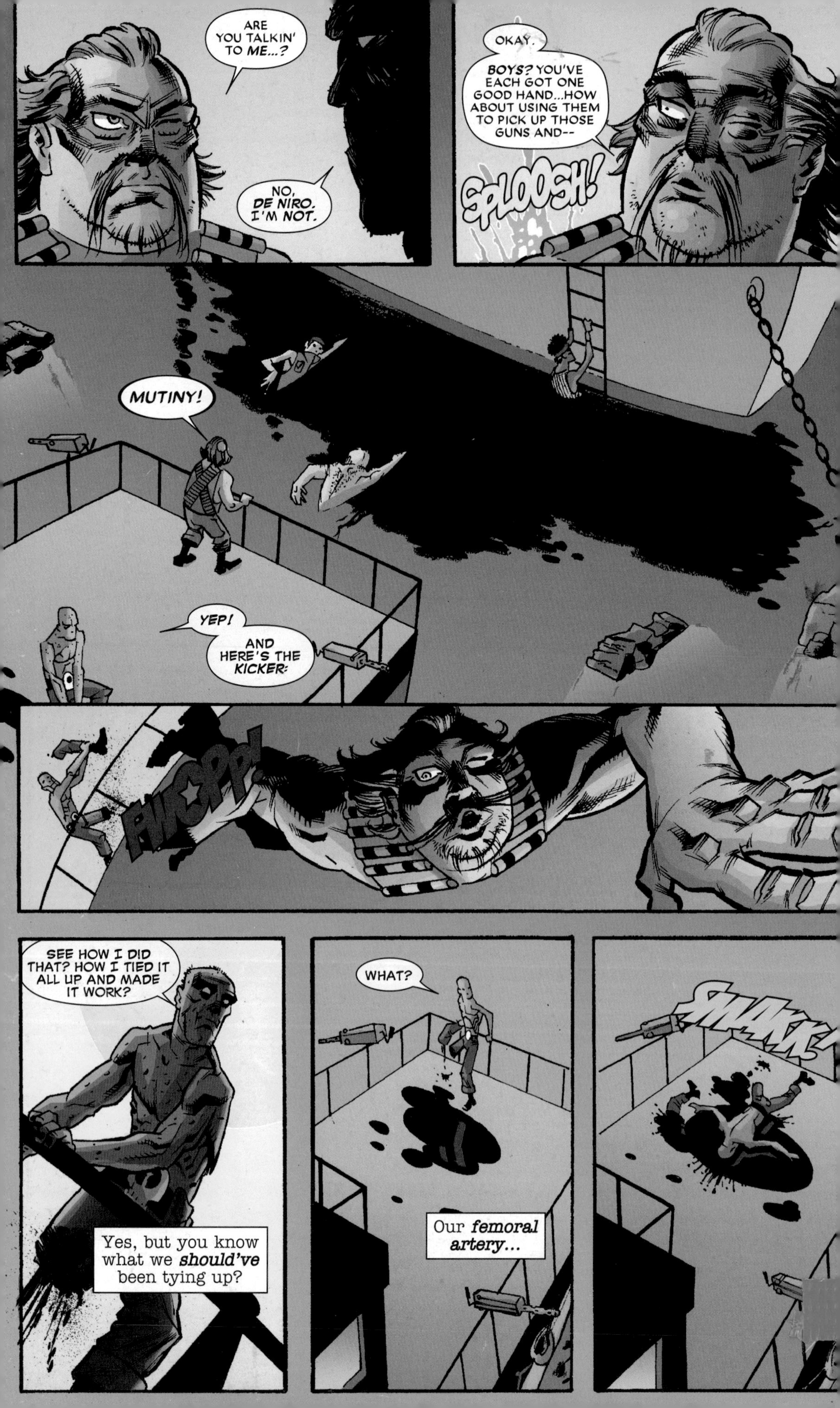

ARE YOU TALKIN' TO *ME*...?
NO, *DE NIRO.* I'M *NOT.*
OKAY.
*BOYS?* YOU'VE EACH GOT ONE GOOD HAND...HOW ABOUT USING THEM TO PICK UP THOSE GUNS AND--
SPLOOSH!
*MUTINY!*
*YEP!*
AND HERE'S THE *KICKER:*
FWOPP!
SEE HOW I DID THAT? HOW I TIED IT ALL UP AND MADE IT WORK?
Yes, but you know what we ***should've*** been tying up?
WHAT?
Our ***femoral artery***...
SMAKK!

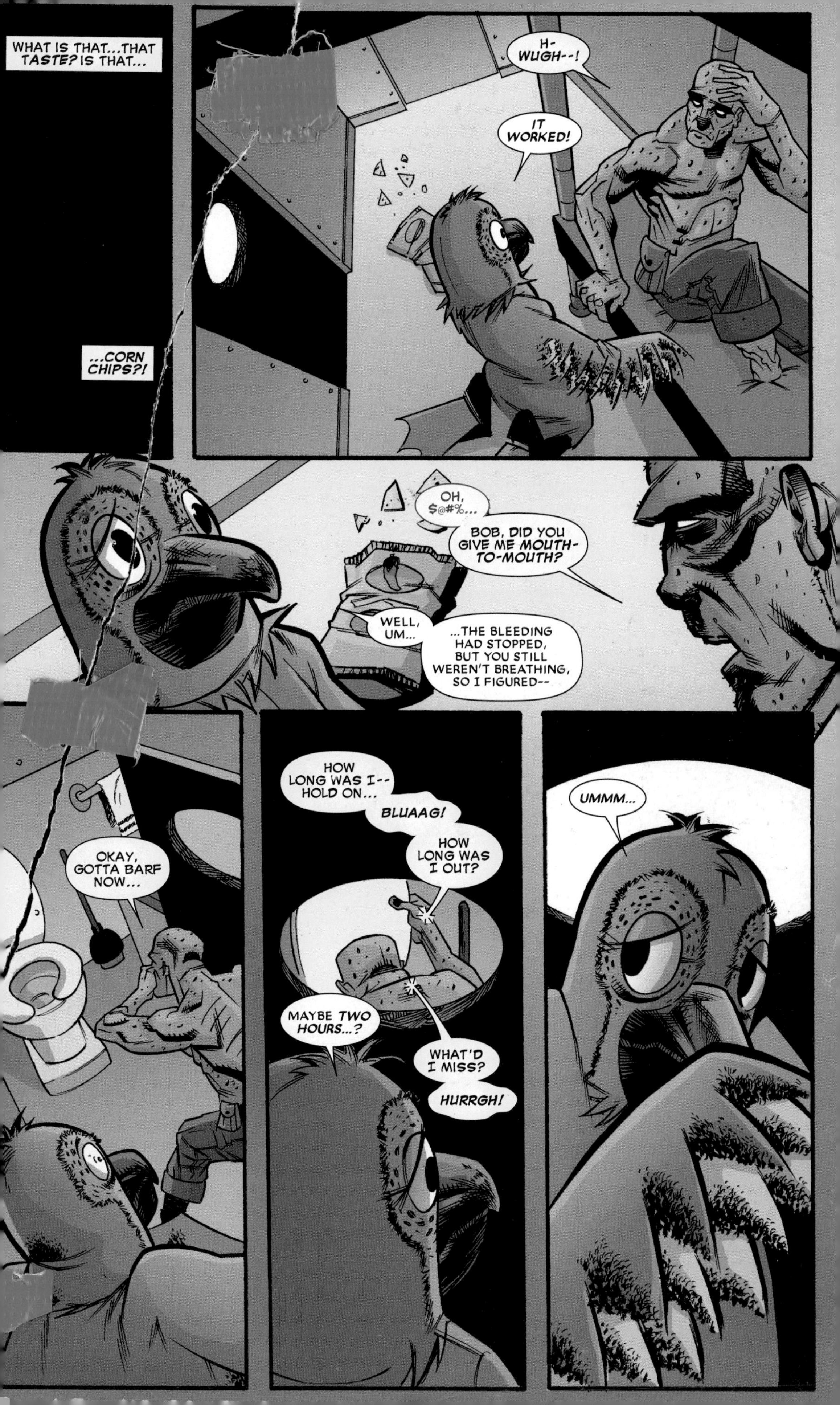
WHAT IS THAT...THAT TASTE? IS THAT...
...CORN CHIPS?!
H-WUGH--!
IT WORKED!
OH, $@#%...
BOB, DID YOU GIVE ME MOUTH-TO-MOUTH?
WELL, UM...
...THE BLEEDING HAD STOPPED, BUT YOU STILL WEREN'T BREATHING, SO I FIGURED--
OKAY, GOTTA BARF NOW...
HOW LONG WAS I-- HOLD ON...
BLUAAG!
HOW LONG WAS I OUT?
MAYBE TWO HOURS...?
WHAT'D I MISS?
HURRGH!
UMMM...

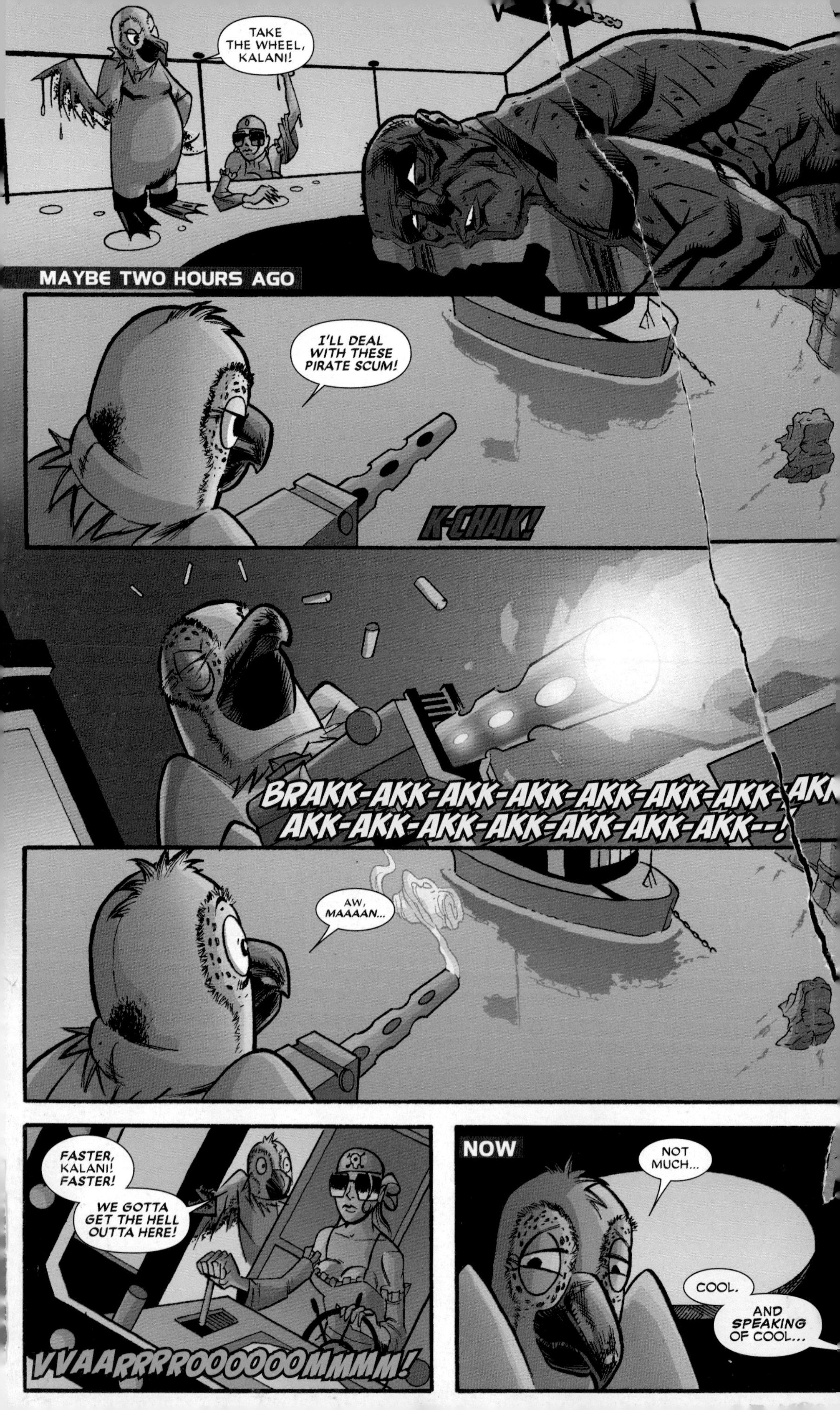

TAKE THE WHEEL, KALANI!
MAYBE TWO HOURS AGO
I'LL DEAL WITH THESE PIRATE SCUM!
K-CHAK!
BRAKK-AKK-AKK-AKK-AKK-AKK-AKK-AKK-AKK-AKK-AKK-AKK-AKK-AKK-AKK--!
AW, MAAAAN...
FASTER, KALANI! FASTER!
WE GOTTA GET THE HELL OUTTA HERE!
VVAARRRROOOOOOMMMMM!
NOW
NOT MUCH...
COOL.
AND SPEAKING OF COOL...

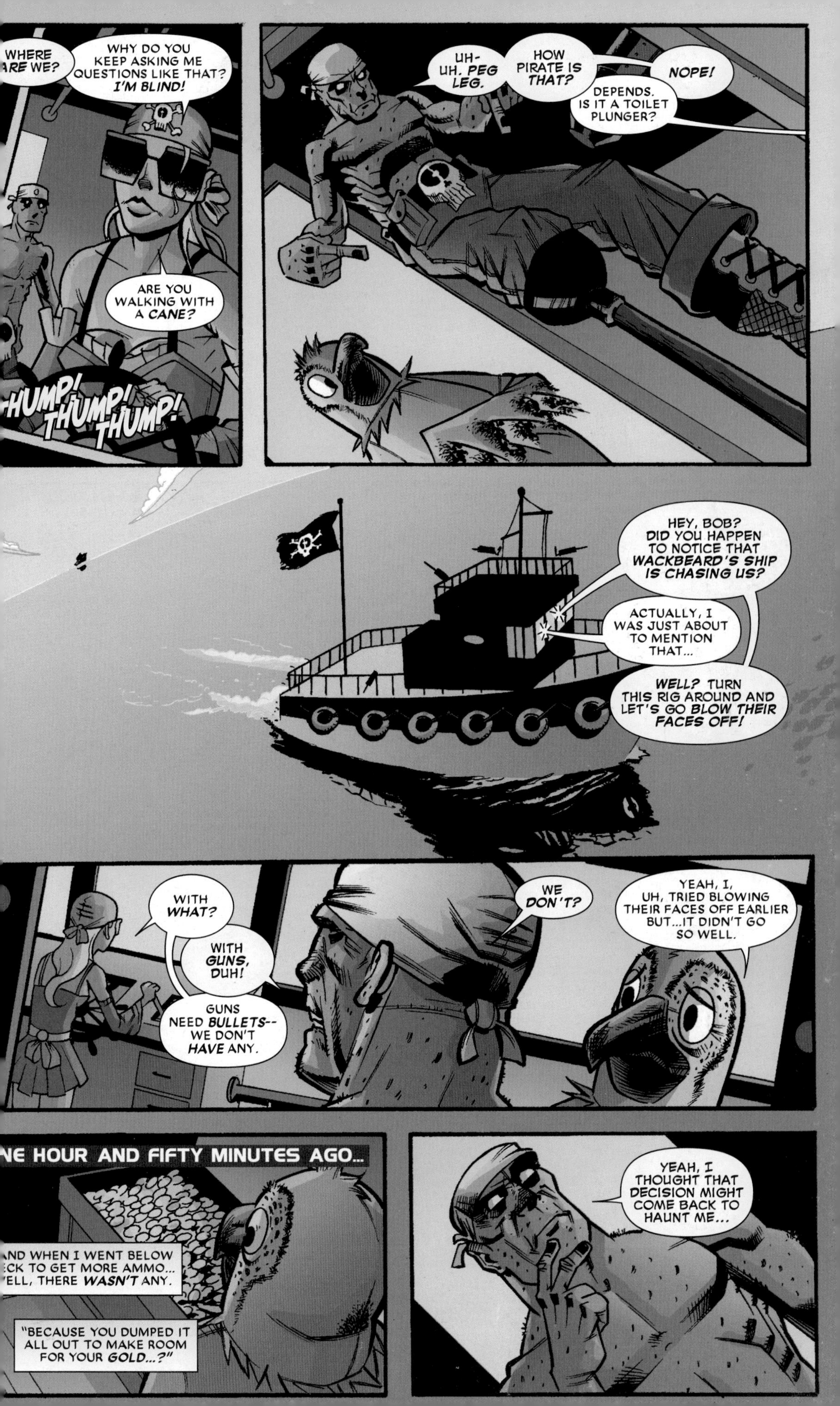
WHERE ARE WE?
WHY DO YOU KEEP ASKING ME QUESTIONS LIKE THAT? I'M BLIND!
ARE YOU WALKING WITH A CANE?
HUMP! THUMP! THUMP!
UH-UH. PEG LEG.
HOW PIRATE IS THAT?
NOPE!
DEPENDS. IS IT A TOILET PLUNGER?
HEY, BOB? DID YOU HAPPEN TO NOTICE THAT WACKBEARD'S SHIP IS CHASING US?
ACTUALLY, I WAS JUST ABOUT TO MENTION THAT...
WELL? TURN THIS RIG AROUND AND LET'S GO BLOW THEIR FACES OFF!
WITH WHAT?
WITH GUNS, DUH!
GUNS NEED BULLETS-- WE DON'T HAVE ANY.
WE DON'T?
YEAH, I, UH, TRIED BLOWING THEIR FACES OFF EARLIER BUT...IT DIDN'T GO SO WELL.
NE HOUR AND FIFTY MINUTES AGO...
ND WHEN I WENT BELOW CK TO GET MORE AMMO... ELL, THERE WASN'T ANY.
"BECAUSE YOU DUMPED IT ALL OUT TO MAKE ROOM FOR YOUR GOLD...?"
YEAH, I THOUGHT THAT DECISION MIGHT COME BACK TO HAUNT ME...

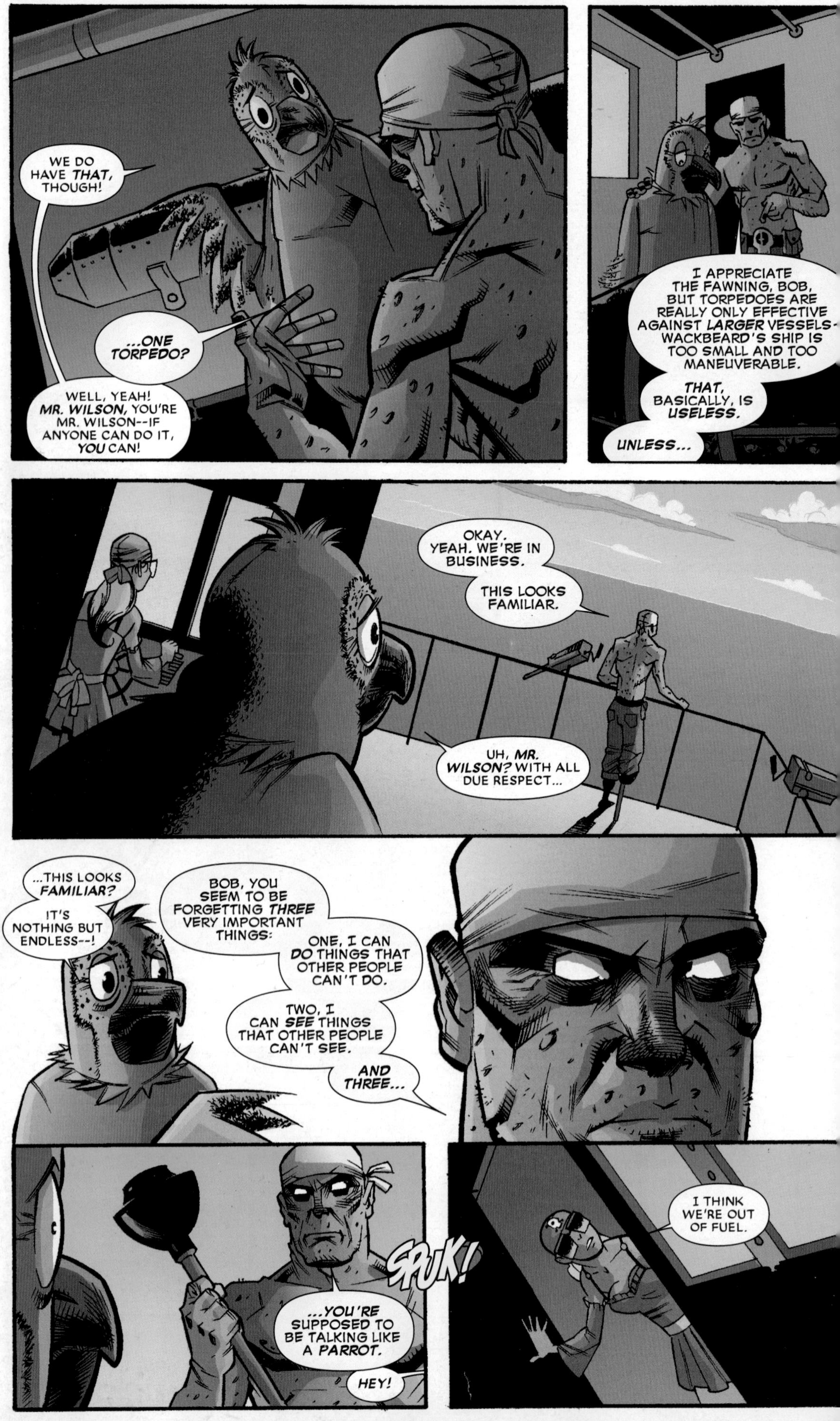
WE DO HAVE THAT, THOUGH!
...ONE TORPEDO?
WELL, YEAH! MR. WILSON, YOU'RE MR. WILSON--IF ANYONE CAN DO IT, YOU CAN!
I APPRECIATE THE FAWNING, BOB, BUT TORPEDOES ARE REALLY ONLY EFFECTIVE AGAINST LARGER VESSELS-WACKBEARD'S SHIP IS TOO SMALL AND TOO MANEUVERABLE.
THAT, BASICALLY, IS USELESS.
UNLESS...
OKAY. YEAH. WE'RE IN BUSINESS.
THIS LOOKS FAMILIAR.
UH, MR. WILSON? WITH ALL DUE RESPECT...
...THIS LOOKS FAMILIAR?
IT'S NOTHING BUT ENDLESS--!
BOB, YOU SEEM TO BE FORGETTING THREE VERY IMPORTANT THINGS:
ONE, I CAN DO THINGS THAT OTHER PEOPLE CAN'T DO.
TWO, I CAN SEE THINGS THAT OTHER PEOPLE CAN'T SEE.
AND THREE...
SPUK!
...YOU'RE SUPPOSED TO BE TALKING LIKE A PARROT.
HEY!
I THINK WE'RE OUT OF FUEL.

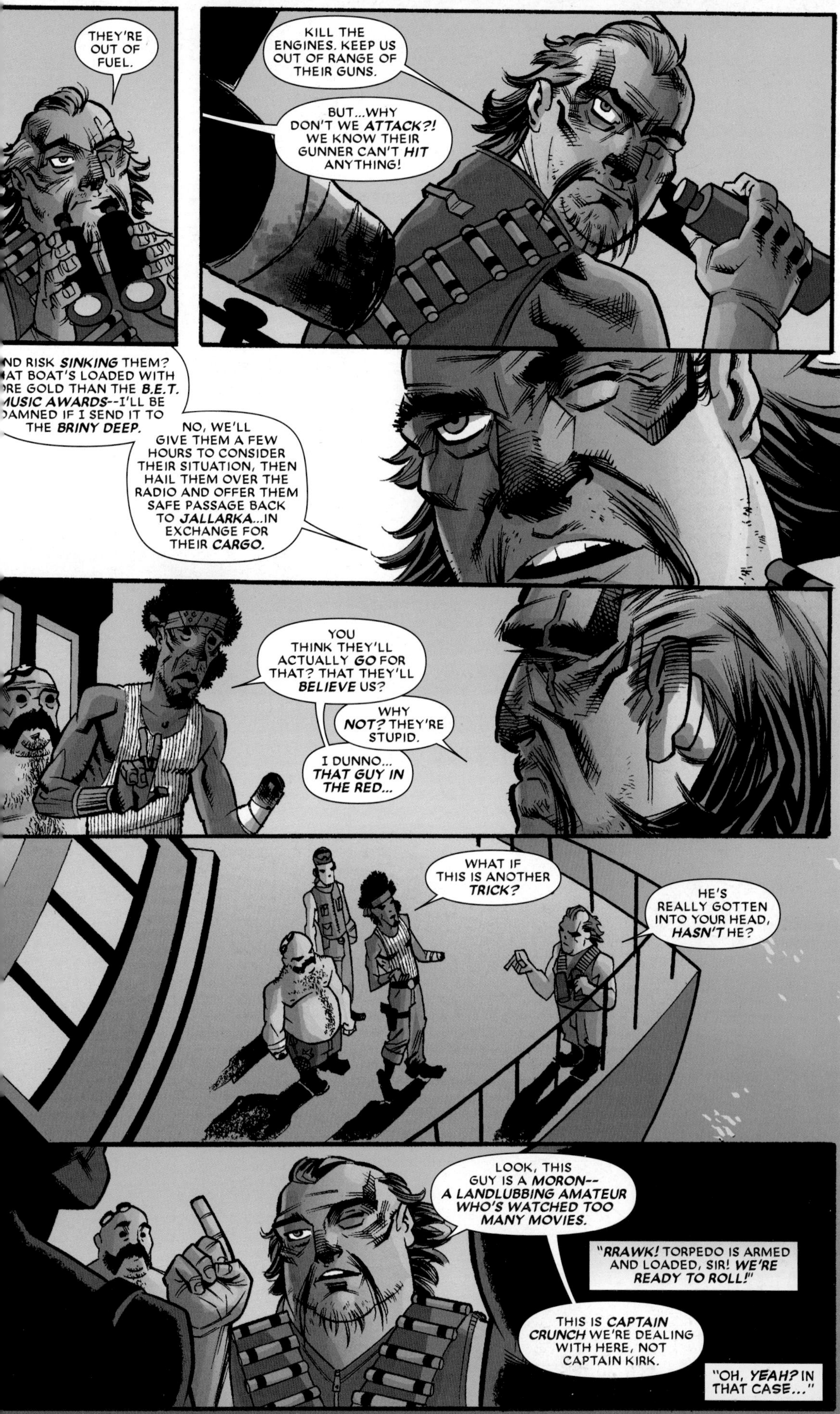

THEY'RE OUT OF FUEL.
KILL THE ENGINES. KEEP US OUT OF RANGE OF THEIR GUNS.
BUT...WHY DON'T WE ATTACK?! WE KNOW THEIR GUNNER CAN'T HIT ANYTHING!
ND RISK SINKING THEM? AT BOAT'S LOADED WITH RE GOLD THAN THE B.E.T. MUSIC AWARDS--I'LL BE DAMNED IF I SEND IT TO THE BRINY DEEP.
NO, WE'LL GIVE THEM A FEW HOURS TO CONSIDER THEIR SITUATION, THEN HAIL THEM OVER THE RADIO AND OFFER THEM SAFE PASSAGE BACK TO JALLARKA...IN EXCHANGE FOR THEIR CARGO.
YOU THINK THEY'LL ACTUALLY GO FOR THAT? THAT THEY'LL BELIEVE US?
WHY NOT? THEY'RE STUPID.
I DUNNO... THAT GUY IN THE RED...
WHAT IF THIS IS ANOTHER TRICK?
HE'S REALLY GOTTEN INTO YOUR HEAD, HASN'T HE?
LOOK, THIS GUY IS A MORON-- A LANDLUBBING AMATEUR WHO'S WATCHED TOO MANY MOVIES.
"RRAWK! TORPEDO IS ARMED AND LOADED, SIR! WE'RE READY TO ROLL!"
THIS IS CAPTAIN CRUNCH WE'RE DEALING WITH HERE, NOT CAPTAIN KIRK.
"OH, YEAH? IN THAT CASE..."

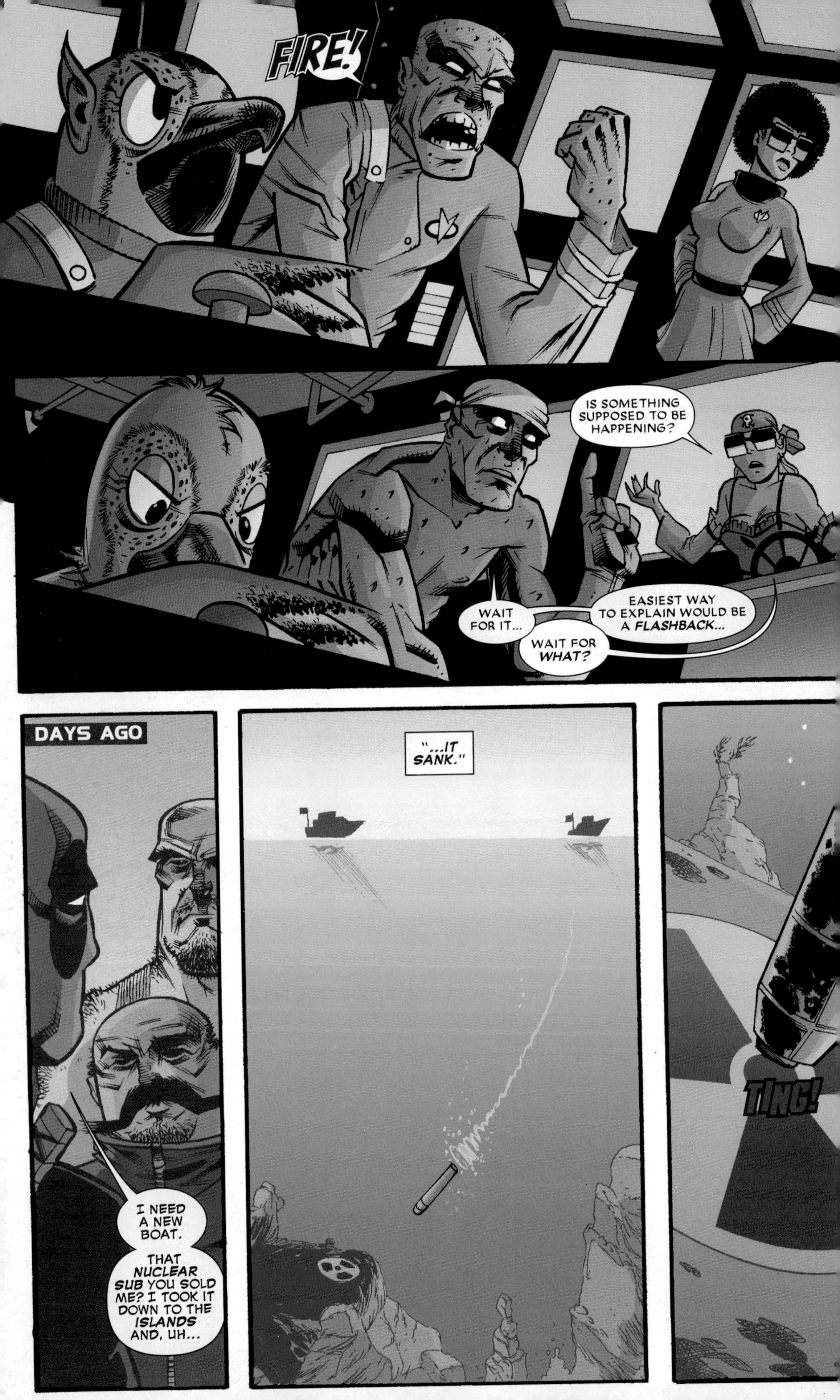

FIRE!
IS SOMETHING SUPPOSED TO BE HAPPENING?
WAIT FOR IT...
EASIEST WAY TO EXPLAIN WOULD BE A FLASHBACK...
WAIT FOR WHAT?
DAYS AGO
I NEED A NEW BOAT.
THAT NUCLEAR SUB YOU SOLD ME? I TOOK IT DOWN TO THE ISLANDS AND, UH...
"...IT SANK."
TING!

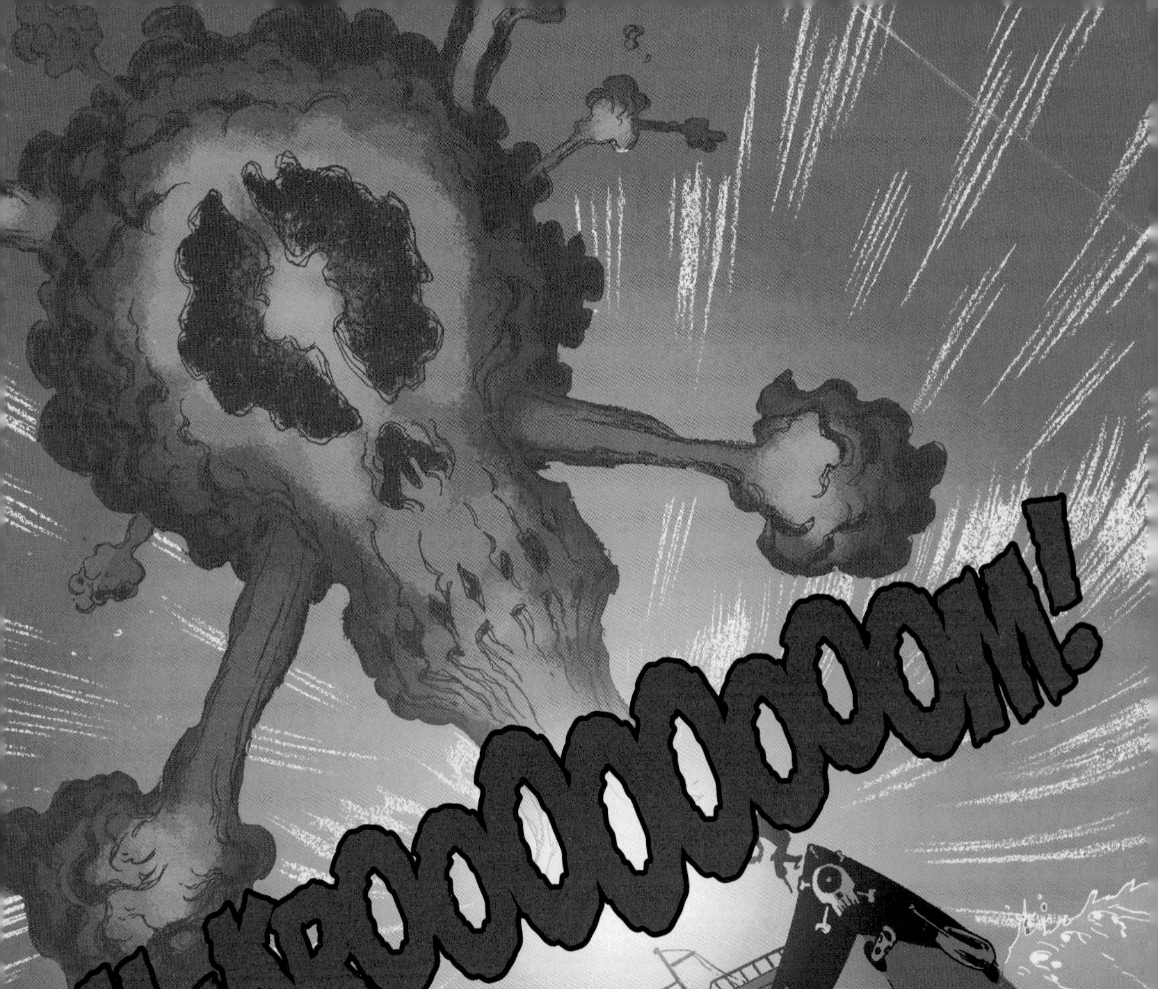
WAH-KROOOOOOOOOM!

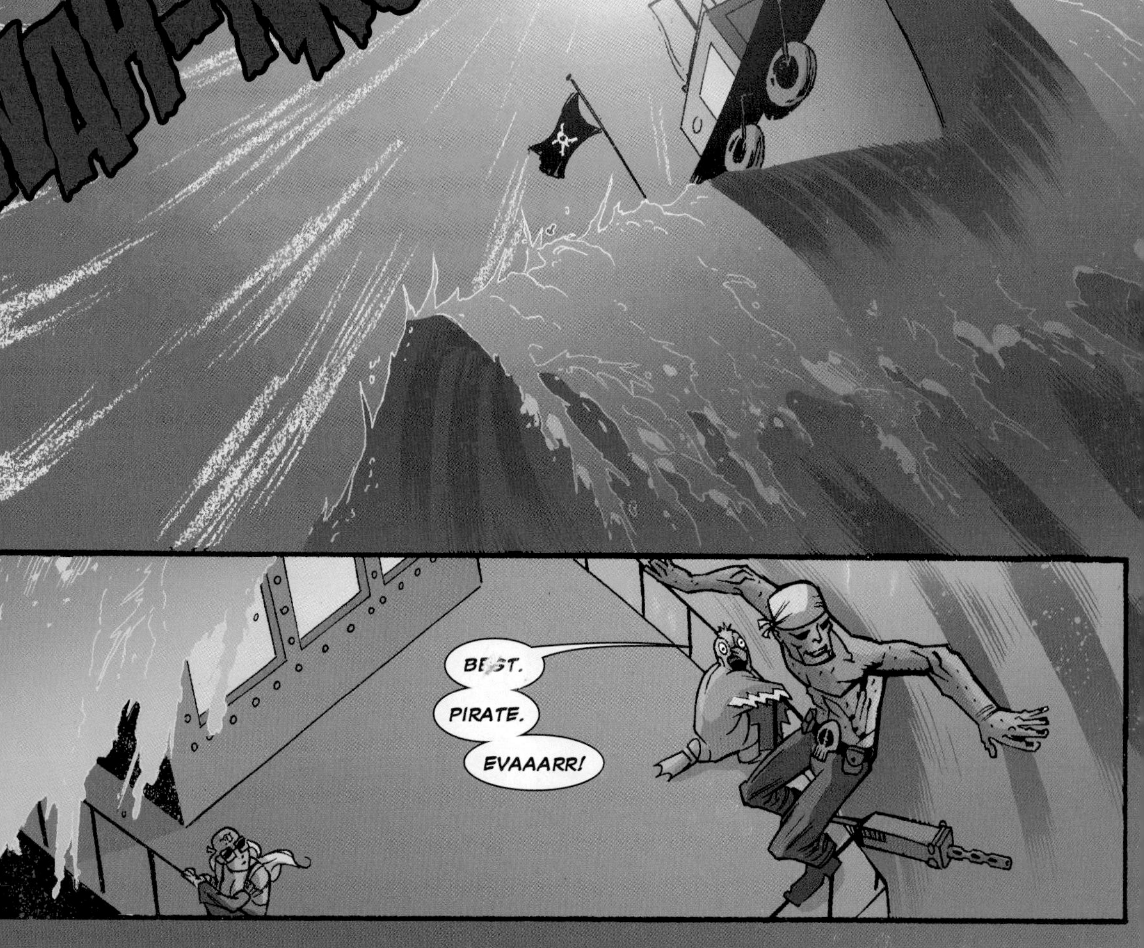
BEST.
PIRATE.
EVAAARR!

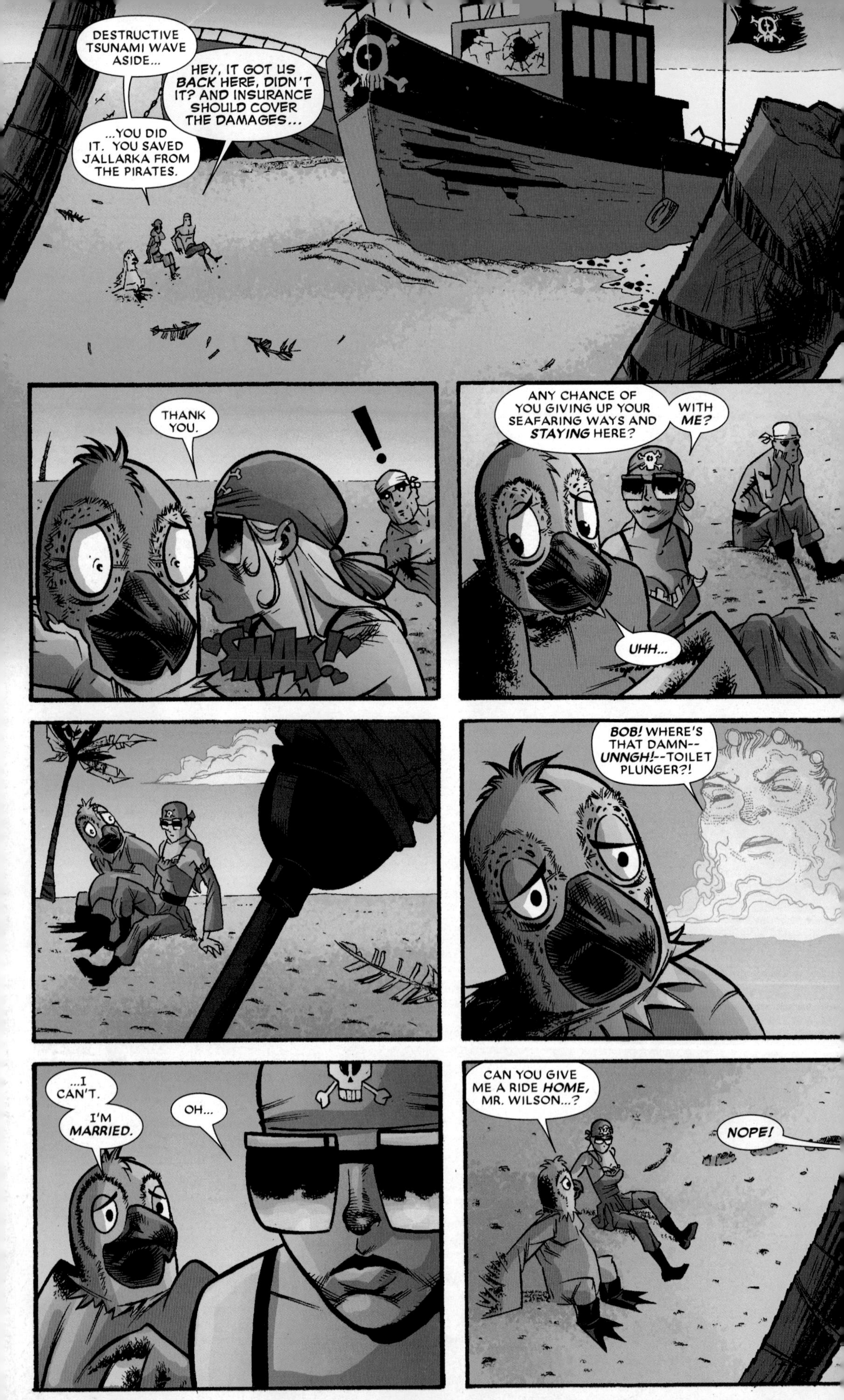
DESTRUCTIVE TSUNAMI WAVE ASIDE...
...YOU DID IT. YOU SAVED JALLARKA FROM THE PIRATES.
HEY, IT GOT US *BACK* HERE, DIDN'T IT? AND INSURANCE SHOULD COVER THE DAMAGES...
THANK YOU.
!
SMAK!
ANY CHANCE OF YOU GIVING UP YOUR SEAFARING WAYS AND *STAYING* HERE?
WITH *ME?*
*UHH...*
*BOB!* WHERE'S THAT DAMN-- *UNNGH!*--TOILET PLUNGER?!
...I CAN'T.
I'M *MARRIED.*
OH...
CAN YOU GIVE ME A RIDE *HOME,* MR. WILSON...?
*NOPE!*

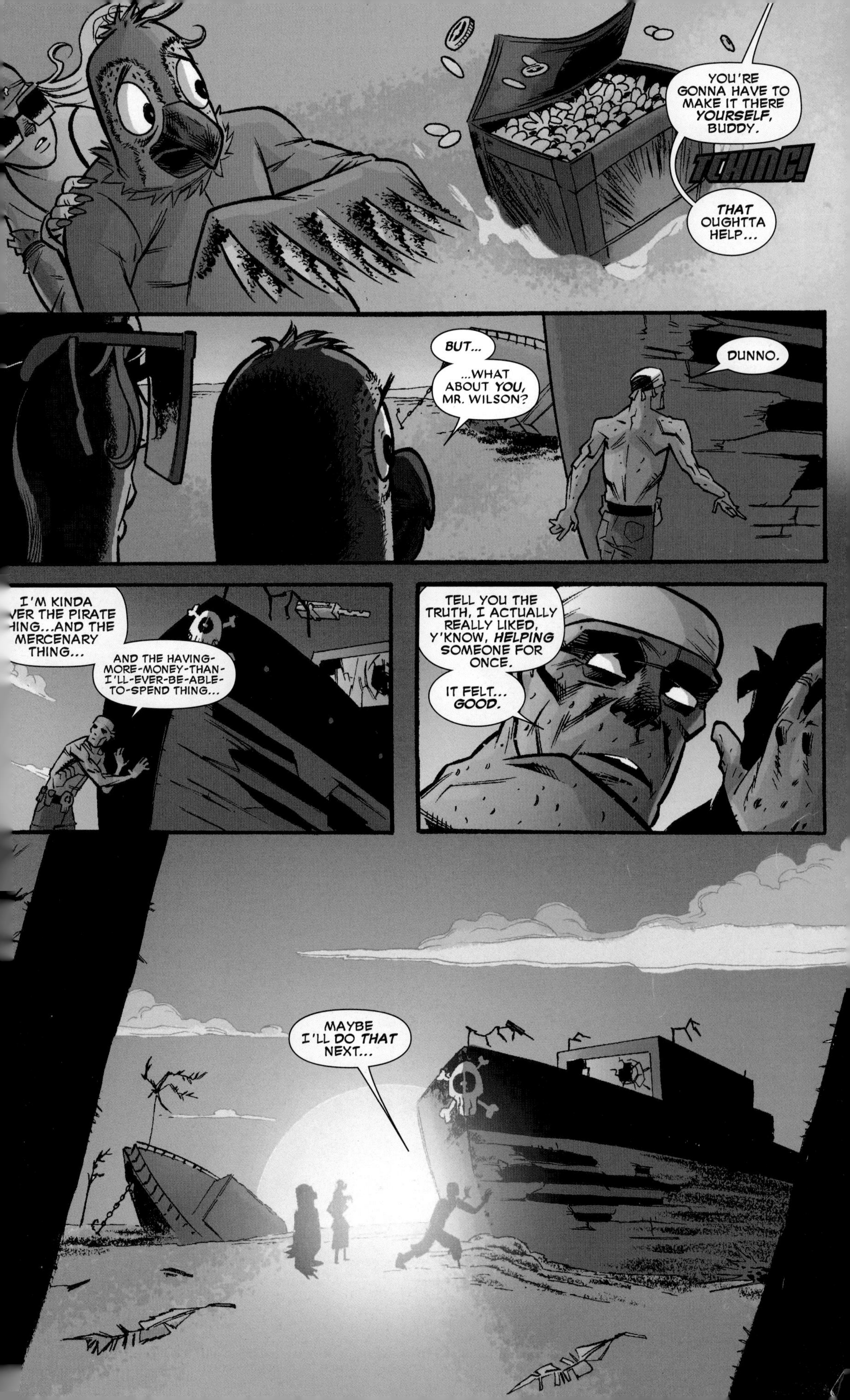
YOU'RE GONNA HAVE TO MAKE IT THERE *YOURSELF*, BUDDY.
TCHING!
*THAT* OUGHTTA HELP...
*BUT...*
...WHAT ABOUT *YOU*, MR. WILSON?
DUNNO.
I'M KINDA VER THE PIRATE HING...AND THE MERCENARY THING...
AND THE HAVING-MORE-MONEY-THAN-I'LL-EVER-BE-ABLE-TO-SPEND THING...
TELL YOU THE TRUTH, I ACTUALLY REALLY LIKED, Y'KNOW, *HELPING* SOMEONE FOR ONCE.
IT FELT... *GOOD.*
MAYBE I'LL DO *THAT* NEXT...

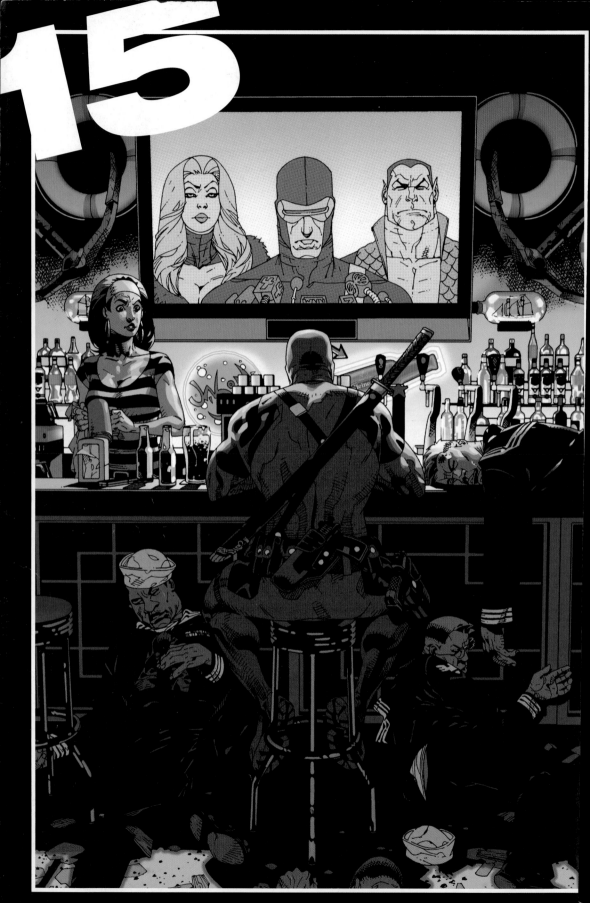

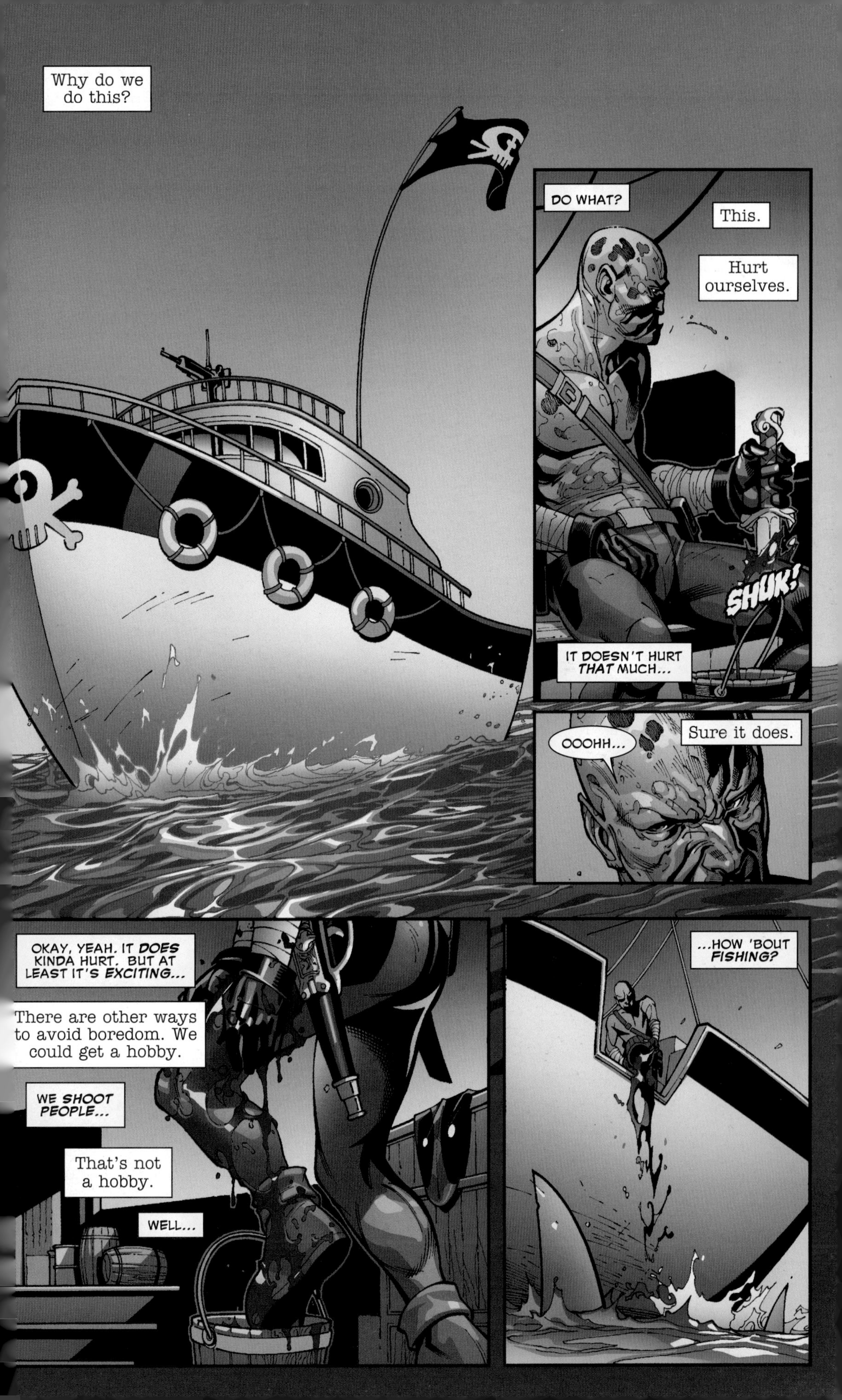

Why do we do this?
DO WHAT?
This.
Hurt ourselves.
SHUK!
IT DOESN'T HURT *THAT* MUCH...
OOOHH...
Sure it does.
OKAY, YEAH. IT *DOES* KINDA HURT. BUT AT LEAST IT'S *EXCITING*...
There are other ways to avoid boredom. We could get a hobby.
WE *SHOOT PEOPLE*...
That's not a hobby.
WELL...
...HOW 'BOUT *FISHING?*

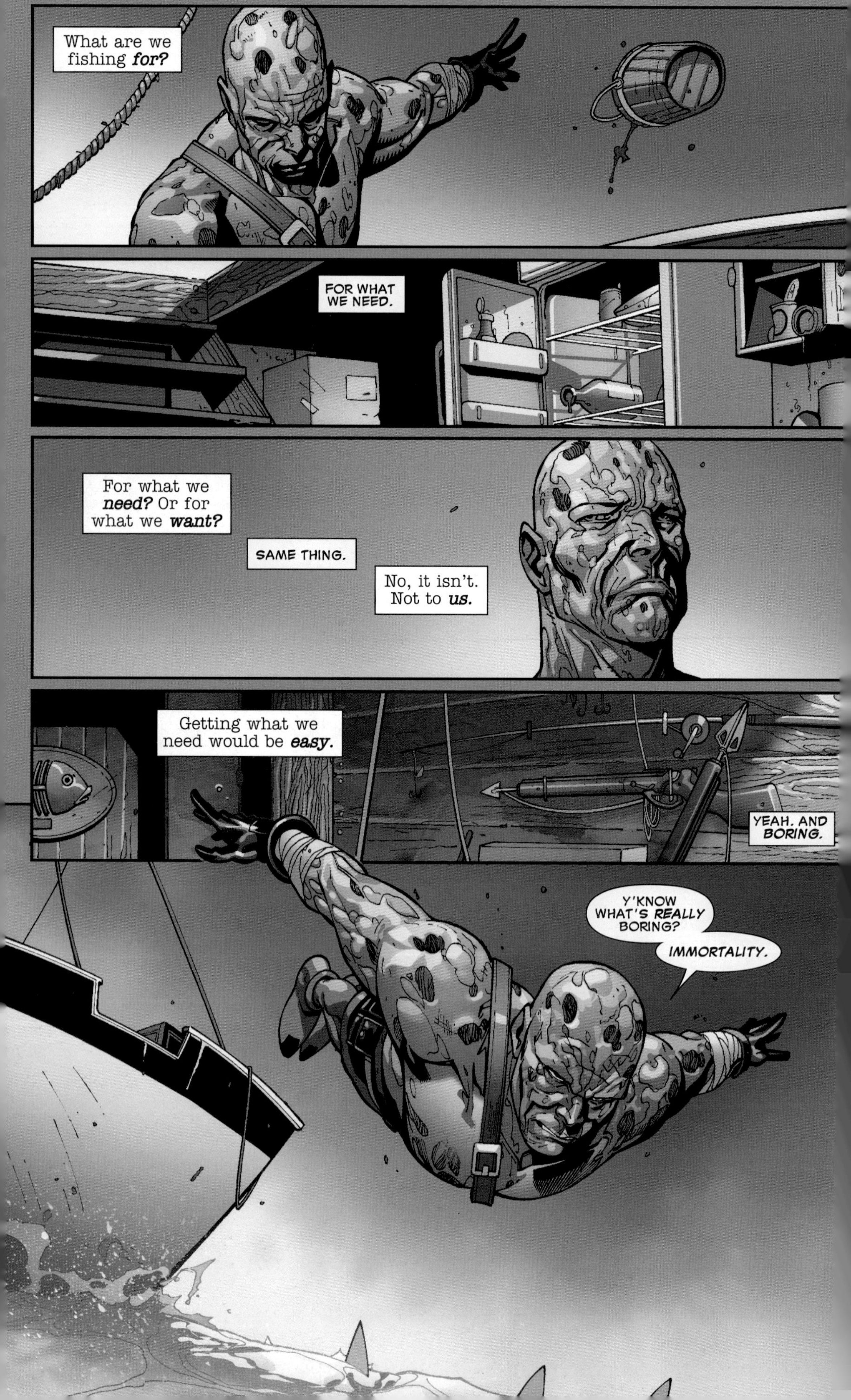

What are we fishing for?
FOR WHAT WE NEED.
For what we need? Or for what we want?
SAME THING.
No, it isn't. Not to us.
Getting what we need would be easy.
YEAH. AND BORING.
Y'KNOW WHAT'S REALLY BORING?
IMMORTALITY.

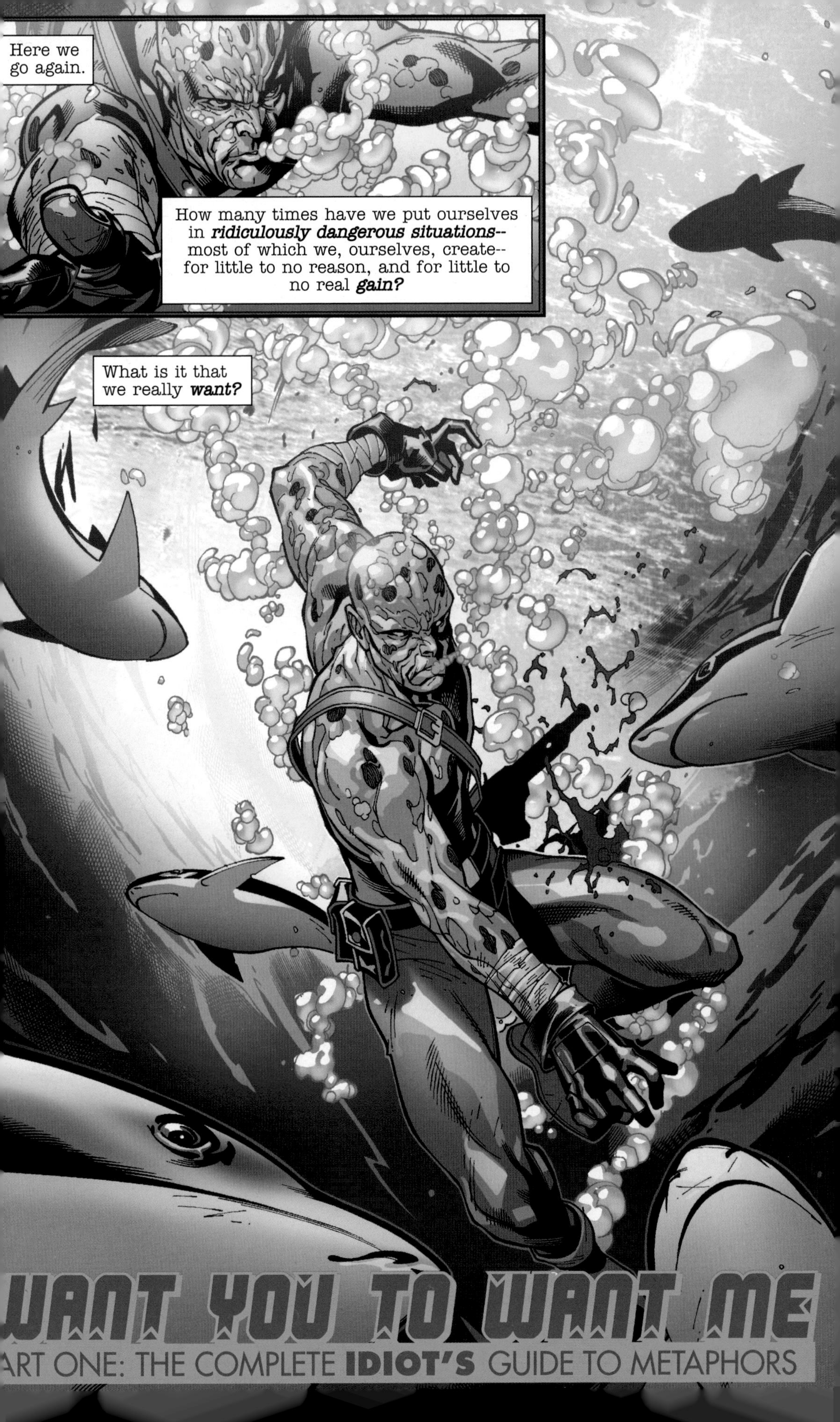

Here we go again.
How many times have we put ourselves in ridiculously dangerous situations-- most of which we, ourselves, create-- for little to no reason, and for little to no real gain?
What is it that we really want?
WANT YOU TO WANT ME
ART ONE: THE COMPLETE IDIOT'S GUIDE TO METAPHORS

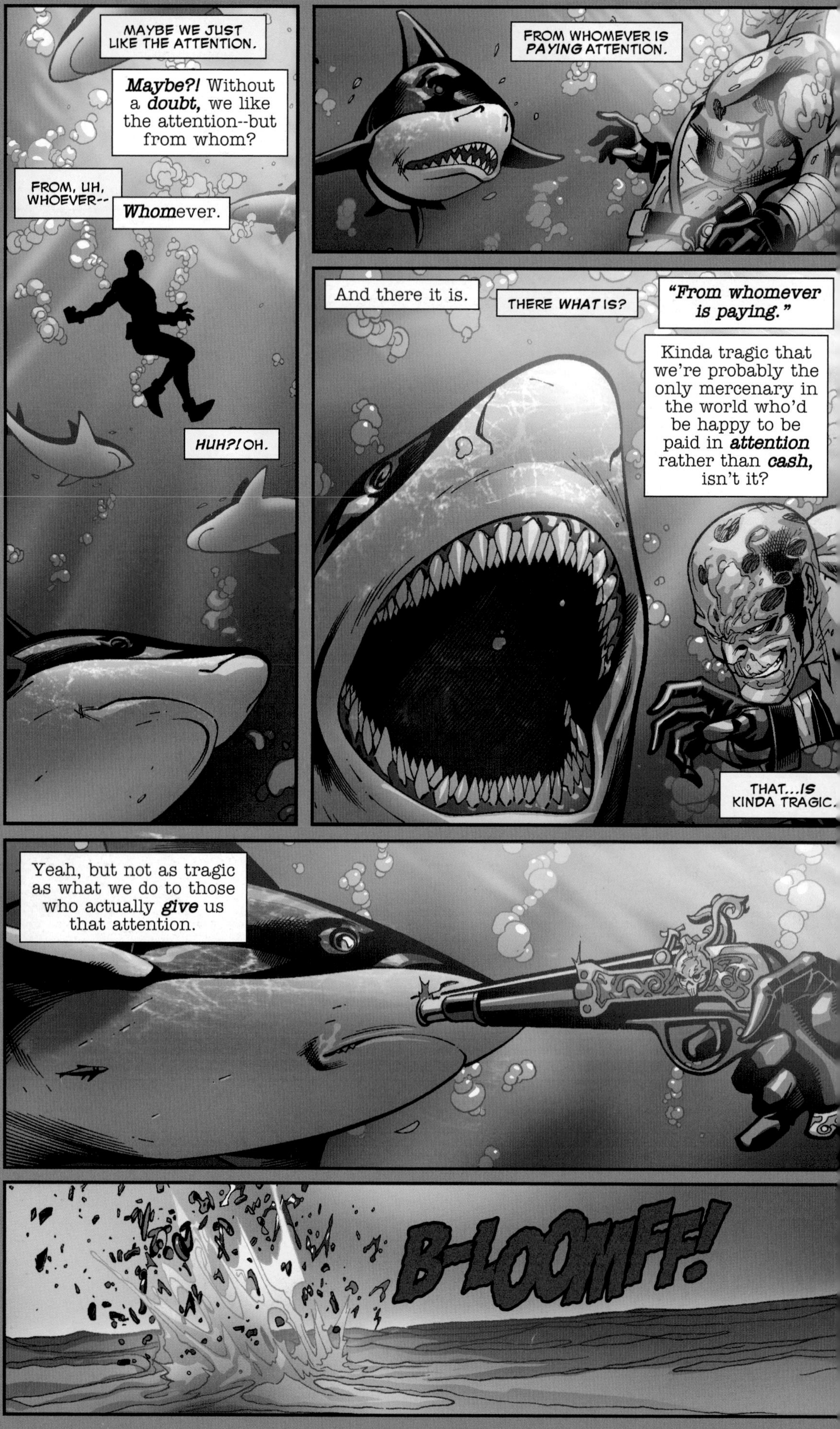
MAYBE WE JUST LIKE THE ATTENTION.
*Maybe?!* Without a **doubt,** we like the attention--but from whom?
FROM, UH, WHOEVER--
**Whom**ever.
HUH?! OH.
FROM WHOMEVER IS *PAYING* ATTENTION.
And there it is.
THERE *WHAT* IS?
*"From whomever is paying."*
Kinda tragic that we're probably the only mercenary in the world who'd be happy to be paid in **attention** rather than **cash,** isn't it?
THAT...*IS* KINDA TRAGIC.
Yeah, but not as tragic as what we do to those who actually ***give*** us that attention.
B-LOOMFF!

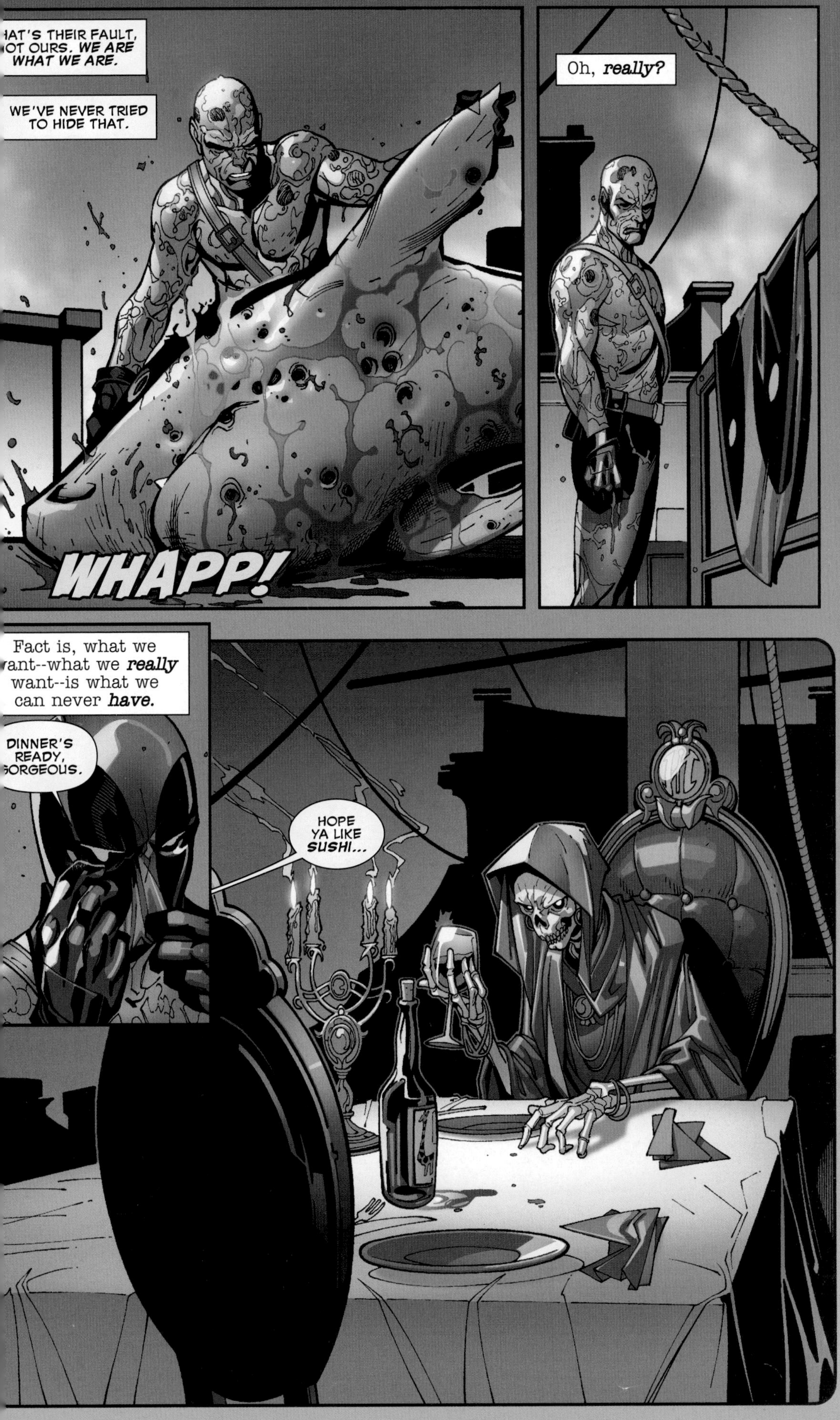

HAT'S THEIR FAULT, OT OURS. WE ARE WHAT WE ARE.
WE'VE NEVER TRIED TO HIDE THAT.
WHAPP!
Oh, really?
Fact is, what we want--what we really want--is what we can never have.
DINNER'S READY, GORGEOUS.
HOPE YA LIKE SUSHI...

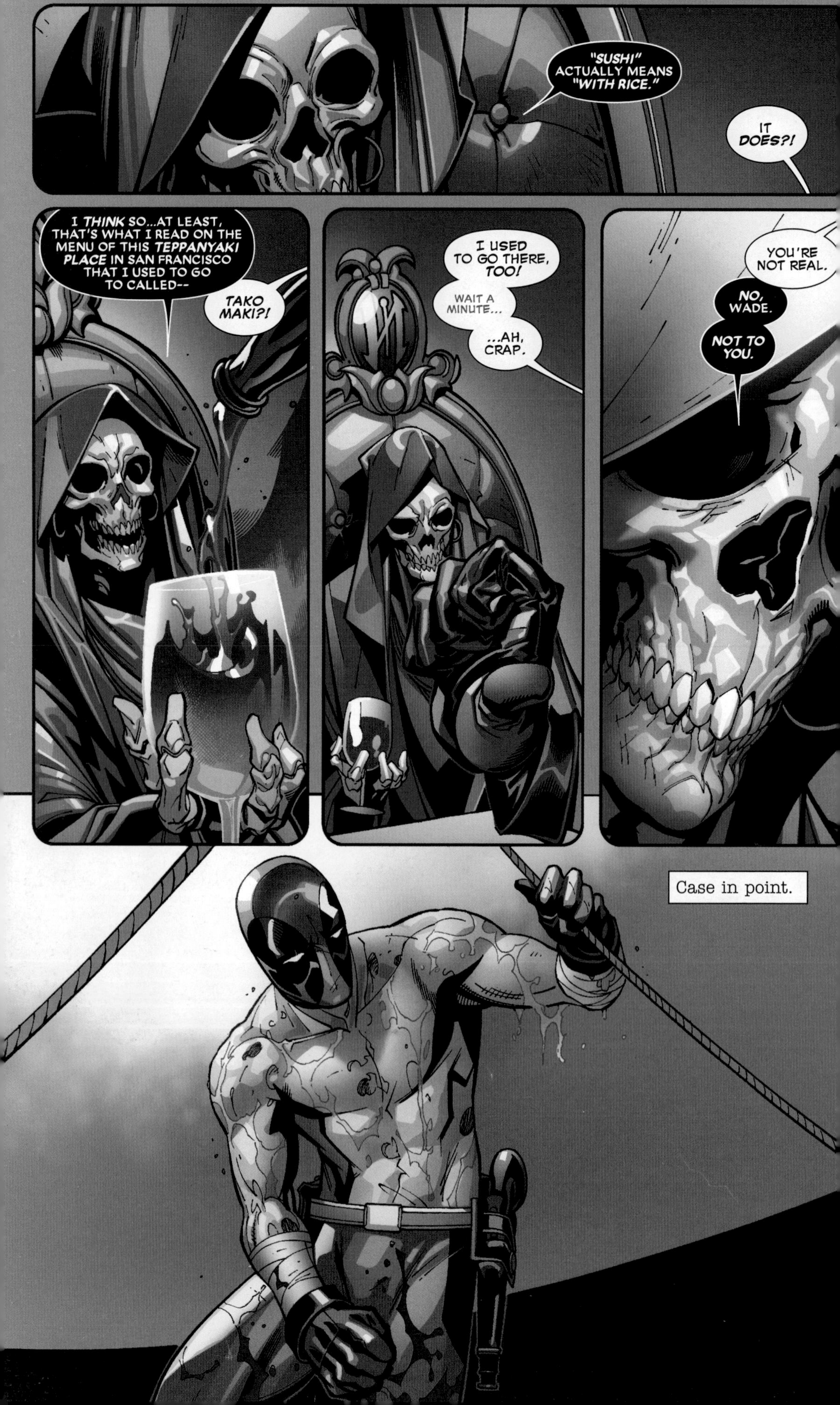
"SUSHI" ACTUALLY MEANS "WITH RICE."
IT DOES?!
I THINK SO...AT LEAST, THAT'S WHAT I READ ON THE MENU OF THIS TEPPANYAKI PLACE IN SAN FRANCISCO THAT I USED TO GO TO CALLED--
TAKO MAKI?!
I USED TO GO THERE, TOO!
WAIT A MINUTE...
...AH, CRAP.
YOU'RE NOT REAL.
NO, WADE.
NOT TO YOU.
Case in point.

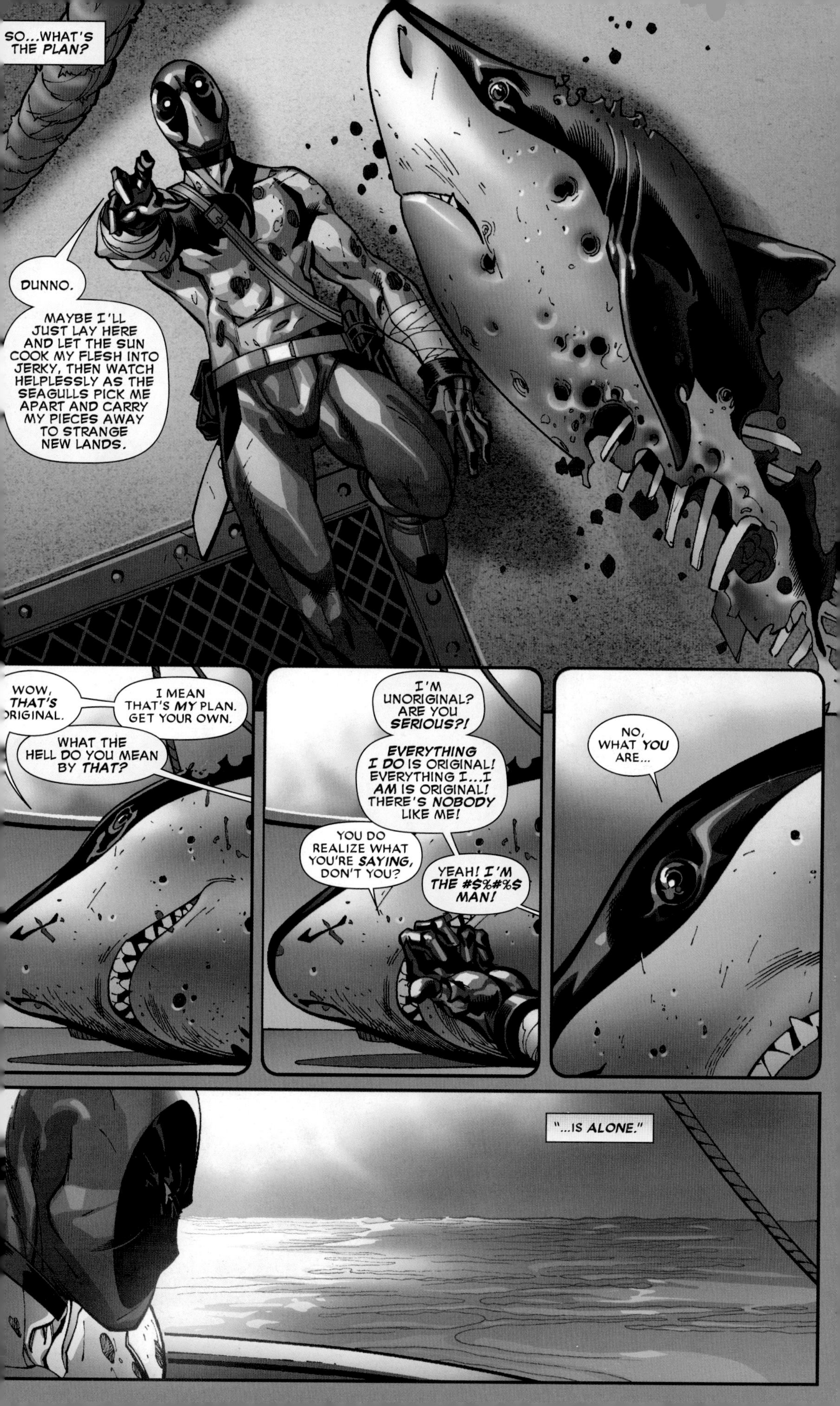
SO...WHAT'S THE *PLAN?*
DUNNO.
MAYBE I'LL JUST LAY HERE AND LET THE SUN COOK MY FLESH INTO JERKY, THEN WATCH HELPLESSLY AS THE SEAGULLS PICK ME APART AND CARRY MY PIECES AWAY TO STRANGE NEW LANDS.
WOW, *THAT'S* ORIGINAL.
I MEAN THAT'S *MY* PLAN. GET YOUR OWN.
WHAT THE HELL *DO* YOU MEAN BY *THAT?*
I'M UNORIGINAL? ARE YOU *SERIOUS?!*
*EVERYTHING I DO* IS ORIGINAL! EVERYTHING I...I *AM* IS ORIGINAL! THERE'S *NOBODY* LIKE ME!
YOU DO REALIZE WHAT YOU'RE *SAYING,* DON'T YOU?
YEAH! *I'M THE #$%#%$ MAN!*
NO, WHAT *YOU* ARE...
"...IS *ALONE.*"

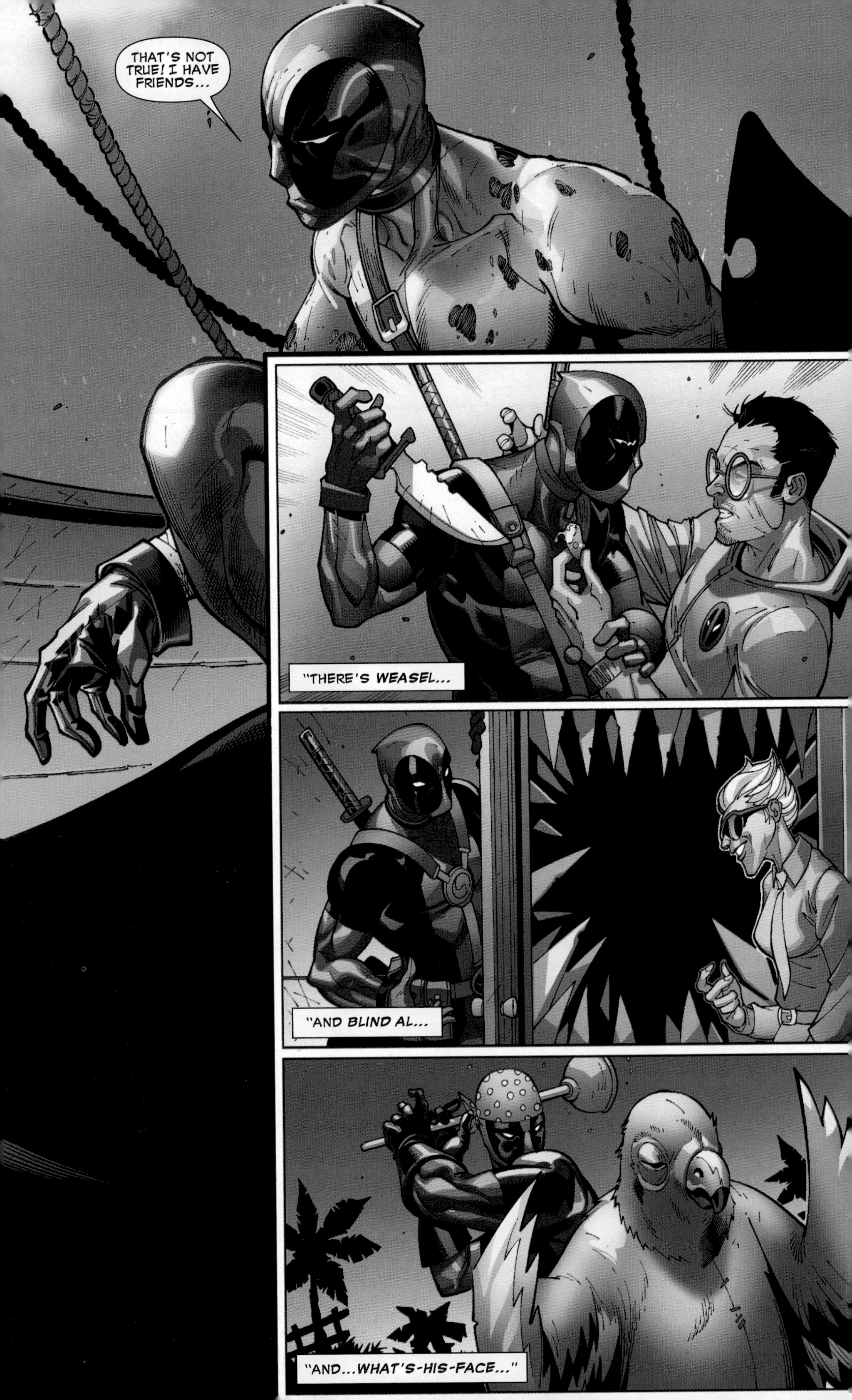
THAT'S NOT TRUE! I HAVE FRIENDS...
"THERE'S WEASEL...
"AND BLIND AL...
"AND...WHAT'S-HIS-FACE..."

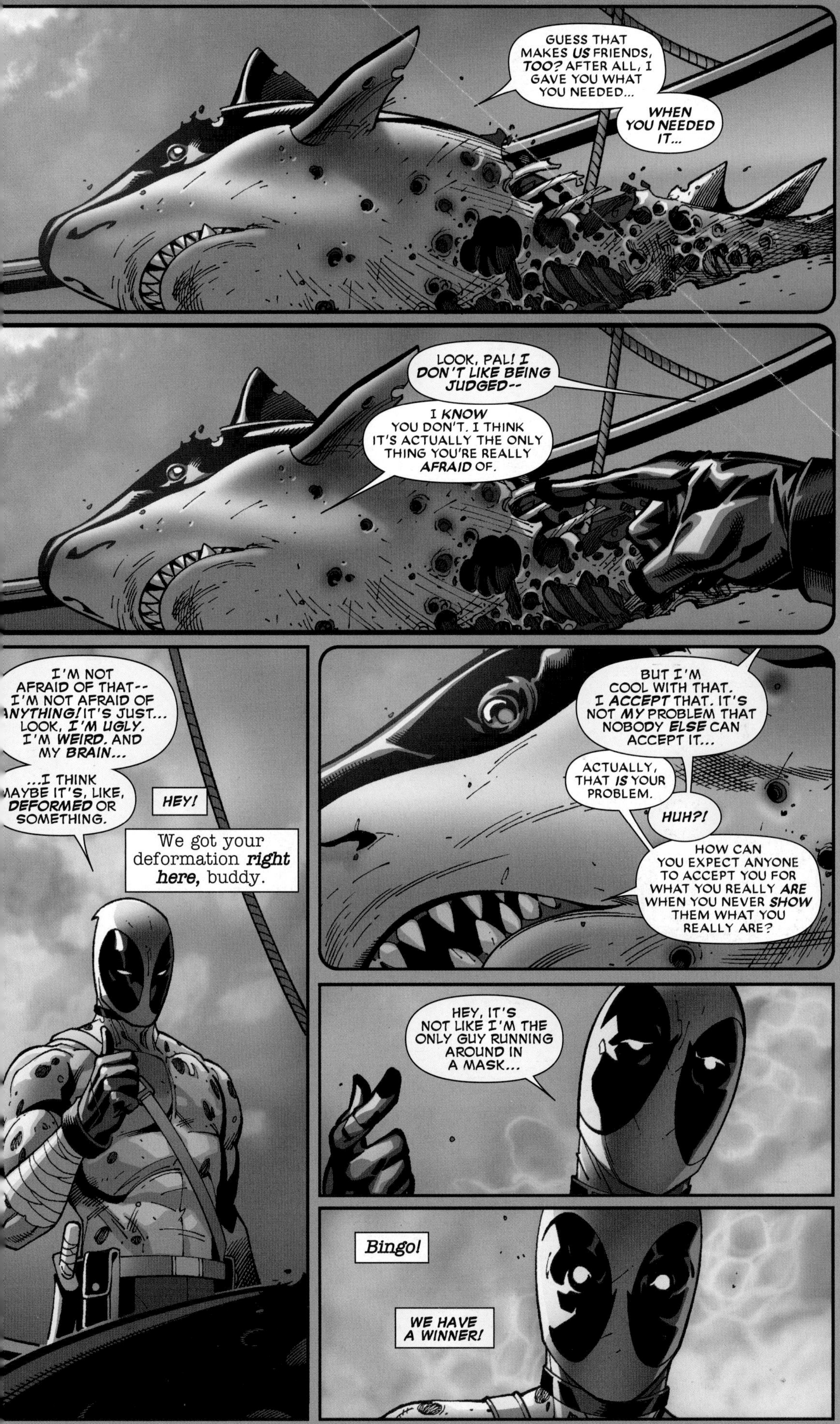
GUESS THAT MAKES US FRIENDS, TOO? AFTER ALL, I GAVE YOU WHAT YOU NEEDED...
WHEN YOU NEEDED IT...
LOOK, PAL! I DON'T LIKE BEING JUDGED--
I KNOW YOU DON'T. I THINK IT'S ACTUALLY THE ONLY THING YOU'RE REALLY AFRAID OF.
I'M NOT AFRAID OF THAT-- I'M NOT AFRAID OF ANYTHING! IT'S JUST... LOOK, I'M UGLY. I'M WEIRD. AND MY BRAIN...
...I THINK MAYBE IT'S, LIKE, DEFORMED OR SOMETHING.
HEY!
We got your deformation right here, buddy.
BUT I'M COOL WITH THAT. I ACCEPT THAT. IT'S NOT MY PROBLEM THAT NOBODY ELSE CAN ACCEPT IT...
ACTUALLY, THAT IS YOUR PROBLEM.
HUH?!
HOW CAN YOU EXPECT ANYONE TO ACCEPT YOU FOR WHAT YOU REALLY ARE WHEN YOU NEVER SHOW THEM WHAT YOU REALLY ARE?
HEY, IT'S NOT LIKE I'M THE ONLY GUY RUNNING AROUND IN A MASK...
Bingo!
WE HAVE A WINNER!

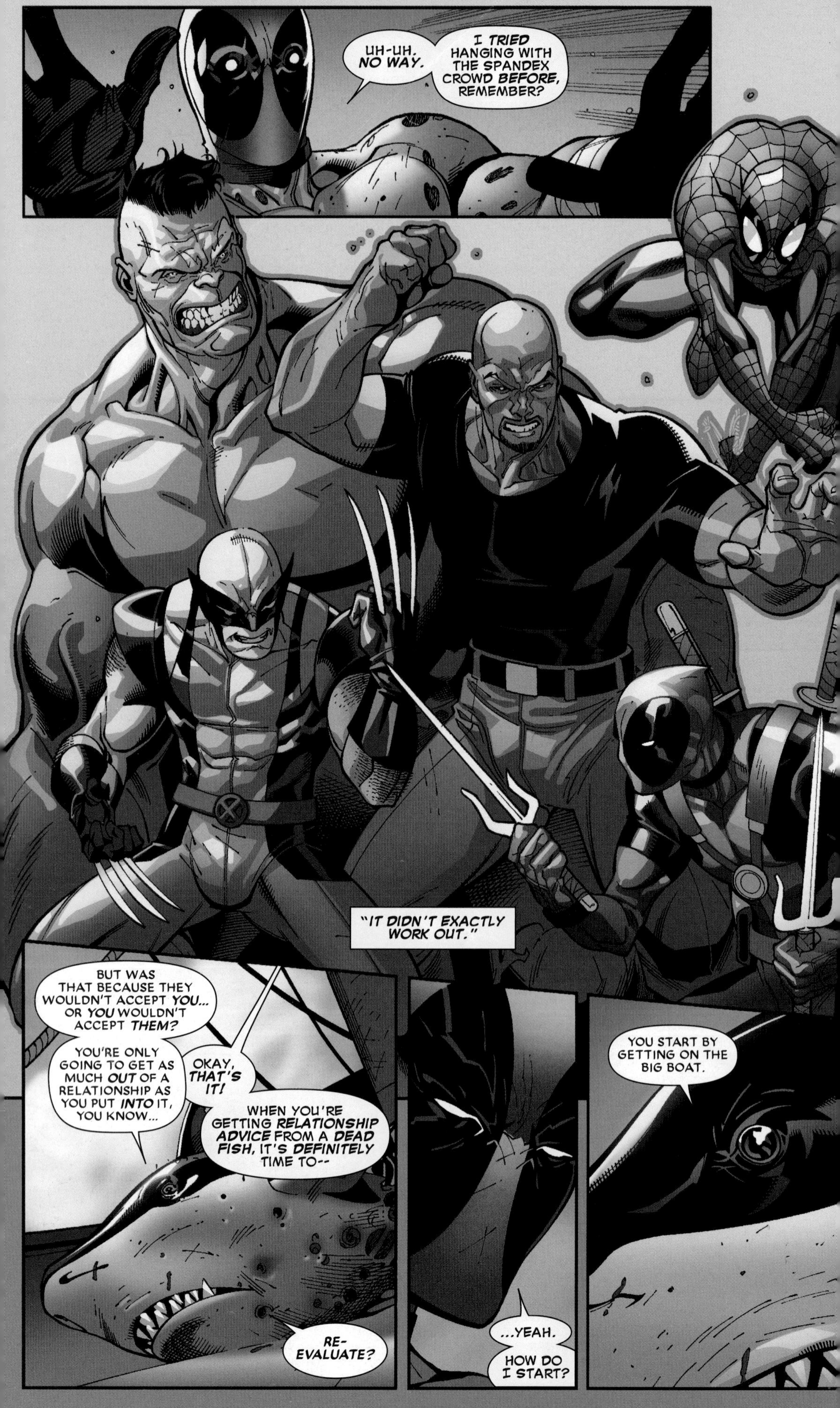
UH-UH. NO WAY.
I TRIED HANGING WITH THE SPANDEX CROWD BEFORE, REMEMBER?
"IT DIDN'T EXACTLY WORK OUT."
BUT WAS THAT BECAUSE THEY WOULDN'T ACCEPT YOU... OR YOU WOULDN'T ACCEPT THEM?
YOU'RE ONLY GOING TO GET AS MUCH OUT OF A RELATIONSHIP AS YOU PUT INTO IT, YOU KNOW...
OKAY, THAT'S IT!
WHEN YOU'RE GETTING RELATIONSHIP ADVICE FROM A DEAD FISH, IT'S DEFINITELY TIME TO--
RE-EVALUATE?
...YEAH.
HOW DO I START?
YOU START BY GETTING ON THE BIG BOAT.

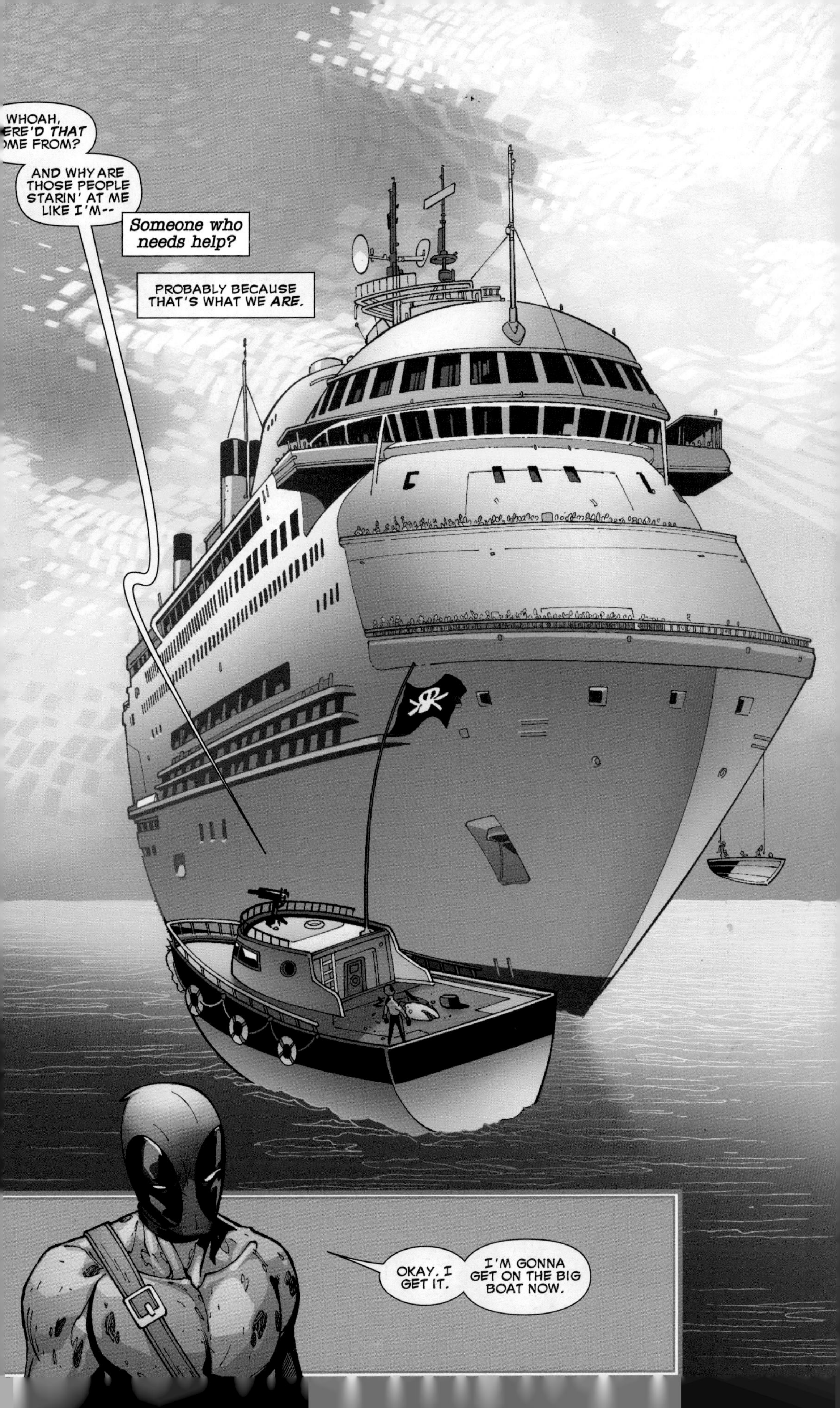

WHOAH,
ERE'D THAT
OME FROM?
AND WHY ARE THOSE PEOPLE STARIN' AT ME LIKE I'M--
Someone who needs help?
PROBABLY BECAUSE THAT'S WHAT WE ARE.
OKAY. I GET IT.
I'M GONNA GET ON THE BIG BOAT NOW.

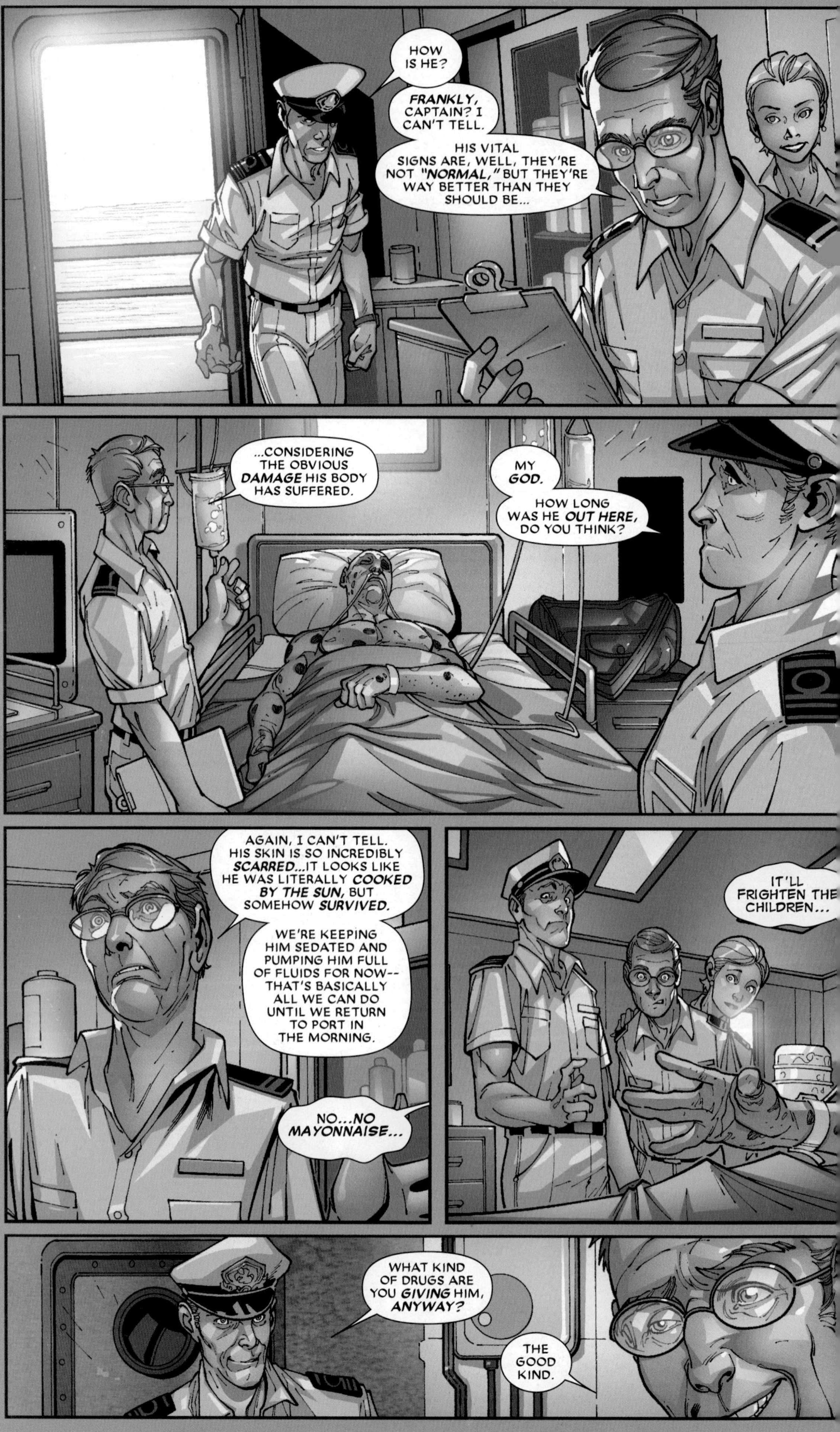
HOW IS HE?
FRANKLY, CAPTAIN? I CAN'T TELL.
HIS VITAL SIGNS ARE, WELL, THEY'RE NOT "NORMAL," BUT THEY'RE WAY BETTER THAN THEY SHOULD BE...
...CONSIDERING THE OBVIOUS DAMAGE HIS BODY HAS SUFFERED.
MY GOD.
HOW LONG WAS HE OUT HERE, DO YOU THINK?
AGAIN, I CAN'T TELL. HIS SKIN IS SO INCREDIBLY SCARRED...IT LOOKS LIKE HE WAS LITERALLY COOKED BY THE SUN, BUT SOMEHOW SURVIVED.
WE'RE KEEPING HIM SEDATED AND PUMPING HIM FULL OF FLUIDS FOR NOW--THAT'S BASICALLY ALL WE CAN DO UNTIL WE RETURN TO PORT IN THE MORNING.
NO...NO MAYONNAISE...
IT'LL FRIGHTEN THE CHILDREN...
WHAT KIND OF DRUGS ARE YOU GIVING HIM, ANYWAY?
THE GOOD KIND.

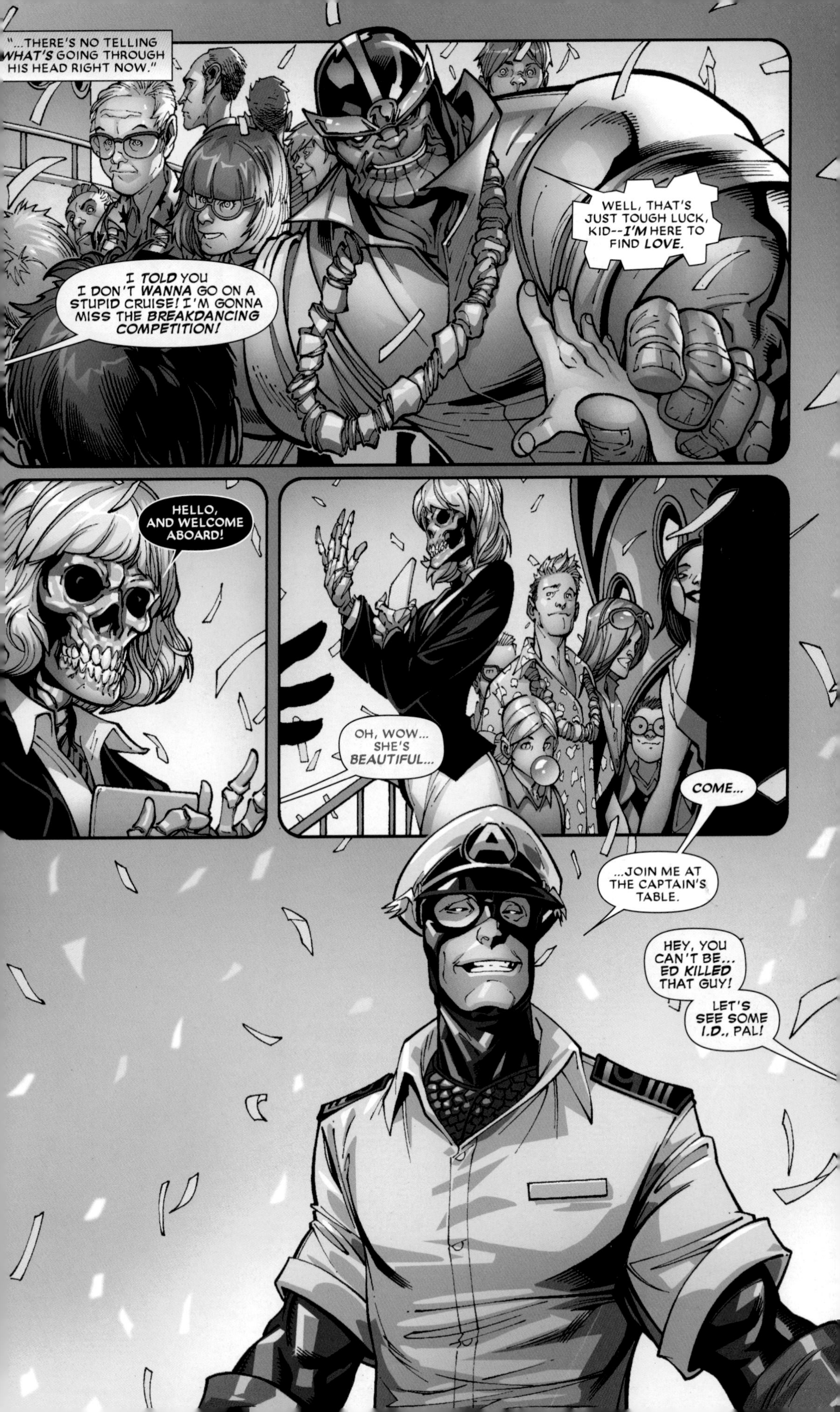
"...THERE'S NO TELLING WHAT'S GOING THROUGH HIS HEAD RIGHT NOW."
I TOLD YOU I DON'T WANNA GO ON A STUPID CRUISE! I'M GONNA MISS THE BREAKDANCING COMPETITION!
WELL, THAT'S JUST TOUGH LUCK, KID--I'M HERE TO FIND LOVE.
HELLO, AND WELCOME ABOARD!
OH, WOW... SHE'S BEAUTIFUL...
COME...
...JOIN ME AT THE CAPTAIN'S TABLE.
HEY, YOU CAN'T BE... ED KILLED THAT GUY!
LET'S SEE SOME I.D., PAL!

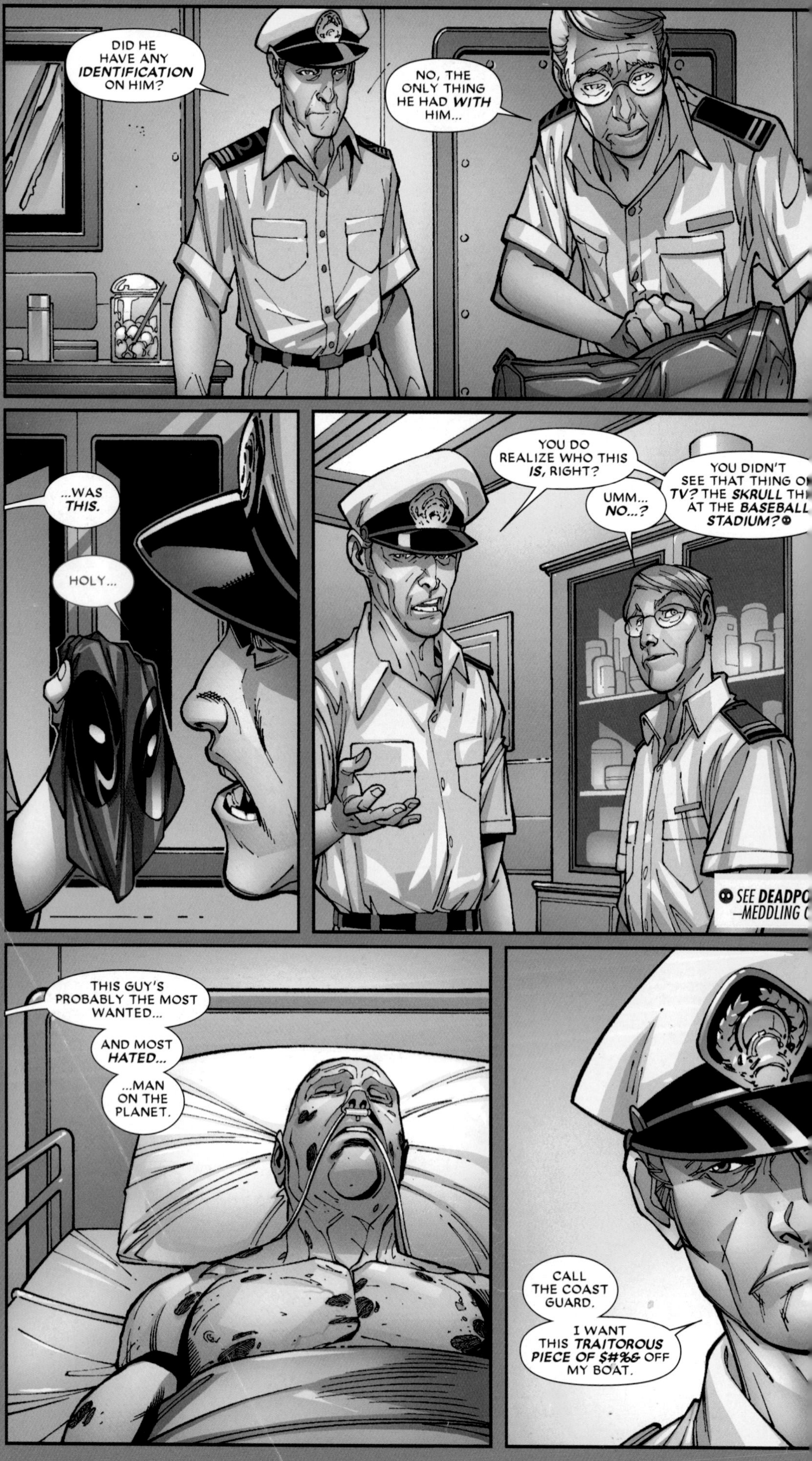
DID HE HAVE ANY IDENTIFICATION ON HIM?
NO, THE ONLY THING HE HAD WITH HIM...
...WAS THIS.
HOLY...
YOU DO REALIZE WHO THIS IS, RIGHT?
UMM... NO...?
YOU DIDN'T SEE THAT THING O TV? THE SKRULL TH AT THE BASEBALL STADIUM?
SEE DEADPO —MEDDLING
THIS GUY'S PROBABLY THE MOST WANTED...
AND MOST HATED...
...MAN ON THE PLANET.
CALL THE COAST GUARD.
I WANT THIS TRAITOROUS PIECE OF $#%& OFF MY BOAT.

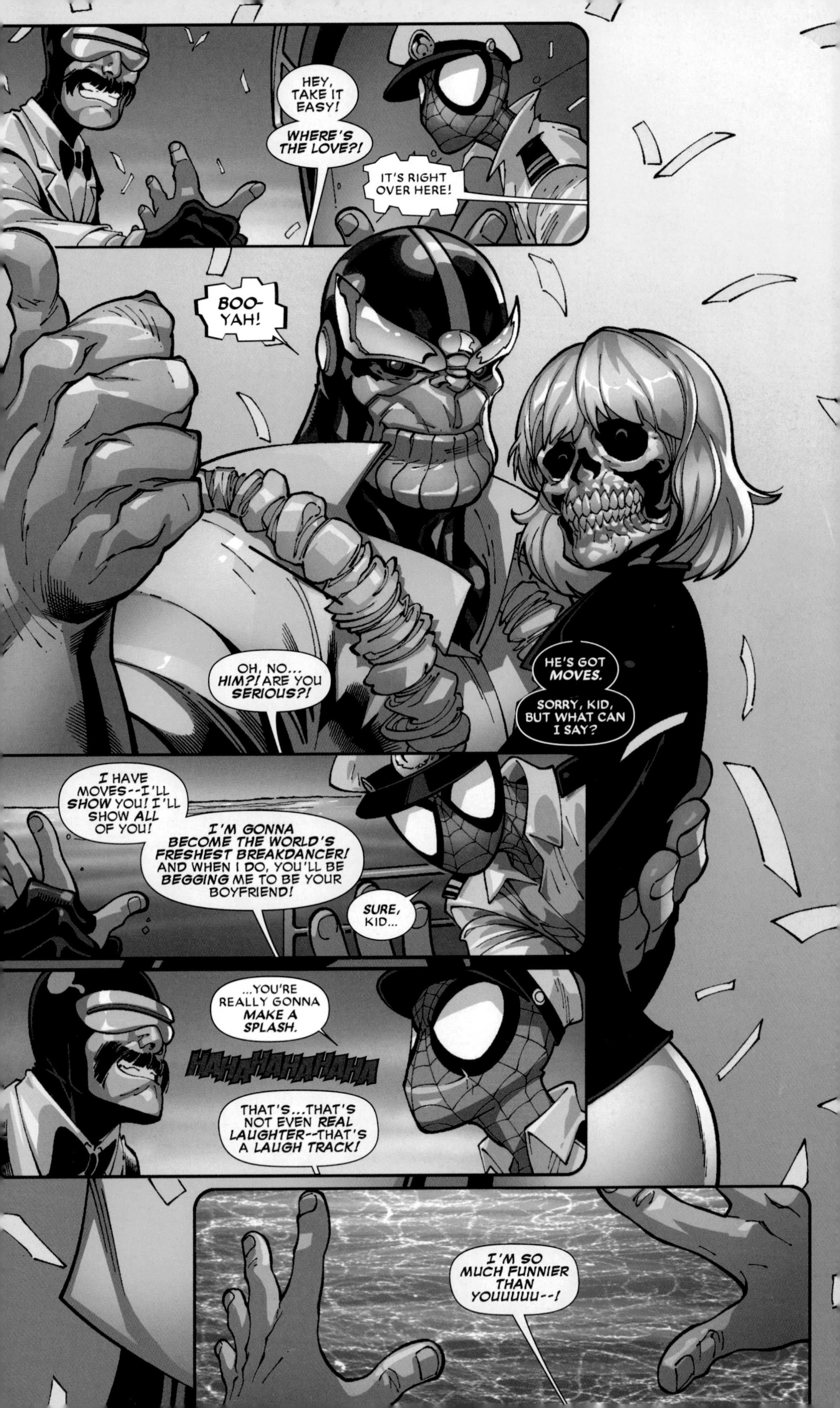
HEY, TAKE IT EASY!
WHERE'S THE LOVE?!
IT'S RIGHT OVER HERE!
BOO-YAH!
OH, NO... HIM?! ARE YOU SERIOUS?!
HE'S GOT MOVES.
SORRY, KID, BUT WHAT CAN I SAY?
I HAVE MOVES--I'LL SHOW YOU! I'LL SHOW ALL OF YOU!
I'M GONNA BECOME THE WORLD'S FRESHEST BREAKDANCER! AND WHEN I DO, YOU'LL BE BEGGING ME TO BE YOUR BOYFRIEND!
SURE, KID...
...YOU'RE REALLY GONNA MAKE A SPLASH.
HAHAHAHAHAHAHA
THAT'S...THAT'S NOT EVEN REAL LAUGHTER--THAT'S A LAUGH TRACK!
I'M SO MUCH FUNNIER THAN YOUUUUU--!

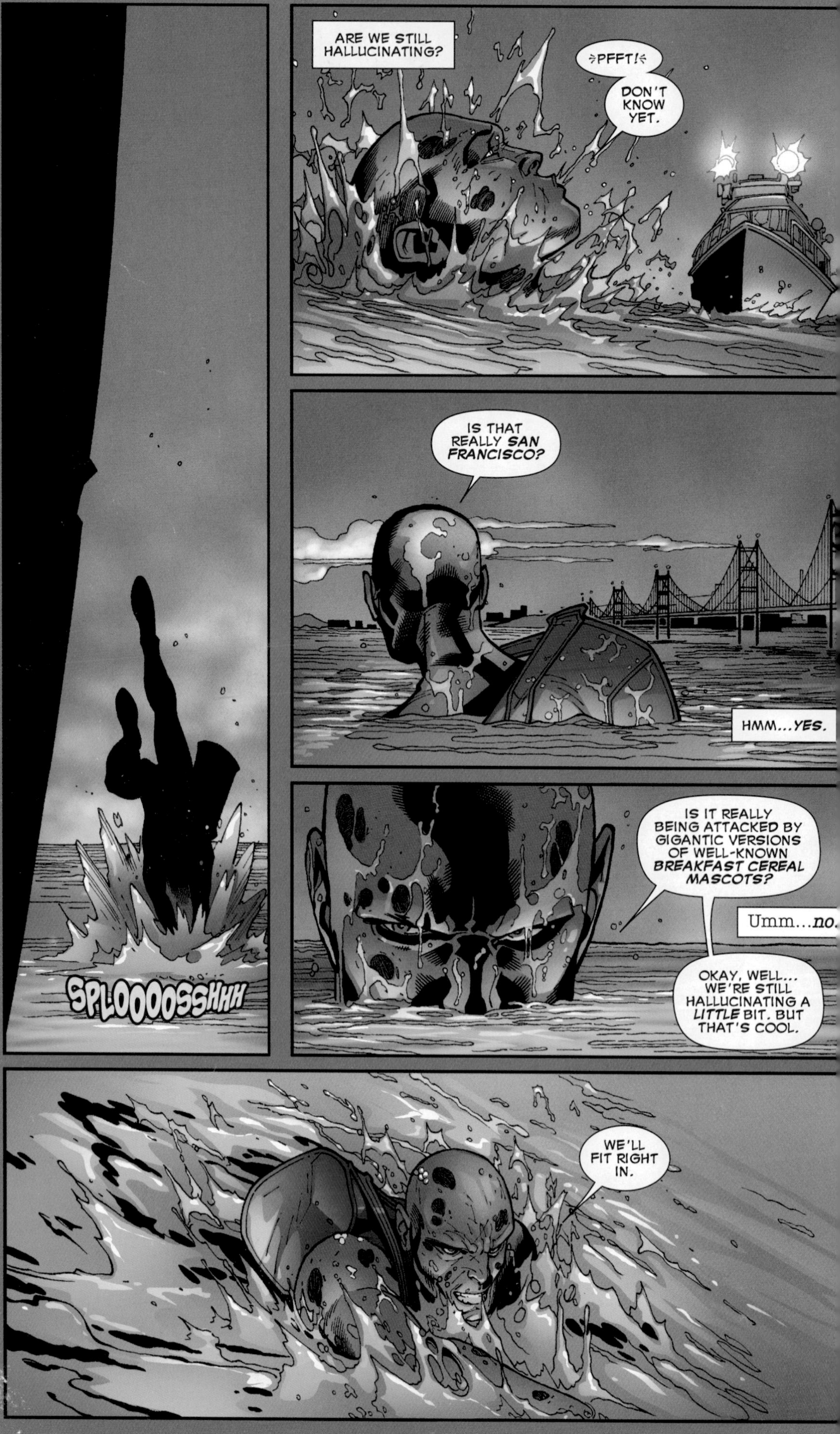
ARE WE STILL HALLUCINATING?
PFFT! DON'T KNOW YET.
IS THAT REALLY SAN FRANCISCO?
HMM...YES.
IS IT REALLY BEING ATTACKED BY GIGANTIC VERSIONS OF WELL-KNOWN BREAKFAST CEREAL MASCOTS?
Umm...no.
OKAY, WELL... WE'RE STILL HALLUCINATING A LITTLE BIT. BUT THAT'S COOL.
SPLOOOOSSHHH
WE'LL FIT RIGHT IN.

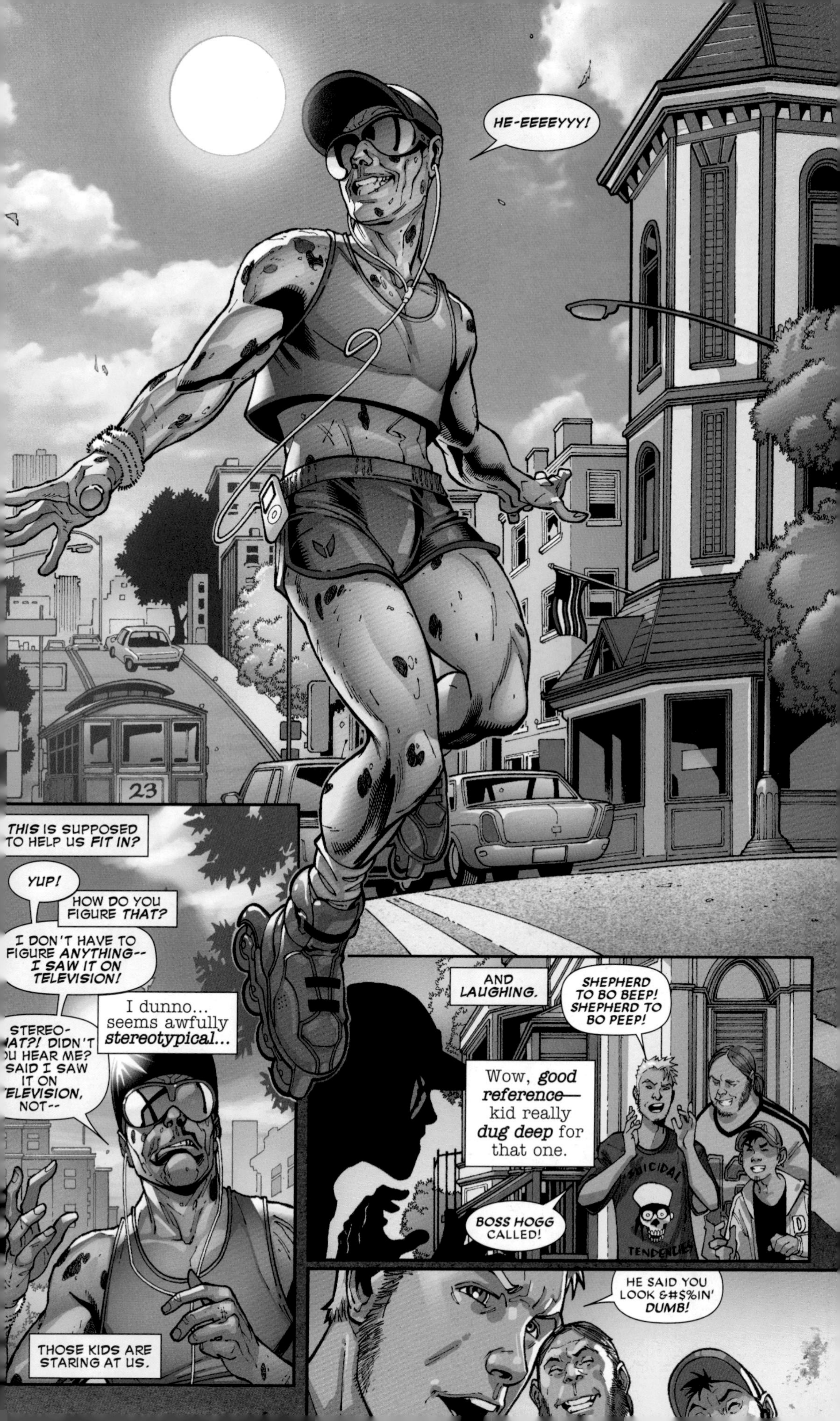
HE-EEEEYYY!
THIS IS SUPPOSED TO HELP US FIT IN?
YUP!
HOW DO YOU FIGURE THAT?
I DON'T HAVE TO FIGURE ANYTHING-- I SAW IT ON TELEVISION!
I dunno... seems awfully stereotypical...
STEREO-
AT?! DIDN'T
U HEAR ME?
SAID I SAW
IT ON
ELEVISION,
NOT--
THOSE KIDS ARE STARING AT US.
AND LAUGHING.
SHEPHERD TO BO BEEP! SHEPHERD TO BO PEEP!
Wow, good reference— kid really dug deep for that one.
BOSS HOGG CALLED!
HE SAID YOU LOOK &#$%IN' DUMB!

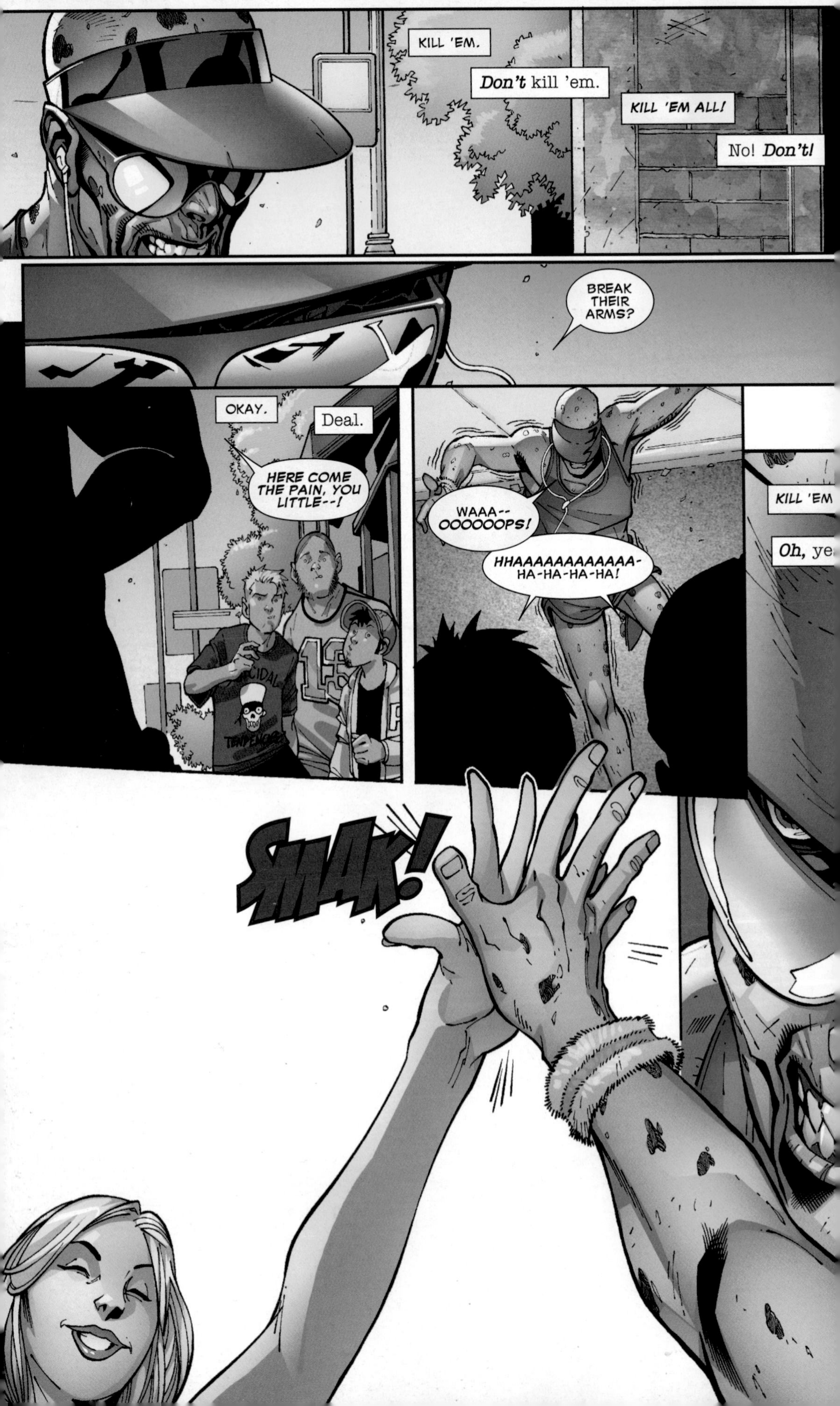
KILL 'EM.
Don't kill 'em.
KILL 'EM ALL!
No! Don't!
BREAK THEIR ARMS?
OKAY.
Deal.
HERE COME THE PAIN, YOU LITTLE--!
WAAA-- OOOOOOPS!
HHAAAAAAAAAAAAA-HA-HA-HA-HA!
KILL 'EM
SMAK!

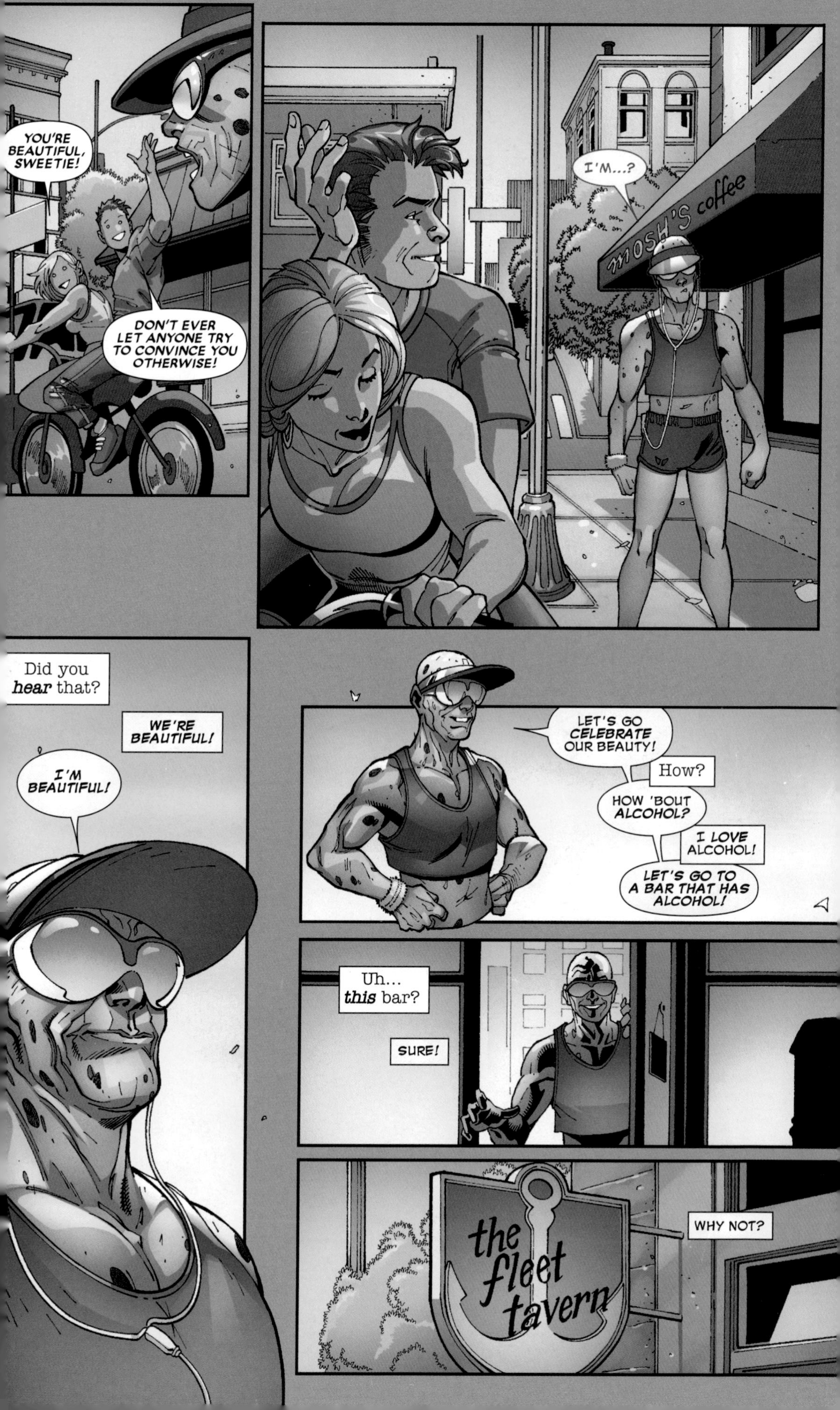
YOU'RE BEAUTIFUL, SWEETIE!
DON'T EVER LET ANYONE TRY TO CONVINCE YOU OTHERWISE!
I'M...?
MOSH'S coffee
Did you hear that?
WE'RE BEAUTIFUL!
I'M BEAUTIFUL!
LET'S GO CELEBRATE OUR BEAUTY!
How?
HOW 'BOUT ALCOHOL?
I LOVE ALCOHOL!
LET'S GO TO A BAR THAT HAS ALCOHOL!
Uh... this bar?
SURE!
the fleet tavern
WHY NOT?

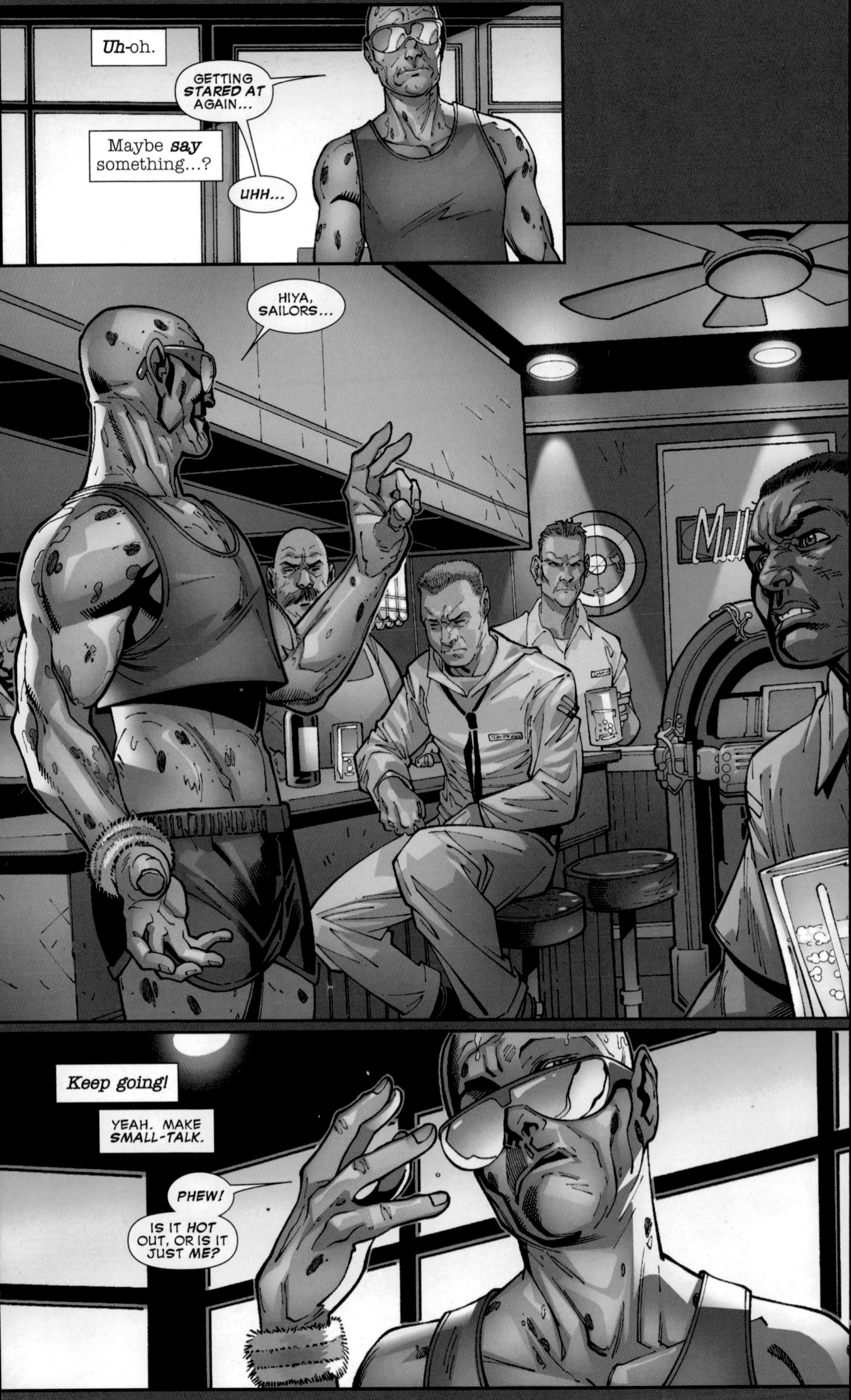
*Uh*-oh.
GETTING *STARED AT* AGAIN...
Maybe *say* something...?
UHH...
HIYA, SAILORS...
*Keep going!*
YEAH. MAKE *SMALL-TALK.*
*PHEW!*
IS IT *HOT* OUT, OR IS IT JUST *ME?*

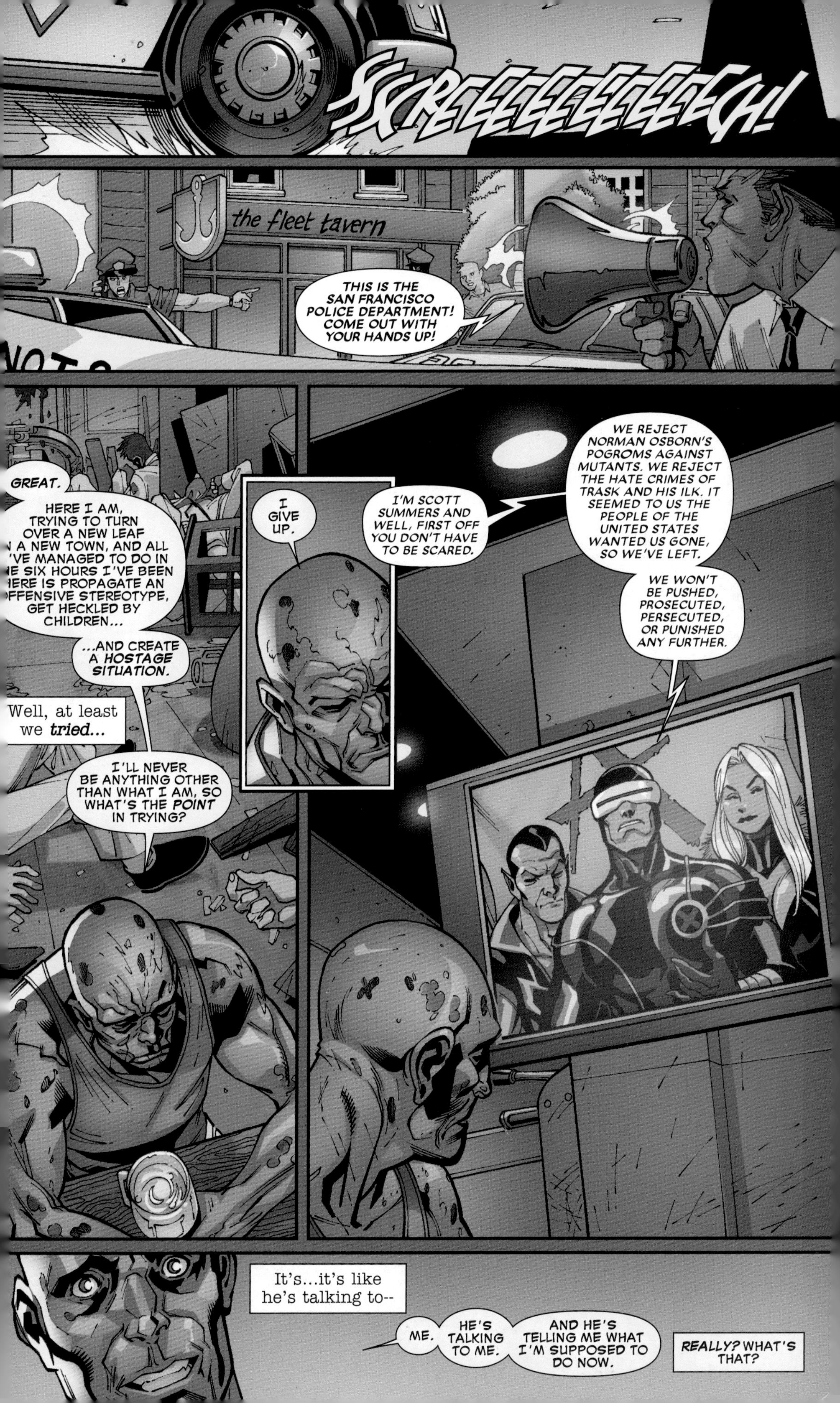
SSCREEEEEEEEEEECH!
the fleet tavern
THIS IS THE SAN FRANCISCO POLICE DEPARTMENT! COME OUT WITH YOUR HANDS UP!
GREAT.
HERE I AM, TRYING TO TURN OVER A NEW LEAF IN A NEW TOWN, AND ALL I'VE MANAGED TO DO IN THE SIX HOURS I'VE BEEN HERE IS PROPAGATE AN OFFENSIVE STEREOTYPE, GET HECKLED BY CHILDREN...
...AND CREATE A HOSTAGE SITUATION.
Well, at least we tried...
I'LL NEVER BE ANYTHING OTHER THAN WHAT I AM, SO WHAT'S THE POINT IN TRYING?
I GIVE UP.
I'M SCOTT SUMMERS AND WELL, FIRST OFF YOU DON'T HAVE TO BE SCARED.
WE REJECT NORMAN OSBORN'S POGROMS AGAINST MUTANTS. WE REJECT THE HATE CRIMES OF TRASK AND HIS ILK. IT SEEMED TO US THE PEOPLE OF THE UNITED STATES WANTED US GONE, SO WE'VE LEFT.
WE WON'T BE PUSHED, PROSECUTED, PERSECUTED, OR PUNISHED ANY FURTHER.
It's...it's like he's talking to--
ME.
HE'S TALKING TO ME.
AND HE'S TELLING ME WHAT I'M SUPPOSED TO DO NOW.
REALLY? WHAT'S THAT?

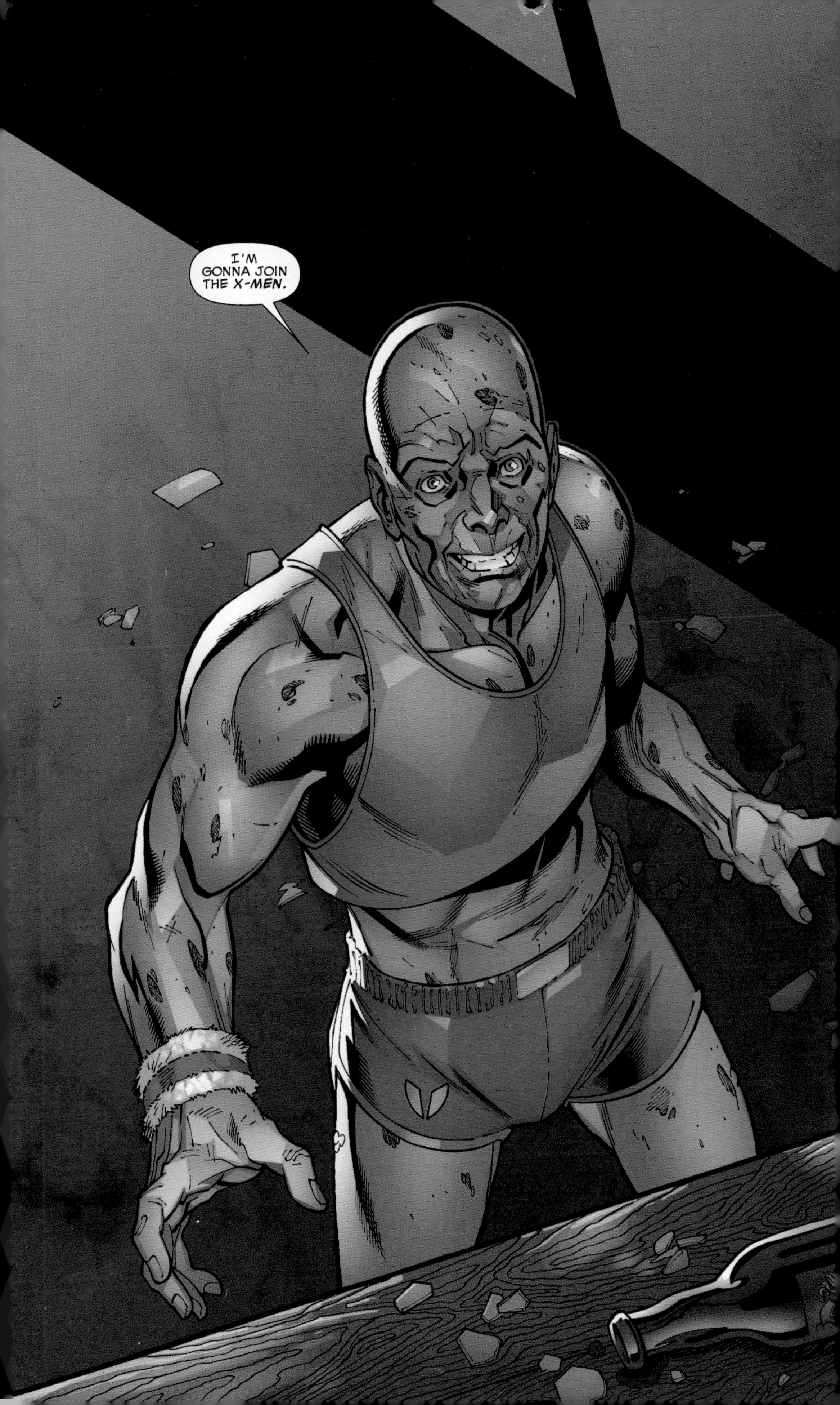
I'M GONNA JOIN THE X-MEN.

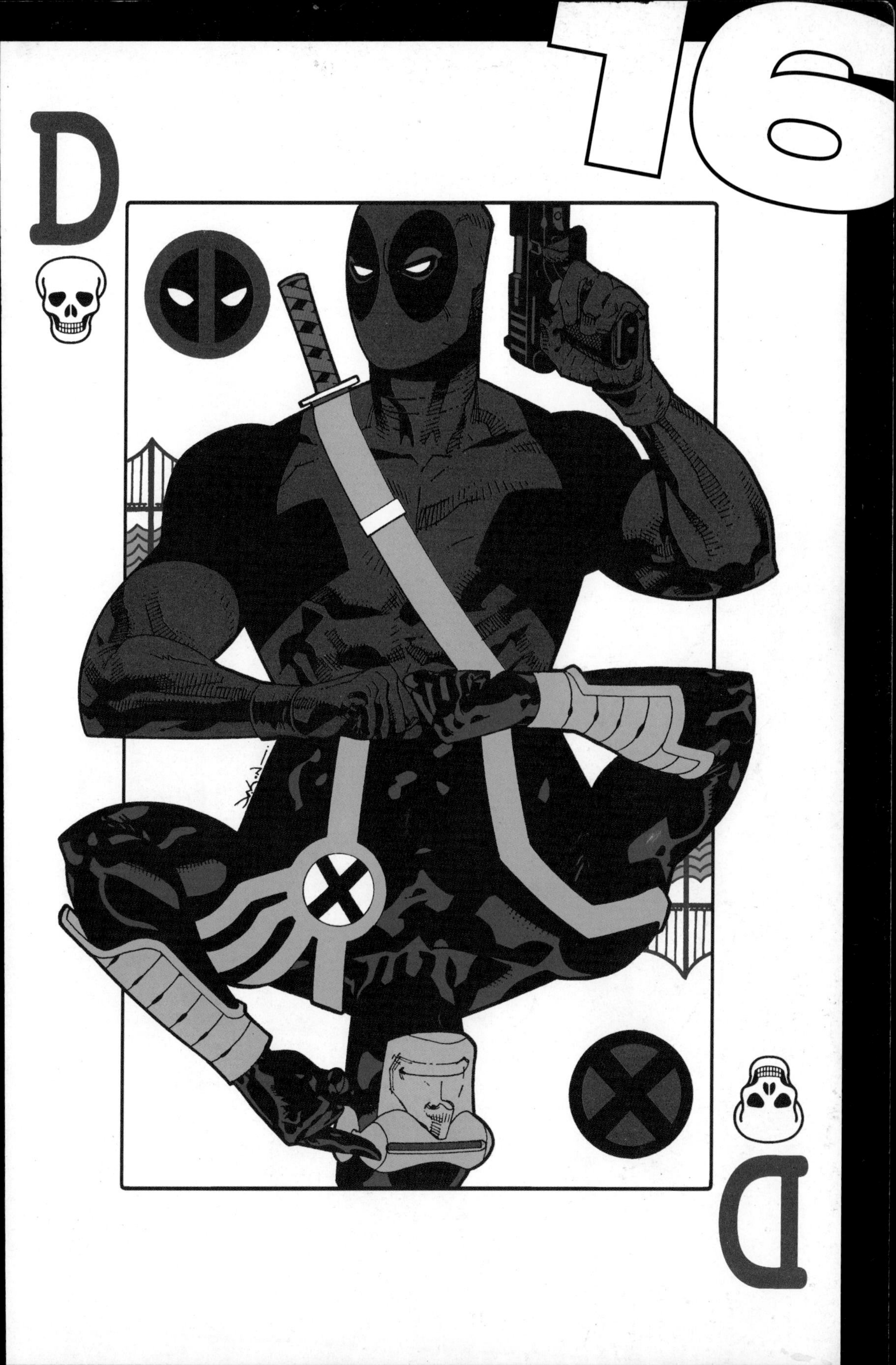
16
D
D

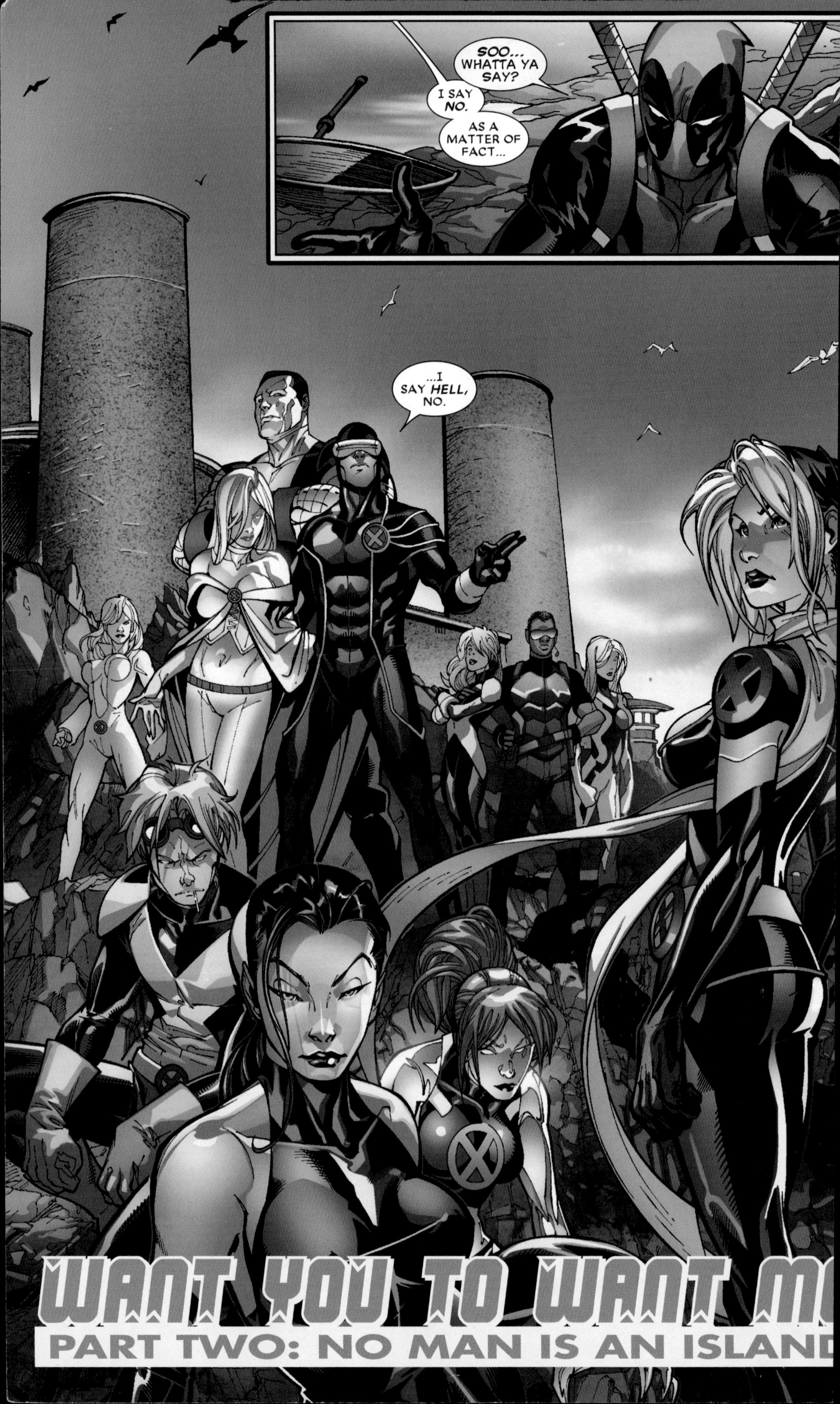
SOO... WHATTA YA SAY?
I SAY NO.
AS A MATTER OF FACT...
...I SAY HELL, NO.
WANT YOU TO WANT ME
PART TWO: NO MAN IS AN ISLAND

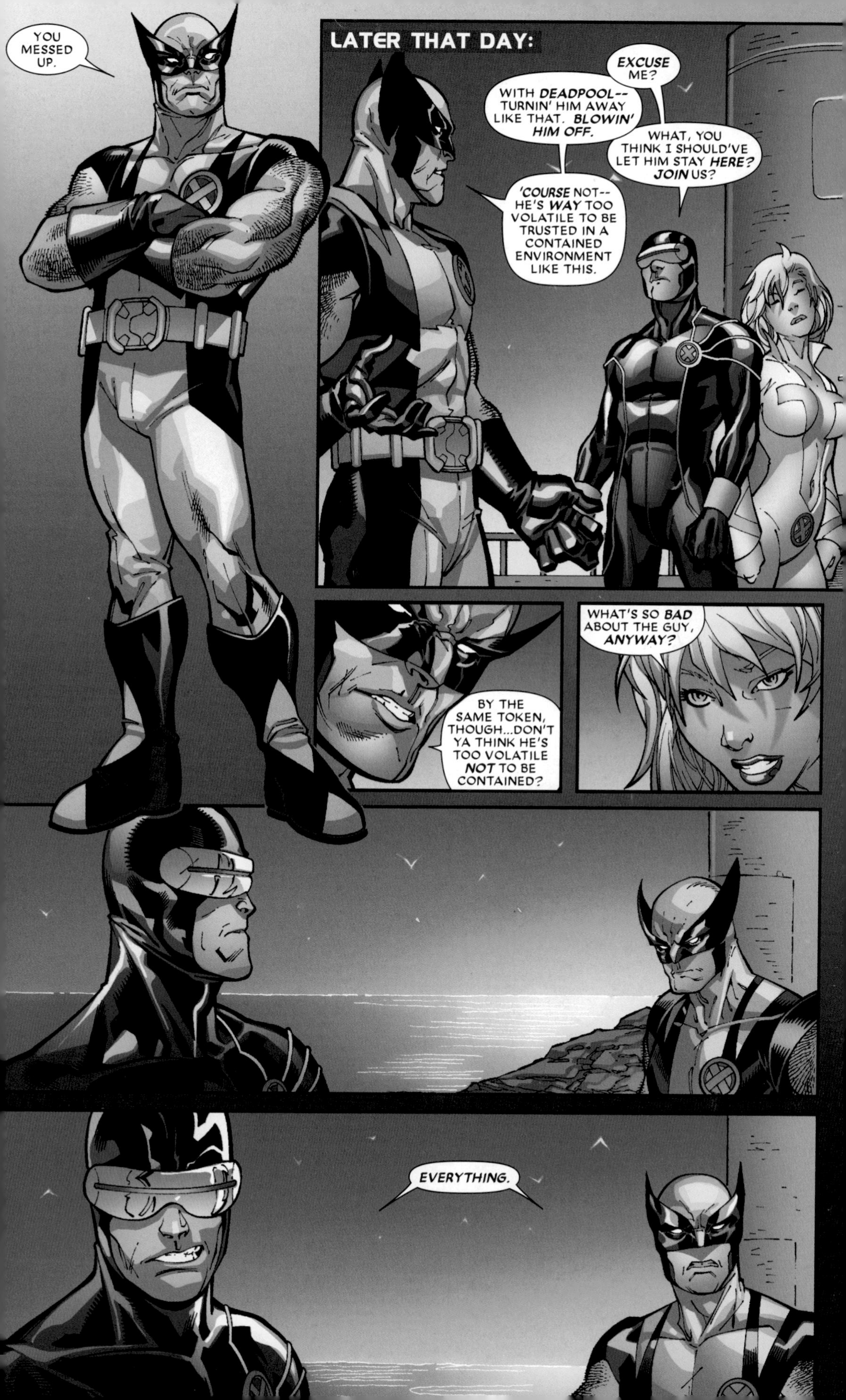

YOU MESSED UP.
LATER THAT DAY:
EXCUSE ME?
WITH DEADPOOL-- TURNIN' HIM AWAY LIKE THAT. BLOWIN' HIM OFF.
WHAT, YOU THINK I SHOULD'VE LET HIM STAY HERE? JOIN US?
'COURSE NOT-- HE'S WAY TOO VOLATILE TO BE TRUSTED IN A CONTAINED ENVIRONMENT LIKE THIS.
BY THE SAME TOKEN, THOUGH...DON'T YA THINK HE'S TOO VOLATILE NOT TO BE CONTAINED?
WHAT'S SO BAD ABOUT THE GUY, ANYWAY?
EVERYTHING.

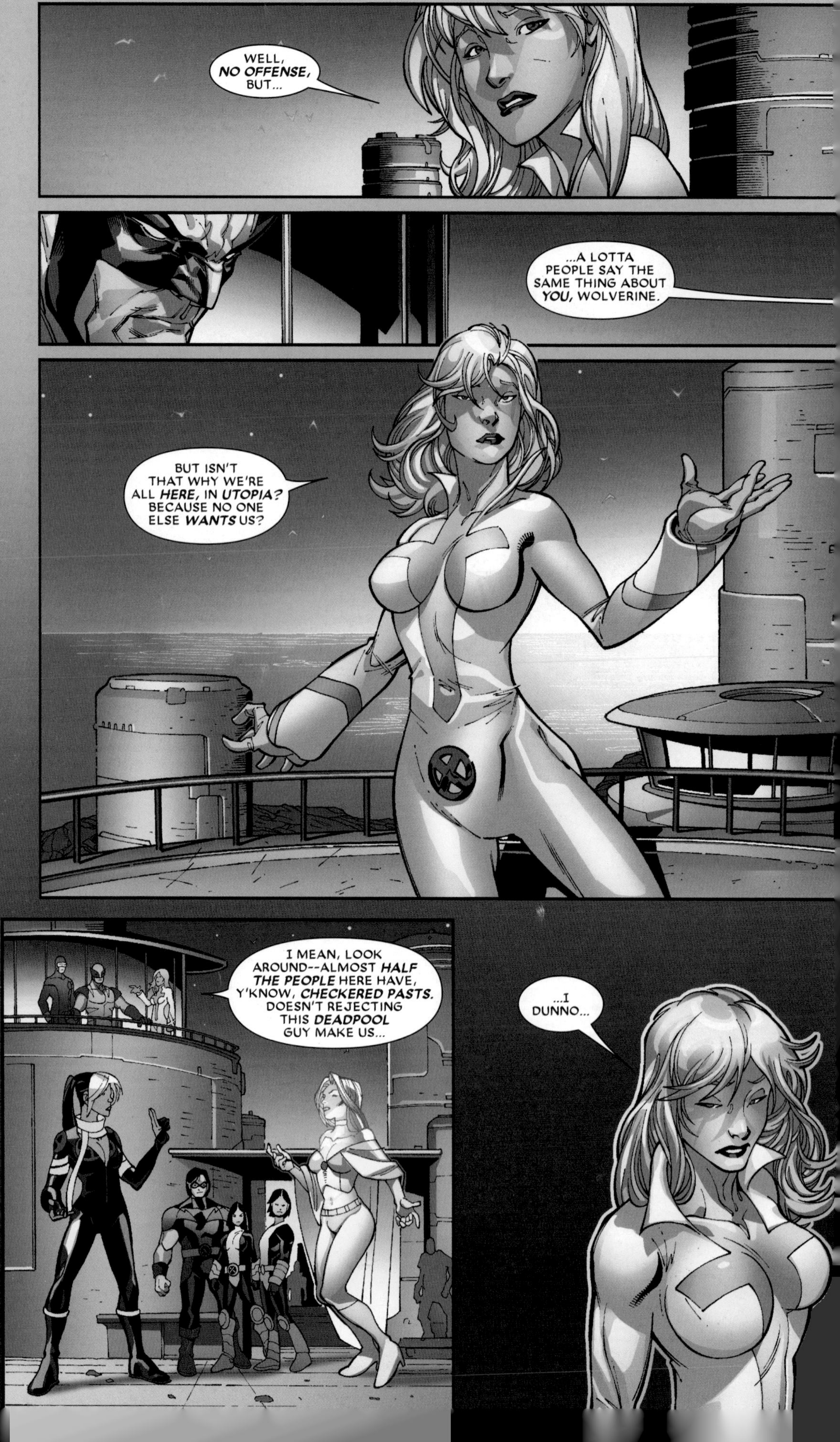
WELL, NO OFFENSE, BUT...
...A LOTTA PEOPLE SAY THE SAME THING ABOUT YOU, WOLVERINE.
BUT ISN'T THAT WHY WE'RE ALL HERE, IN UTOPIA? BECAUSE NO ONE ELSE WANTS US?
I MEAN, LOOK AROUND--ALMOST HALF THE PEOPLE HERE HAVE, Y'KNOW, CHECKERED PASTS. DOESN'T REJECTING THIS DEADPOOL GUY MAKE US...
...I DUNNO...

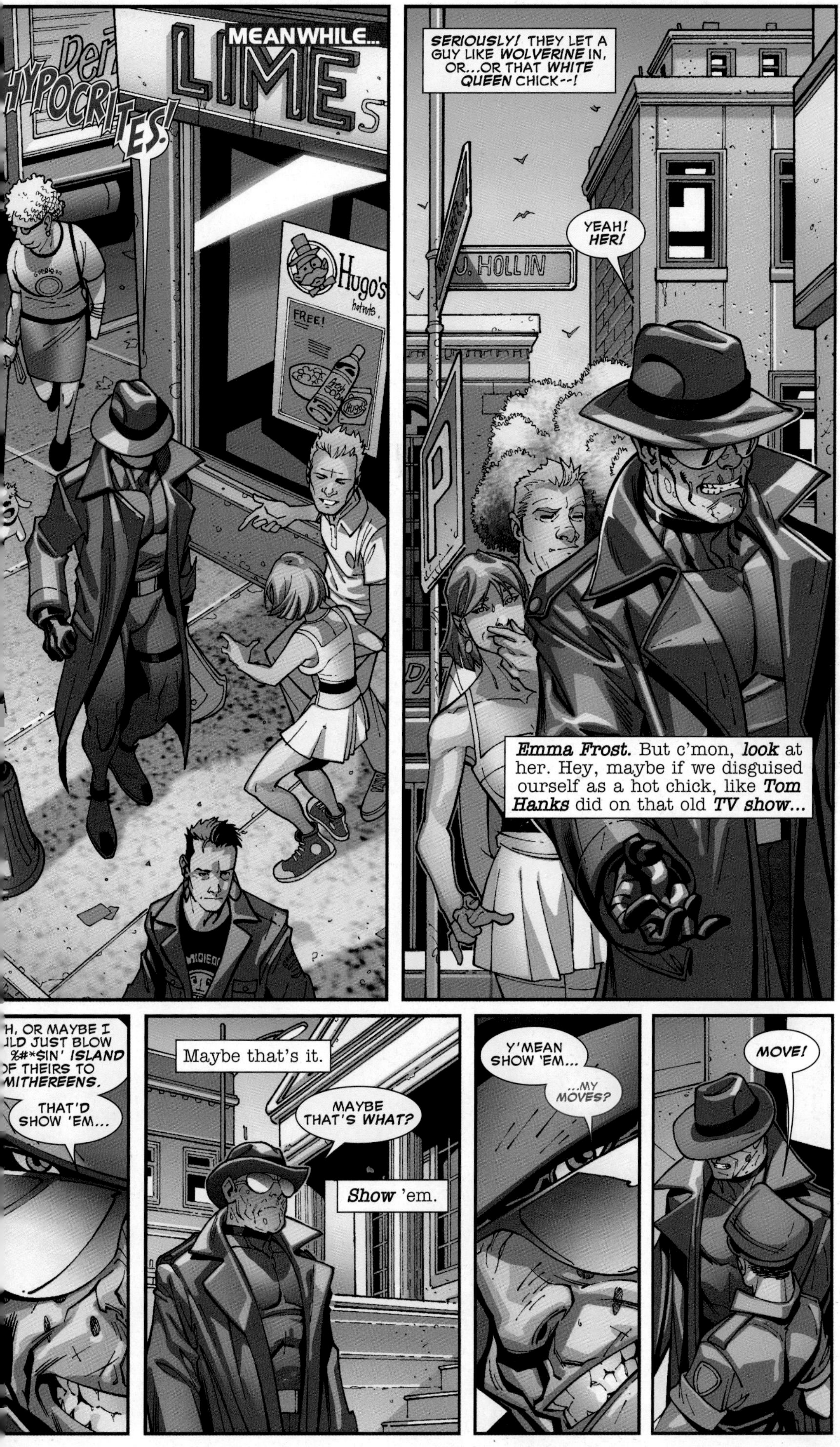
MEANWHILE...
HYPOCRITES!
SERIOUSLY! THEY LET A GUY LIKE WOLVERINE IN, OR...OR THAT WHITE QUEEN CHICK--!
YEAH! HER!
Emma Frost. But c'mon, look at her. Hey, maybe if we disguised ourself as a hot chick, like Tom Hanks did on that old TV show...
H, OR MAYBE I ULD JUST BLOW %#*$IN' ISLAND OF THEIRS TO MITHEREENS.
THAT'D SHOW 'EM...
Maybe that's it.
MAYBE THAT'S WHAT?
Show 'em.
Y'MEAN SHOW 'EM...
...MY MOVES?
MOVE!

**THERE HE IS!**

**THERE WHO IS? ARE THEY TALKING ABOUT US?**

No, they're talking about--

**MR. KINCAID! WHAT WAS THE COURT'S DECISION?**

**THE COURT DECIDED TO DO NOTHING. THE JUDGE SAID THAT, "DUE TO PRESENT CIRCUMSTANCES, THERE'S NOTHING THE COURT CAN DO.**

**ESSENTIALLY, I'VE BEEN TOLD THAT, AS A PARENT, I HAVE NO RIGHTS OR RECOURSE BECAUSE CALIFORNIA LAW EVIDENTLY DOESN'T APPLY TO THE X-MEN'S ISLAND STRONGHOLD.**

**DO YOU BLAME THE X-MEN FOR THIS? WHAT ARE YOUR PERSONAL FEELINGS REGARDING--?**

**LET ME BE CLEAR ON SOMETHING: I'M NOT ANTI-MUTANT, I'M PRO-PARENTAL RIGHTS. MY DAUGHTER IS A MINOR, SHE'S BEEN TRANSFERRED FROM WHAT WAS INITIALLY DESCRIBED TO ME AND MY EX-WIFE AS A "SCHOOL" TO SOME SORT OF...MILITARY COMPOUND, AND I'M BEING BLOCKED FROM VISITING HER. IT'S THAT SIMPLE.**

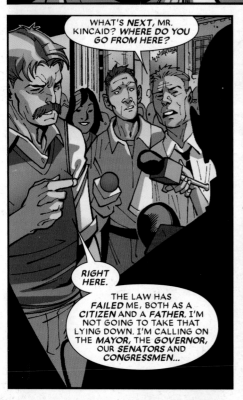

**WHAT'S NEXT, MR. KINCAID? WHERE DO YOU GO FROM HERE?**

**RIGHT HERE.**

**THE LAW HAS FAILED ME, BOTH AS A CITIZEN AND A FATHER. I'M NOT GOING TO TAKE THAT LYING DOWN. I'M CALLING ON THE MAYOR, THE GOVERNOR, OUR SENATORS AND CONGRESSMEN...**

**...AND ESPECIALLY YOU, THE PEOPLE, TO HELP ME DO SOMETHING ABOUT IT!**

"MR. SUMMERS? THERE'S A, UM, SITUATION DEVELOPING..."

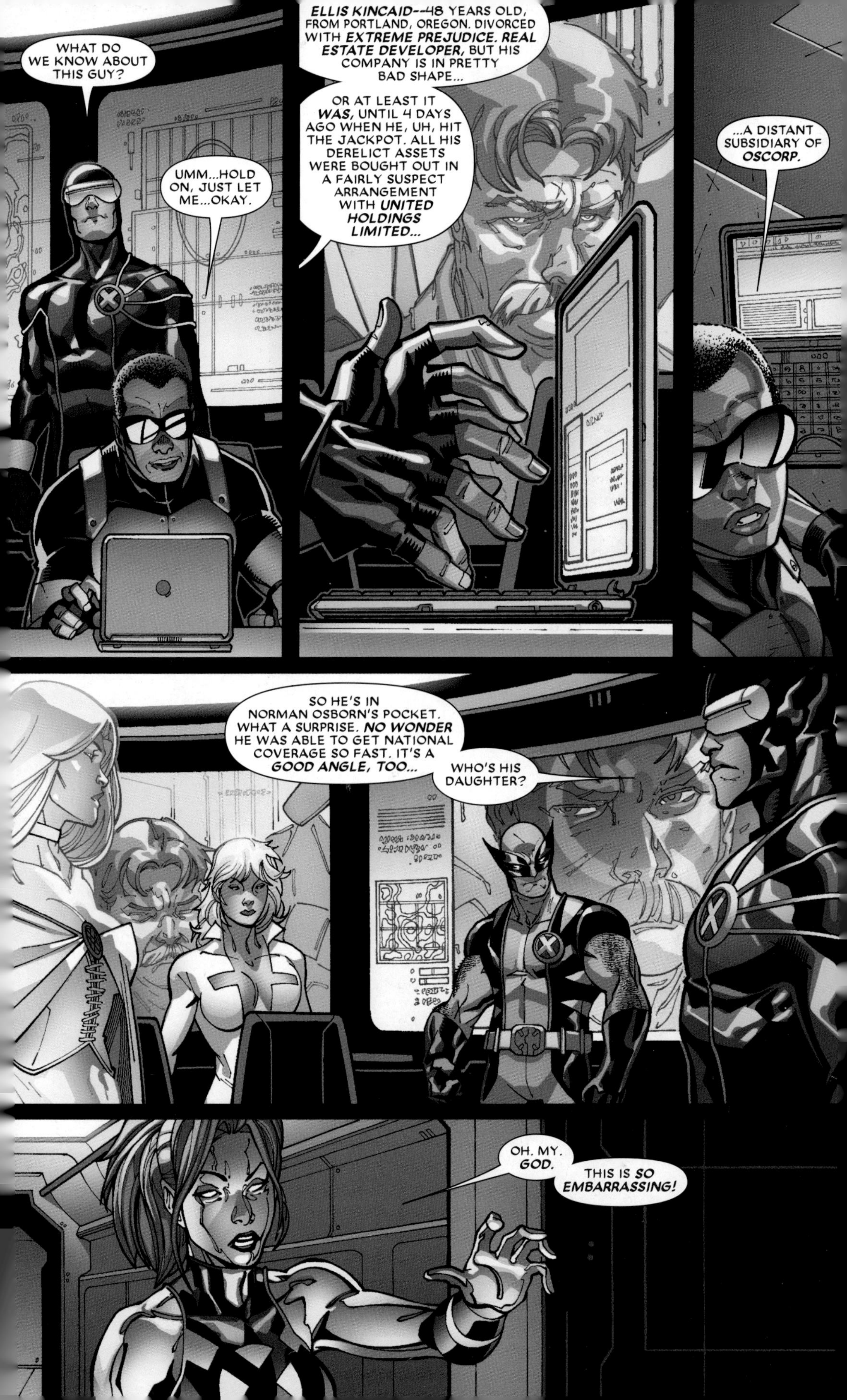
WHAT DO WE KNOW ABOUT THIS GUY?
UMM...HOLD ON, JUST LET ME...OKAY.
ELLIS KINCAID--48 YEARS OLD, FROM PORTLAND, OREGON. DIVORCED WITH EXTREME PREJUDICE. REAL ESTATE DEVELOPER, BUT HIS COMPANY IS IN PRETTY BAD SHAPE...
OR AT LEAST IT WAS, UNTIL 4 DAYS AGO WHEN HE, UH, HIT THE JACKPOT. ALL HIS DERELICT ASSETS WERE BOUGHT OUT IN A FAIRLY SUSPECT ARRANGEMENT WITH UNITED HOLDINGS LIMITED...
...A DISTANT SUBSIDIARY OF OSCORP.
SO HE'S IN NORMAN OSBORN'S POCKET. WHAT A SURPRISE. NO WONDER HE WAS ABLE TO GET NATIONAL COVERAGE SO FAST. IT'S A GOOD ANGLE, TOO...
WHO'S HIS DAUGHTER?
OH. MY. GOD.
THIS IS SO EMBARRASSING!

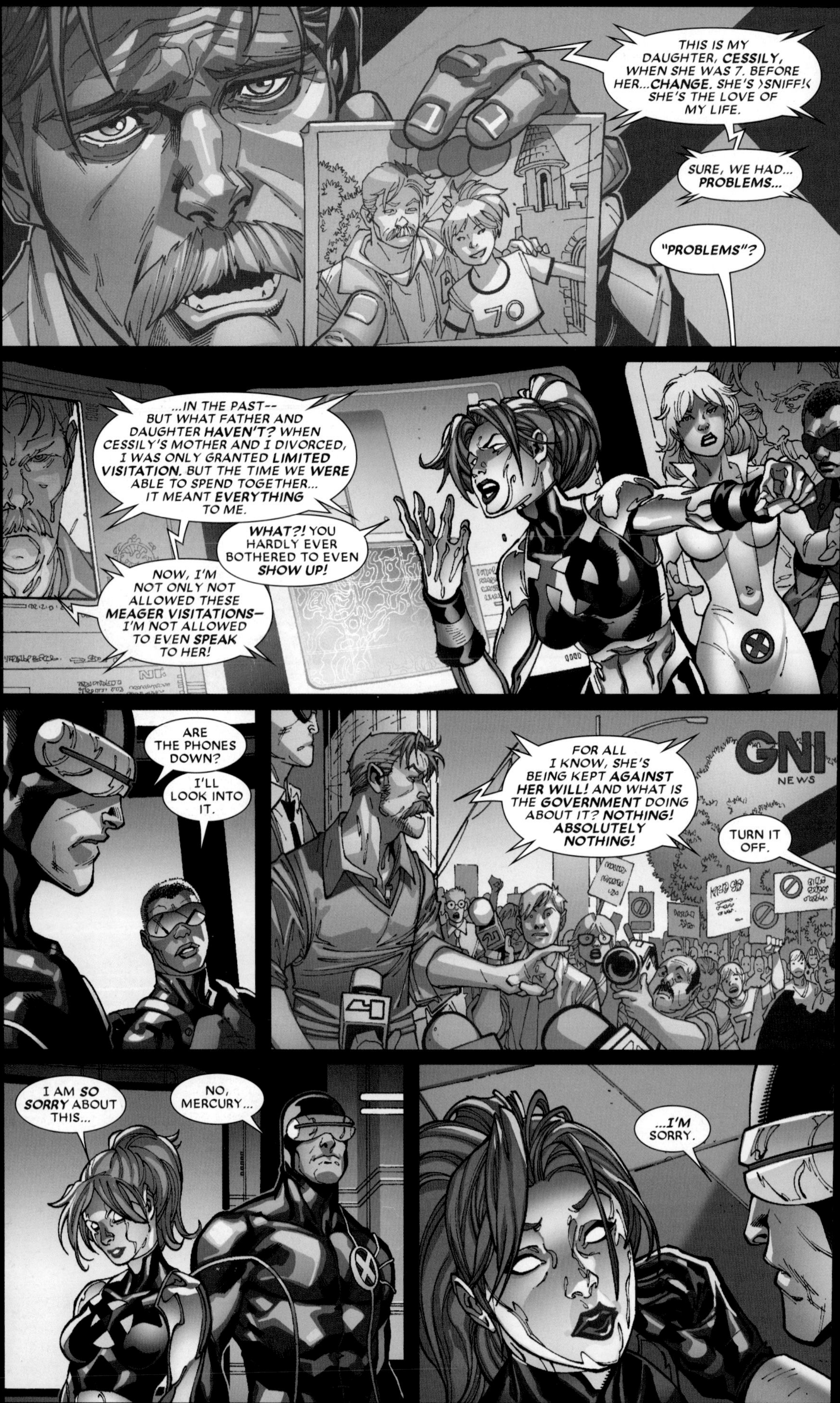

THIS IS MY DAUGHTER, CESSILY, WHEN SHE WAS 7. BEFORE HER...CHANGE. SHE'S ›SNIFF‹ SHE'S THE LOVE OF MY LIFE.
SURE, WE HAD... PROBLEMS...
"PROBLEMS"?
...IN THE PAST-- BUT WHAT FATHER AND DAUGHTER HAVEN'T? WHEN CESSILY'S MOTHER AND I DIVORCED, I WAS ONLY GRANTED LIMITED VISITATION. BUT THE TIME WE WERE ABLE TO SPEND TOGETHER... IT MEANT EVERYTHING TO ME.
WHAT?! YOU HARDLY EVER BOTHERED TO EVEN SHOW UP!
NOW, I'M NOT ONLY NOT ALLOWED THESE MEAGER VISITATIONS-- I'M NOT ALLOWED TO EVEN SPEAK TO HER!
ARE THE PHONES DOWN?
I'LL LOOK INTO IT.
GNI NEWS
FOR ALL I KNOW, SHE'S BEING KEPT AGAINST HER WILL! AND WHAT IS THE GOVERNMENT DOING ABOUT IT? NOTHING! ABSOLUTELY NOTHING!
TURN IT OFF.
I AM SO SORRY ABOUT THIS...
NO, MERCURY...
...I'M SORRY.

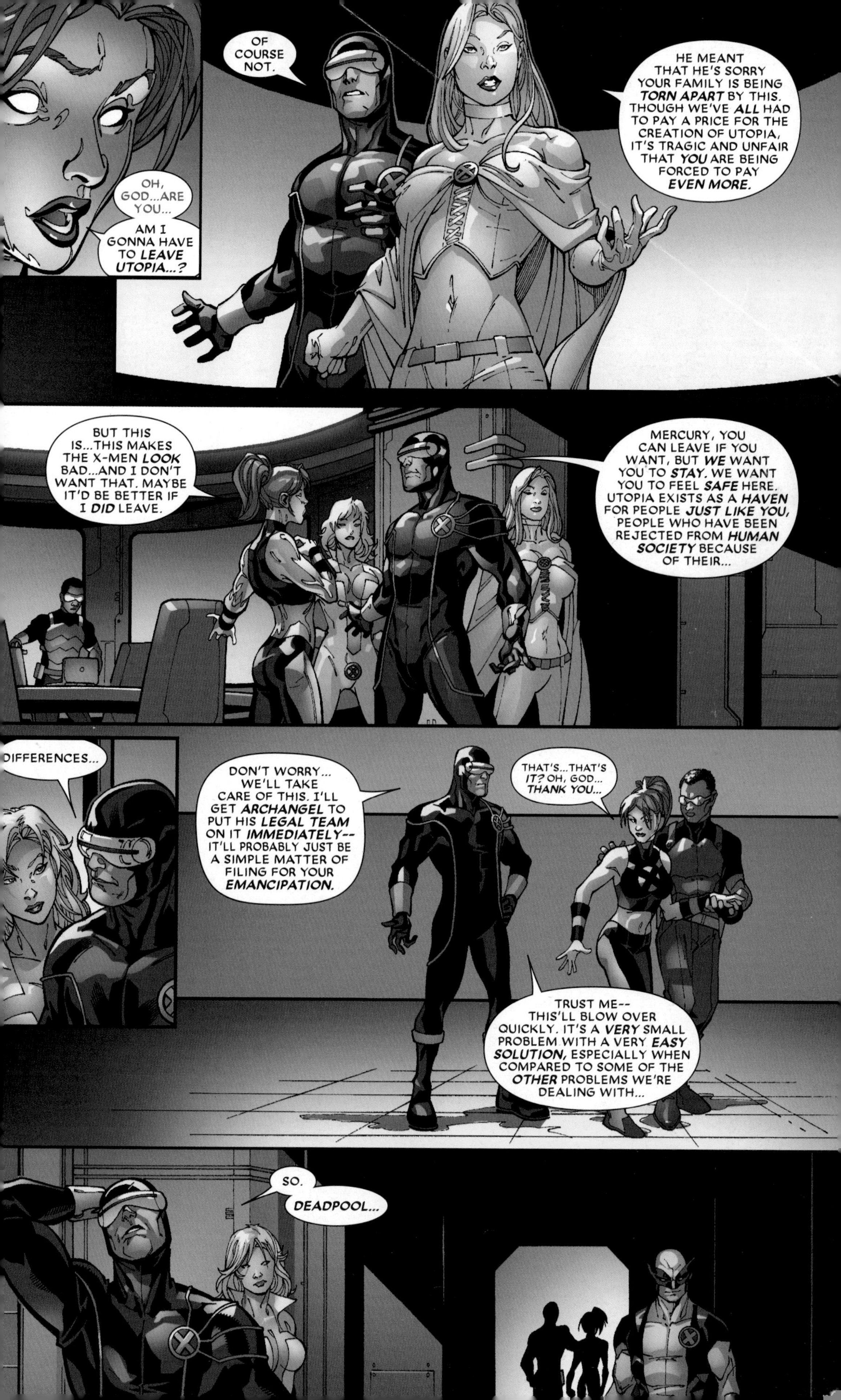
OF COURSE NOT.
HE MEANT THAT HE'S SORRY YOUR FAMILY IS BEING TORN APART BY THIS. THOUGH WE'VE ALL HAD TO PAY A PRICE FOR THE CREATION OF UTOPIA, IT'S TRAGIC AND UNFAIR THAT YOU ARE BEING FORCED TO PAY EVEN MORE.
OH, GOD...ARE YOU...
AM I GONNA HAVE TO LEAVE UTOPIA...?
BUT THIS IS...THIS MAKES THE X-MEN LOOK BAD...AND I DON'T WANT THAT. MAYBE IT'D BE BETTER IF I DID LEAVE.
MERCURY, YOU CAN LEAVE IF YOU WANT, BUT WE WANT YOU TO STAY. WE WANT YOU TO FEEL SAFE HERE. UTOPIA EXISTS AS A HAVEN FOR PEOPLE JUST LIKE YOU, PEOPLE WHO HAVE BEEN REJECTED FROM HUMAN SOCIETY BECAUSE OF THEIR...
DIFFERENCES...
DON'T WORRY... WE'LL TAKE CARE OF THIS. I'LL GET ARCHANGEL TO PUT HIS LEGAL TEAM ON IT IMMEDIATELY-- IT'LL PROBABLY JUST BE A SIMPLE MATTER OF FILING FOR YOUR EMANCIPATION.
THAT'S...THAT'S IT? OH, GOD... THANK YOU...
TRUST ME-- THIS'LL BLOW OVER QUICKLY. IT'S A VERY SMALL PROBLEM WITH A VERY EASY SOLUTION, ESPECIALLY WHEN COMPARED TO SOME OF THE OTHER PROBLEMS WE'RE DEALING WITH...
SO.
DEADPOOL...

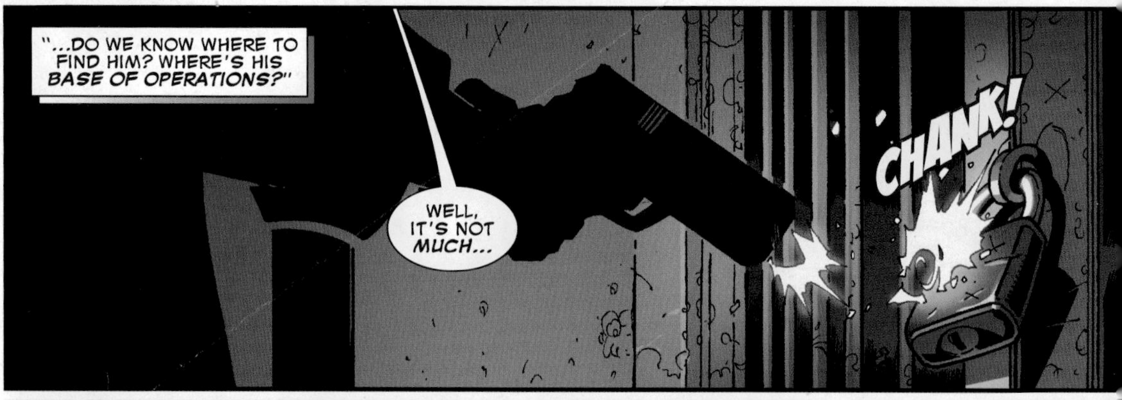
"...DO WE KNOW WHERE TO FIND HIM? WHERE'S HIS BASE OF OPERATIONS?"
WELL, IT'S NOT MUCH...
CHANK!

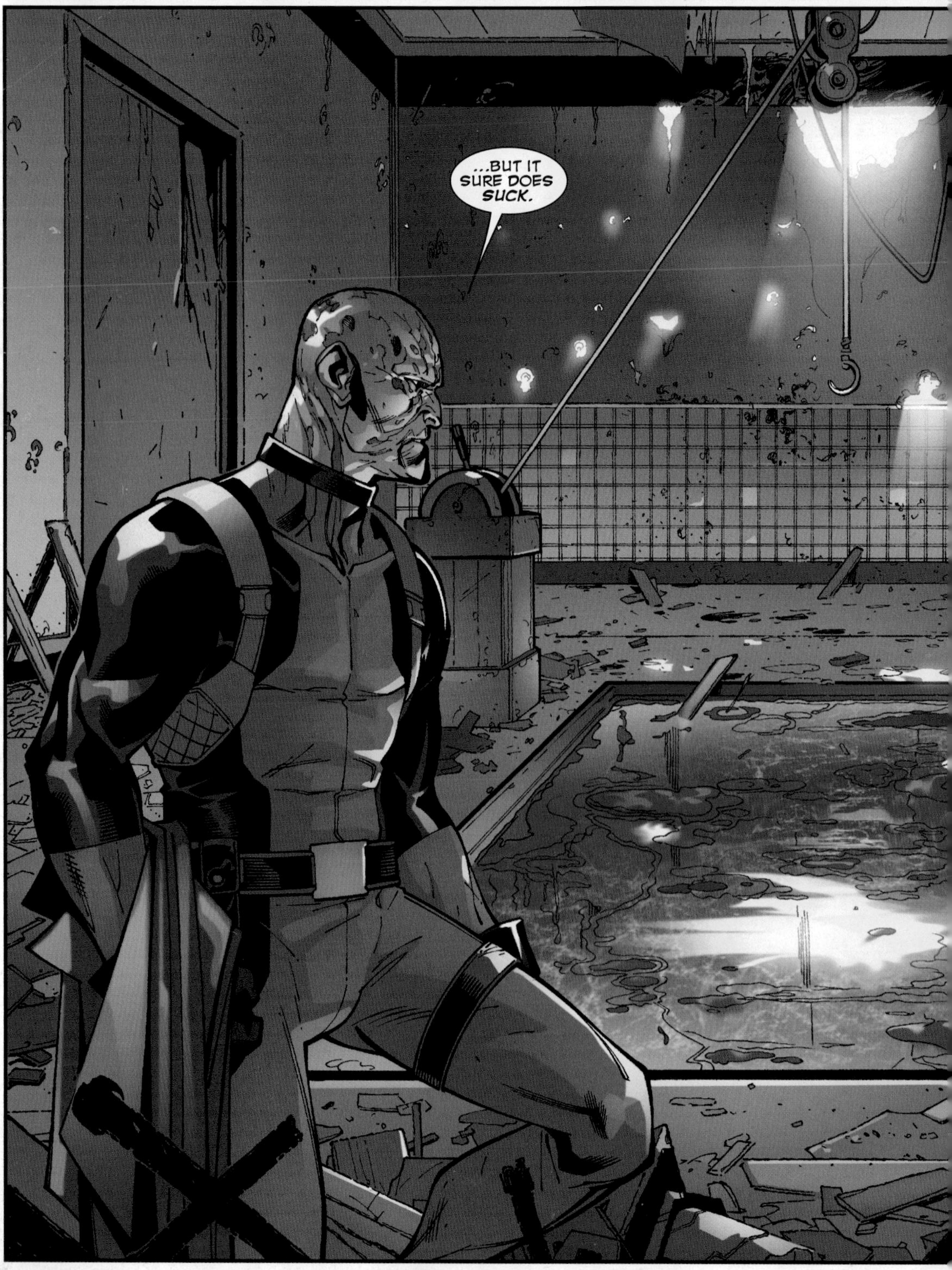
...BUT IT SURE DOES SUCK.

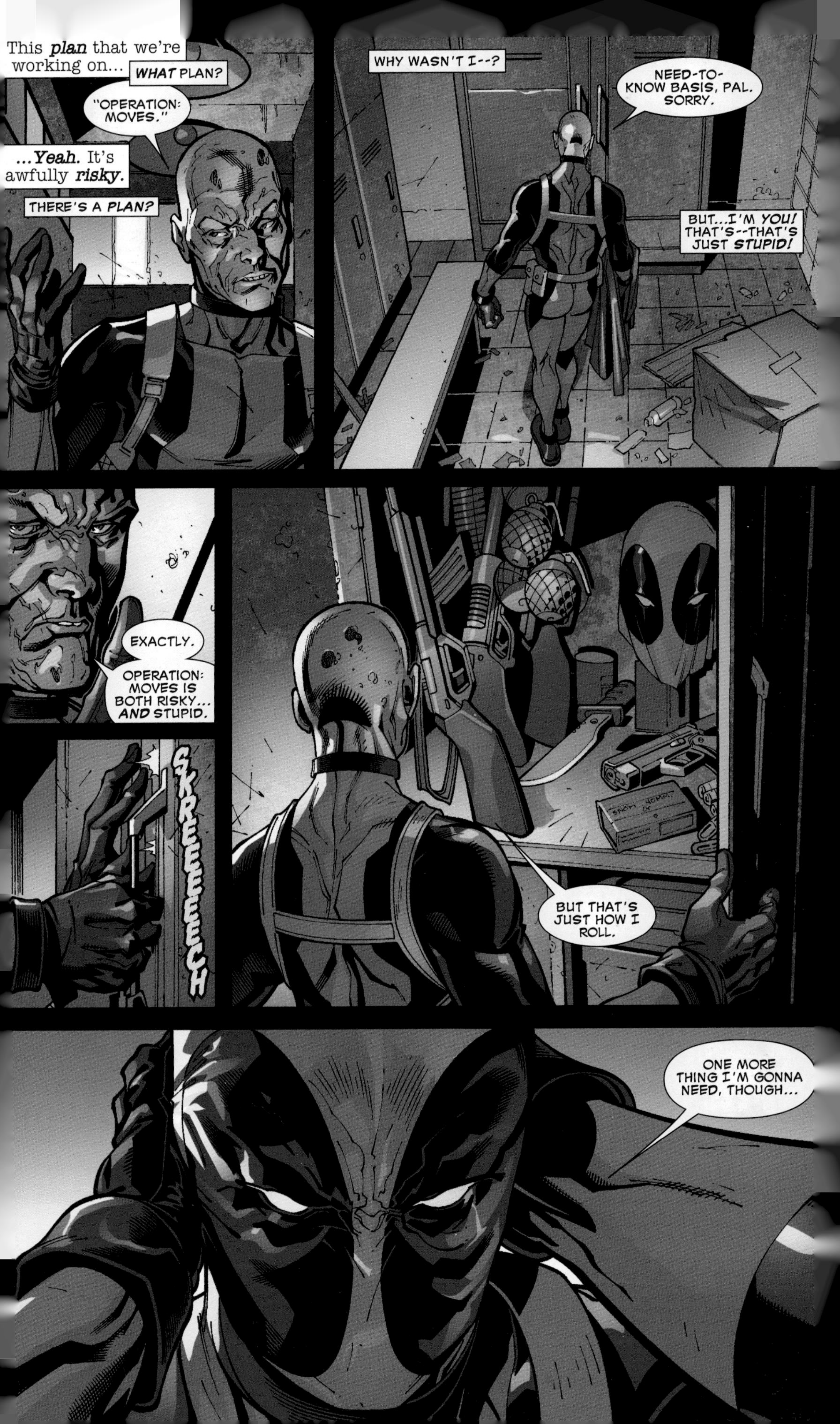

This **plan** that we're working on...
*WHAT* PLAN?
"OPERATION: MOVES."
...**Yeah**. It's awfully **risky**.
THERE'S A *PLAN?*
WHY WASN'T I--?
NEED-TO-KNOW BASIS, PAL. SORRY.
BUT...I'M *YOU!* THAT'S--THAT'S JUST *STUPID!*
EXACTLY.
OPERATION: MOVES IS BOTH RISKY... *AND* STUPID.
SKREEEEECH
BUT THAT'S JUST HOW I ROLL.
ONE MORE THING I'M GONNA NEED, THOUGH...

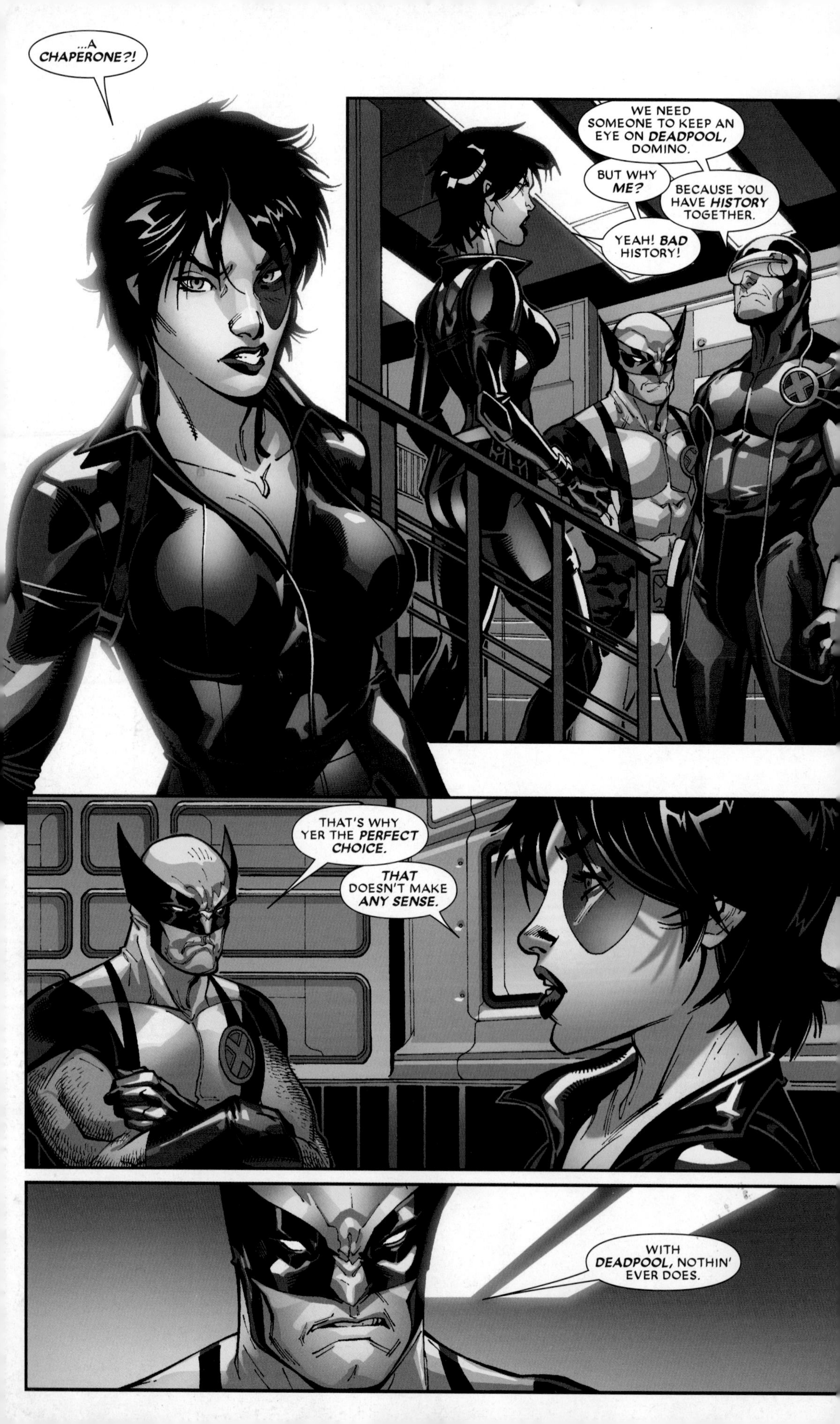
...A CHAPERONE?!
WE NEED SOMEONE TO KEEP AN EYE ON DEADPOOL, DOMINO.
BUT WHY ME?
BECAUSE YOU HAVE HISTORY TOGETHER.
YEAH! BAD HISTORY!
THAT'S WHY YER THE PERFECT CHOICE.
THAT DOESN'T MAKE ANY SENSE.
WITH DEADPOOL, NOTHIN' EVER DOES.

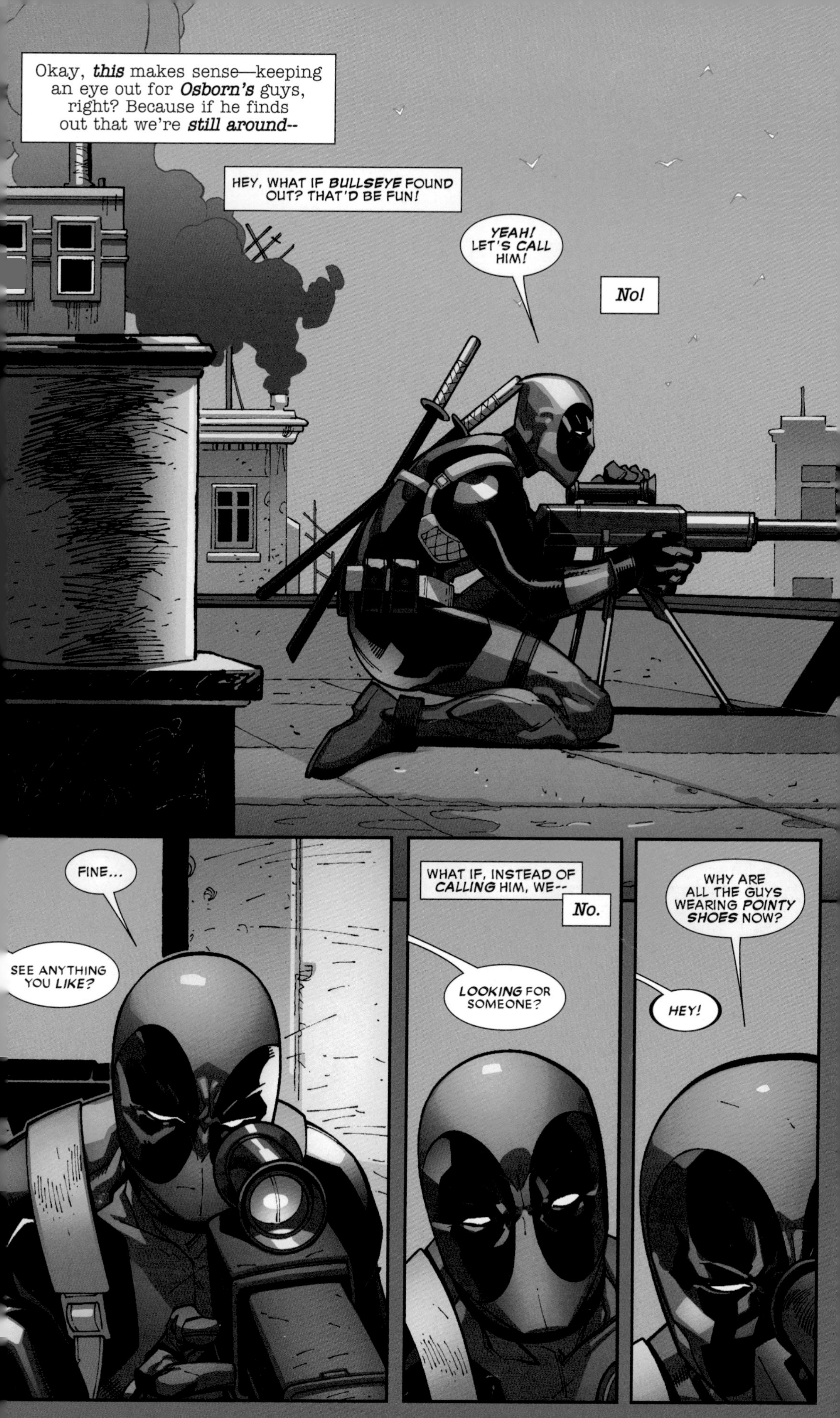
Okay, this makes sense—keeping an eye out for Osborn's guys, right? Because if he finds out that we're still around--
HEY, WHAT IF BULLSEYE FOUND OUT? THAT'D BE FUN!
YEAH! LET'S CALL HIM!
No!
FINE...
SEE ANYTHING YOU LIKE?
WHAT IF, INSTEAD OF CALLING HIM, WE--
No.
LOOKING FOR SOMEONE?
WHY ARE ALL THE GUYS WEARING POINTY SHOES NOW?
HEY!

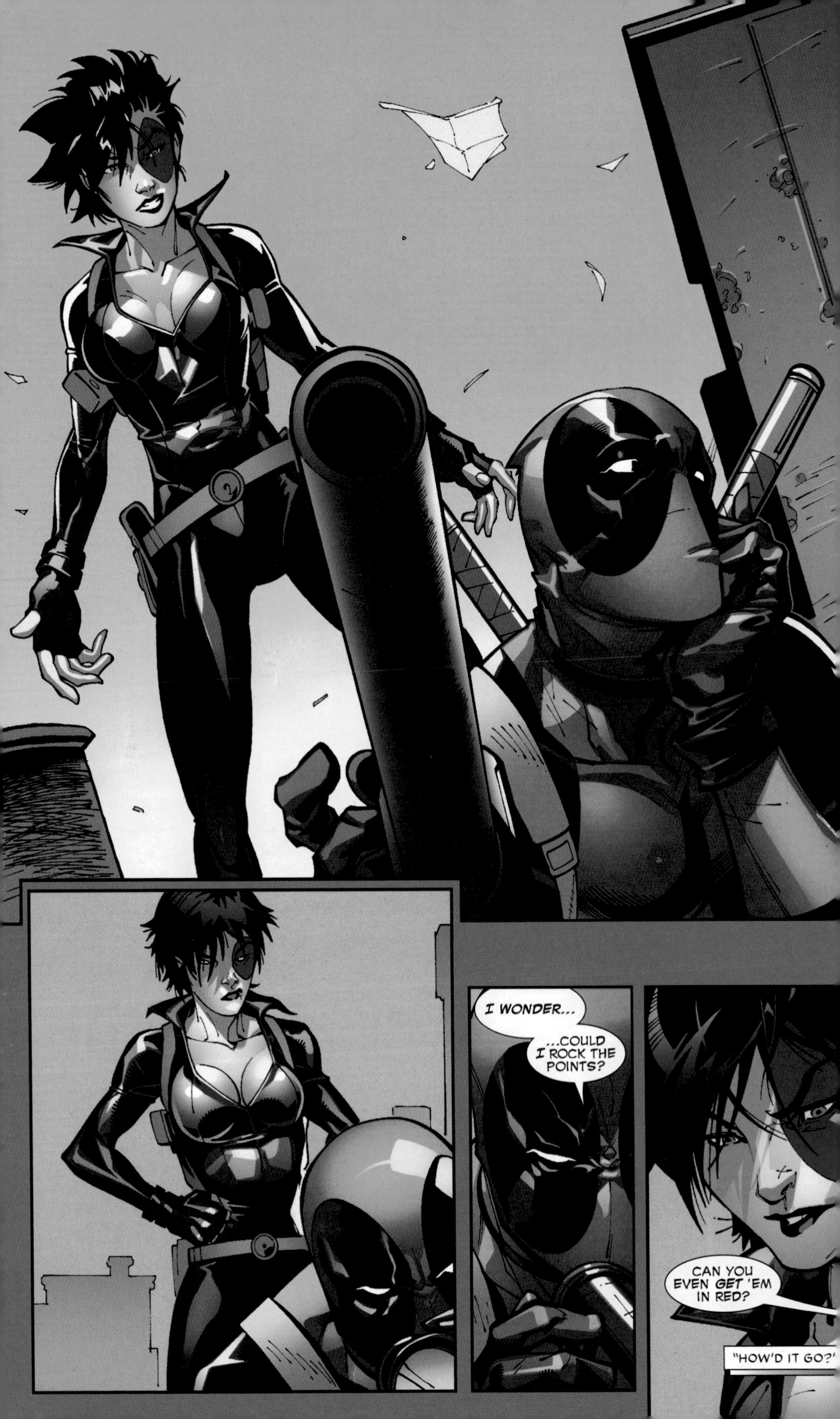
I WONDER...
...COULD I ROCK THE POINTS?
CAN YOU EVEN GET 'EM IN RED?
"HOW'D IT GO?'

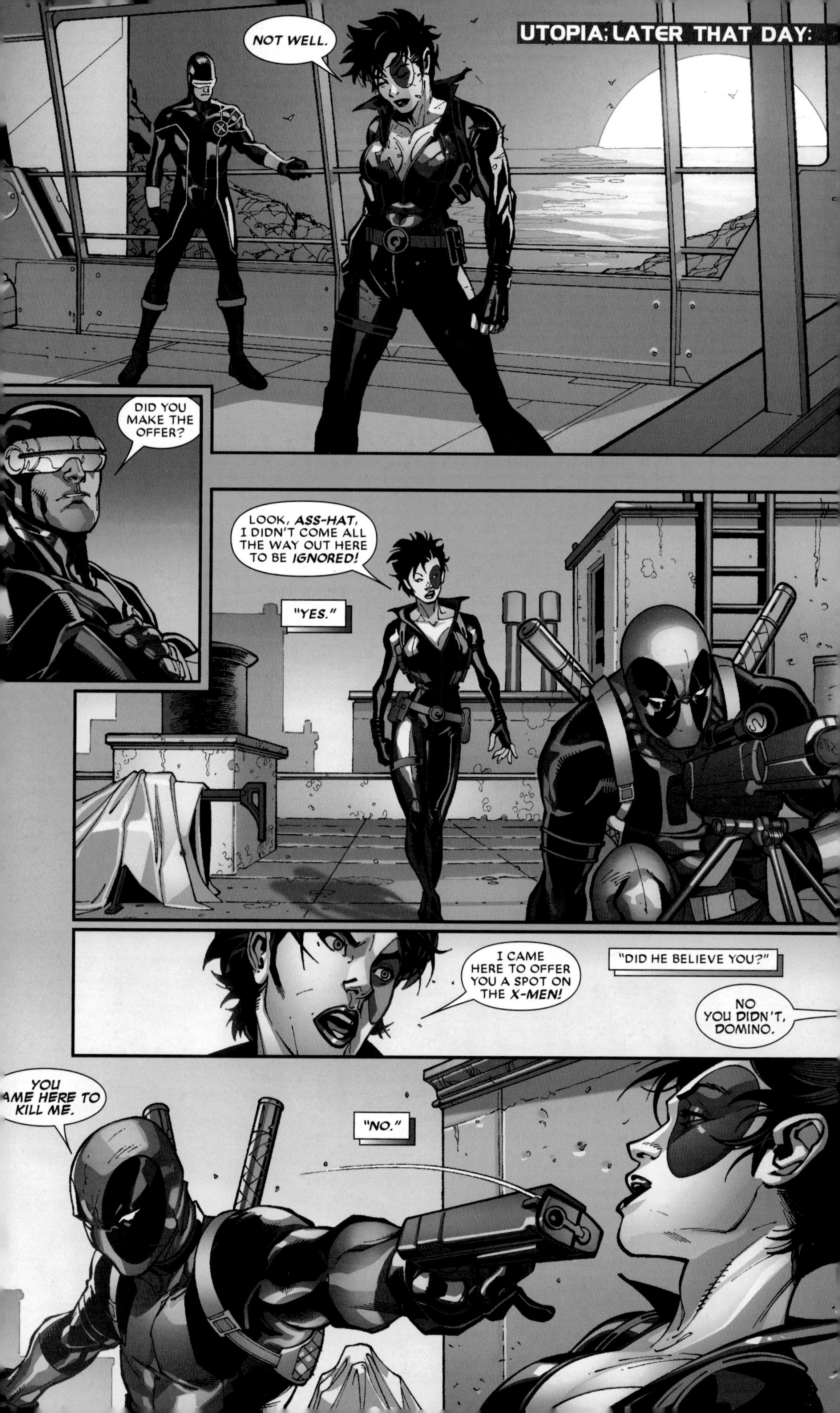
UTOPIA; LATER THAT DAY:
NOT WELL.
DID YOU MAKE THE OFFER?
"YES."
LOOK, ASS-HAT, I DIDN'T COME ALL THE WAY OUT HERE TO BE IGNORED!
I CAME HERE TO OFFER YOU A SPOT ON THE X-MEN!
"DID HE BELIEVE YOU?"
NO YOU DIDN'T, DOMINO.
YOU AME HERE TO KILL ME.
"NO."

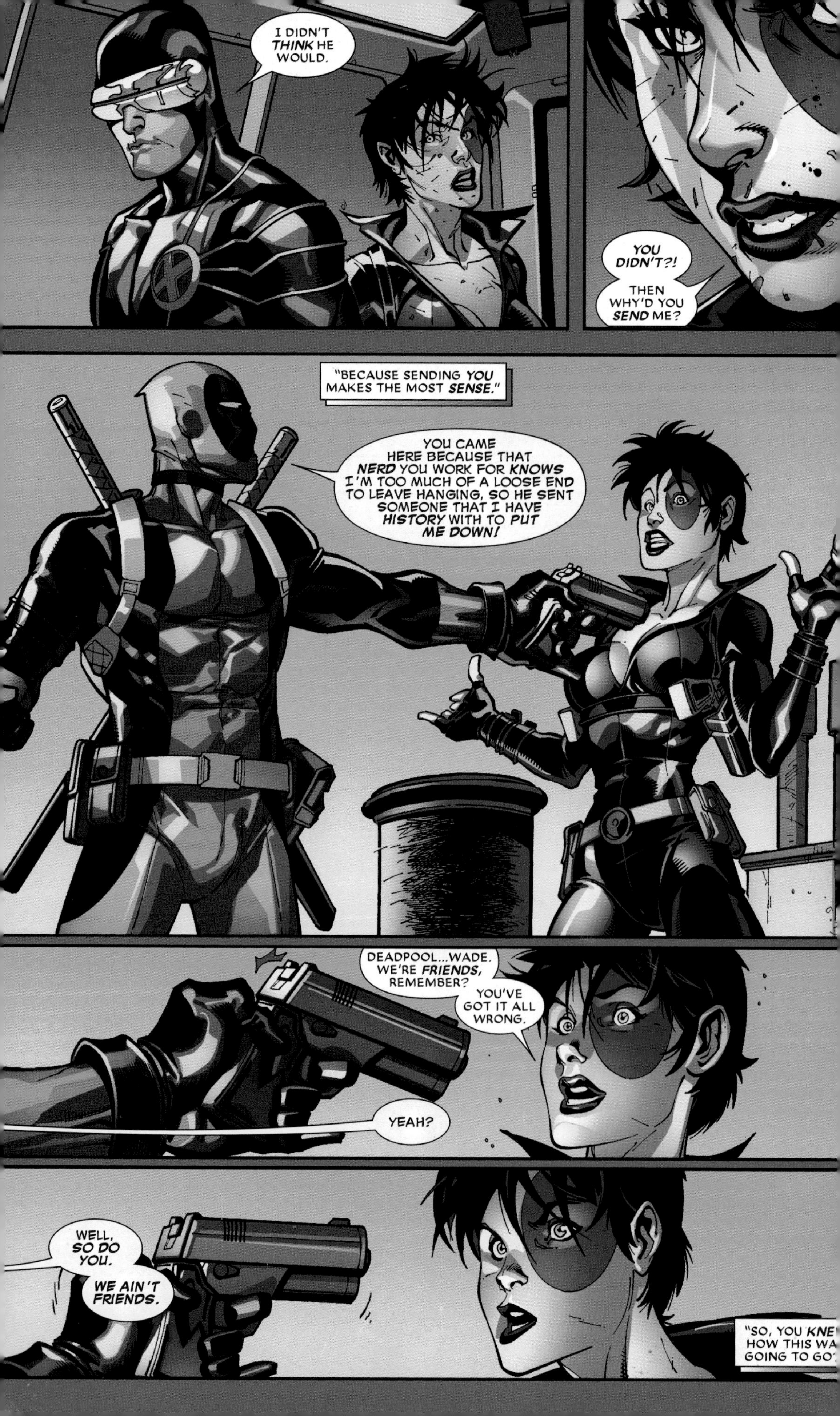
I DIDN'T *THINK* HE WOULD.
*YOU DIDN'T?!*
THEN WHY'D YOU *SEND* ME?
"BECAUSE SENDING *YOU* MAKES THE MOST *SENSE*."
YOU CAME HERE BECAUSE THAT *NERD* YOU WORK FOR *KNOWS* I'M TOO MUCH OF A LOOSE END TO LEAVE HANGING, SO HE SENT SOMEONE THAT I HAVE *HISTORY* WITH TO *PUT ME DOWN!*
DEADPOOL...WADE. WE'RE *FRIENDS*, REMEMBER?
YOU'VE GOT IT ALL WRONG.
YEAH?
WELL, *SO DO YOU.*
*WE AIN'T FRIENDS.*
"SO, YOU KNE HOW THIS WA GOING TO GO

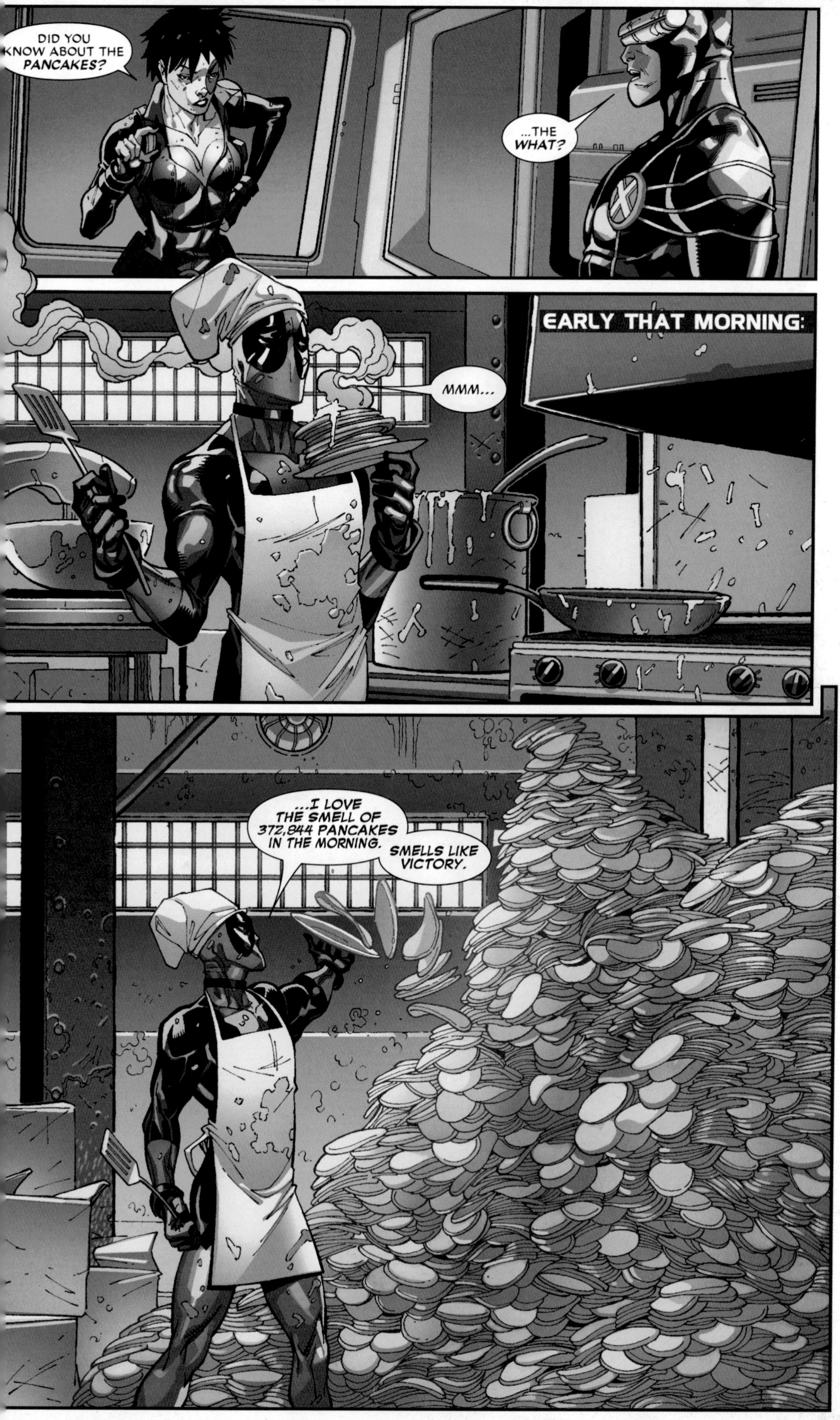
DID YOU KNOW ABOUT THE PANCAKES?
...THE WHAT?
EARLY THAT MORNING:
MMM...
...I LOVE THE SMELL OF 372,844 PANCAKES IN THE MORNING.
SMELLS LIKE VICTORY.

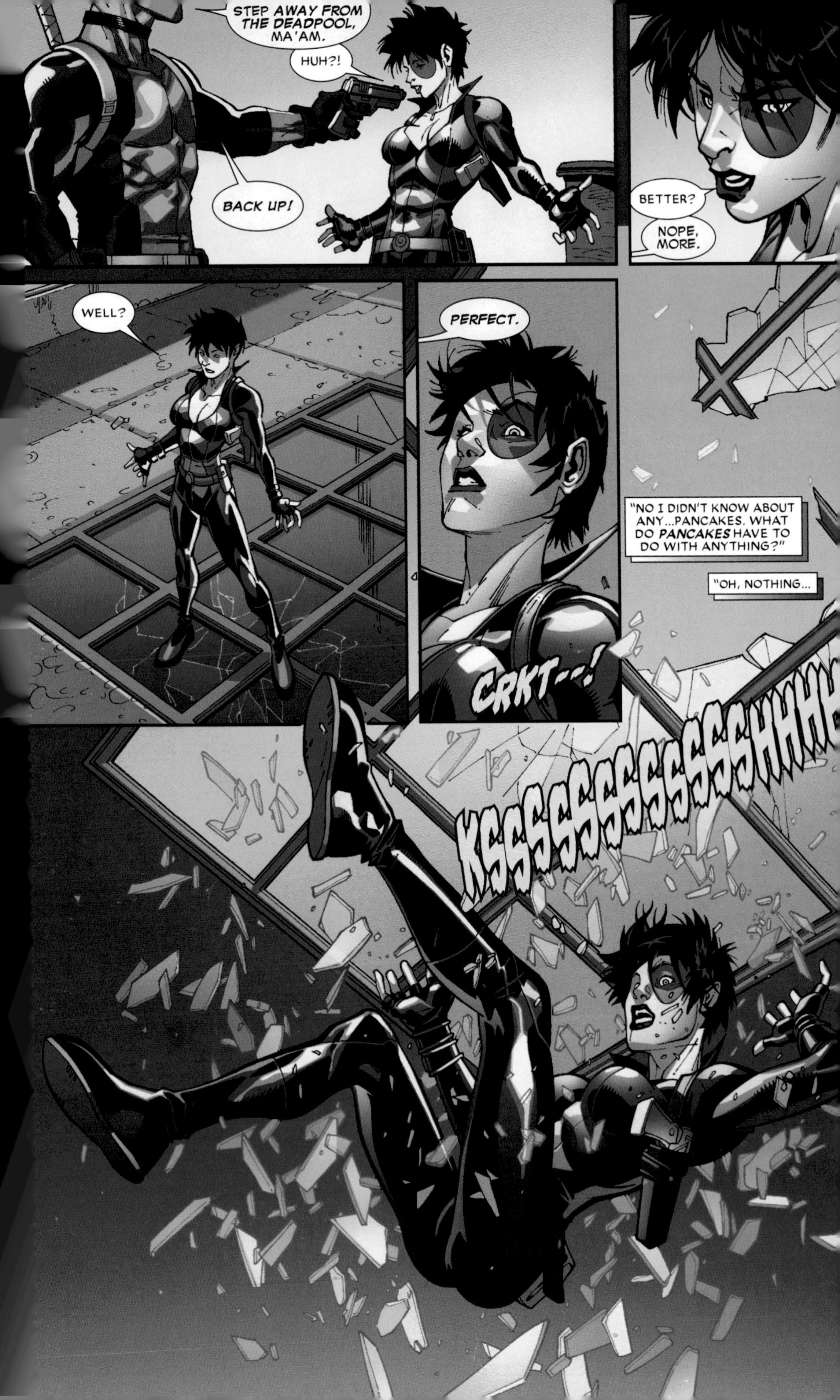
STEP AWAY FROM THE DEADPOOL, MA'AM.
HUH?!
BACK UP!
BETTER?
NOPE, MORE.
WELL?
PERFECT.
"NO I DIDN'T KNOW ABOUT ANY...PANCAKES. WHAT DO PANCAKES HAVE TO DO WITH ANYTHING?"
"OH, NOTHING...
CRKT--!
KSSSSSSSSSSSSSHHH

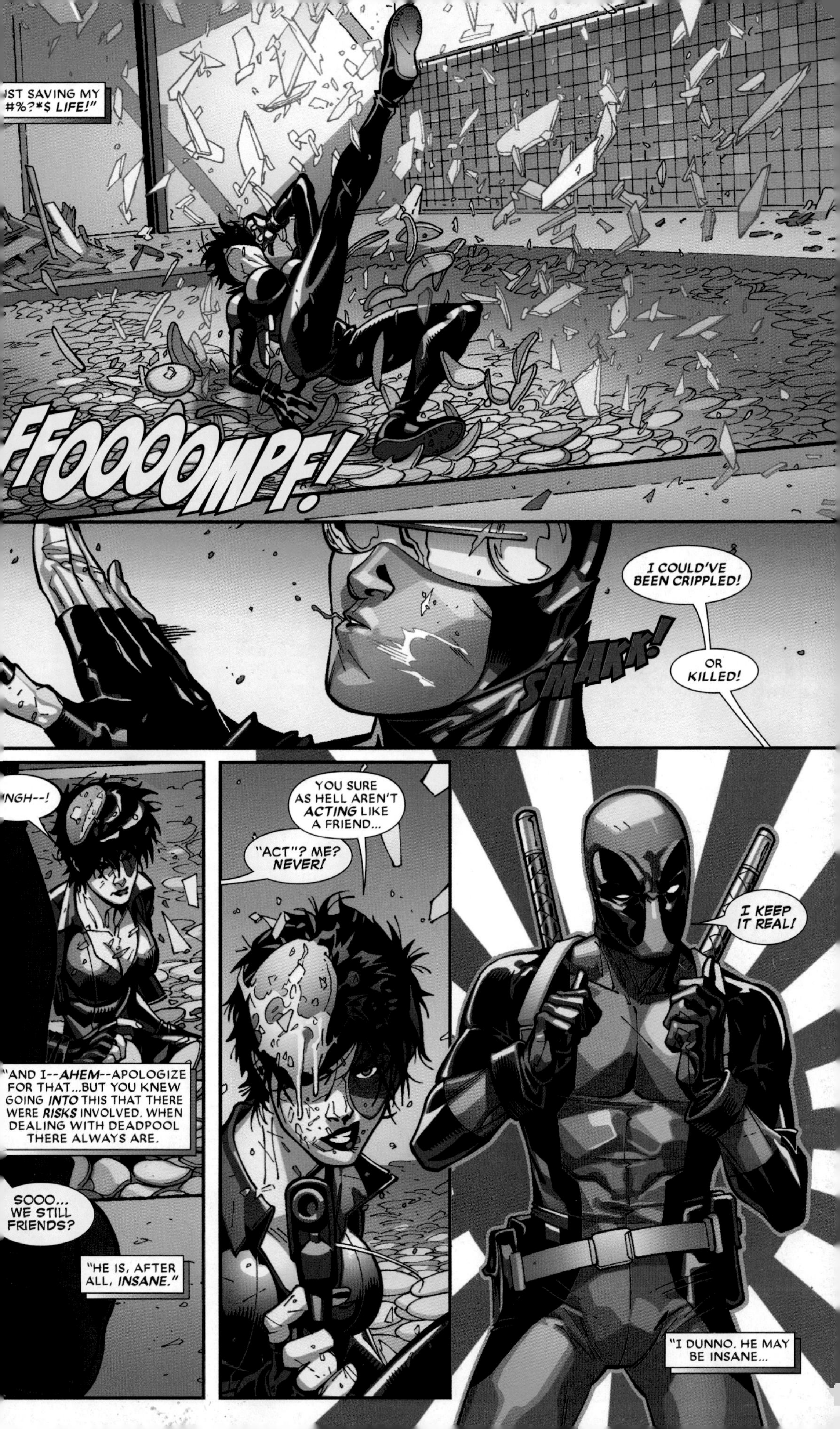
UST SAVING MY #%?*$ LIFE!"
FFOOOOMPF!
I COULD'VE BEEN CRIPPLED!
OR KILLED!
SMAKK!
NGH--!
YOU SURE AS HELL AREN'T ACTING LIKE A FRIEND...
"ACT"? ME? NEVER!
I KEEP IT REAL!
"AND I--AHEM--APOLOGIZE FOR THAT...BUT YOU KNEW GOING INTO THIS THAT THERE WERE RISKS INVOLVED. WHEN DEALING WITH DEADPOOL THERE ALWAYS ARE.
SOOO... WE STILL FRIENDS?
"HE IS, AFTER ALL, INSANE."
"I DUNNO. HE MAY BE INSANE...

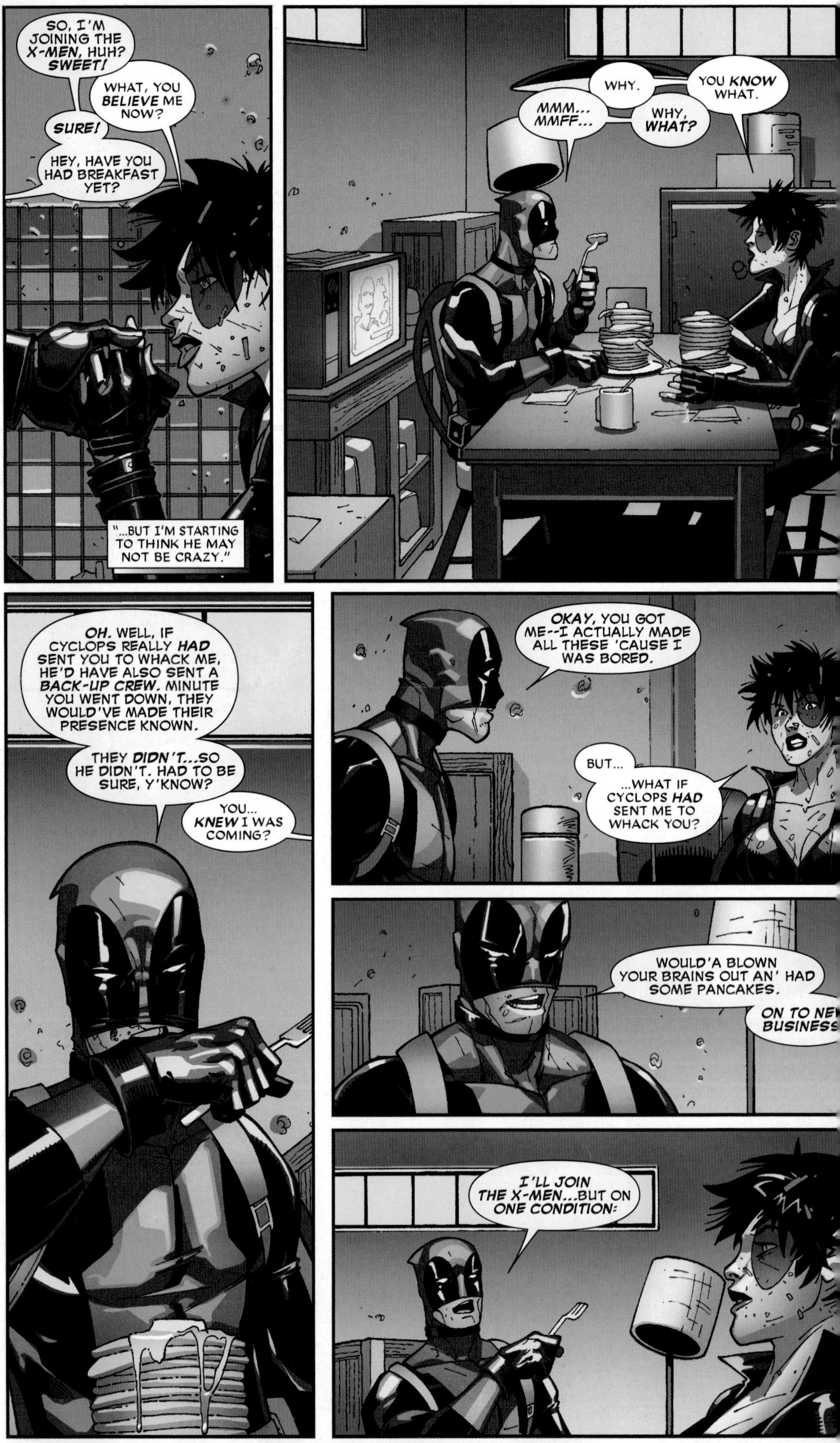
SO, I'M JOINING THE X-MEN, HUH? SWEET!
WHAT, YOU BELIEVE ME NOW?
SURE!
HEY, HAVE YOU HAD BREAKFAST YET?
"...BUT I'M STARTING TO THINK HE MAY NOT BE CRAZY."
MMM... MMFF...
WHY.
WHY, WHAT?
YOU KNOW WHAT.
OH. WELL, IF CYCLOPS REALLY HAD SENT YOU TO WHACK ME, HE'D HAVE ALSO SENT A BACK-UP CREW. MINUTE YOU WENT DOWN, THEY WOULD'VE MADE THEIR PRESENCE KNOWN.
THEY DIDN'T...SO HE DIDN'T. HAD TO BE SURE, Y'KNOW?
YOU... KNEW I WAS COMING?
OKAY, YOU GOT ME--I ACTUALLY MADE ALL THESE 'CAUSE I WAS BORED.
BUT...
...WHAT IF CYCLOPS HAD SENT ME TO WHACK YOU?
WOULD'A BLOWN YOUR BRAINS OUT AN' HAD SOME PANCAKES.
ON TO NE BUSINES
I'LL JOIN THE X-MEN...BUT ON ONE CONDITION:

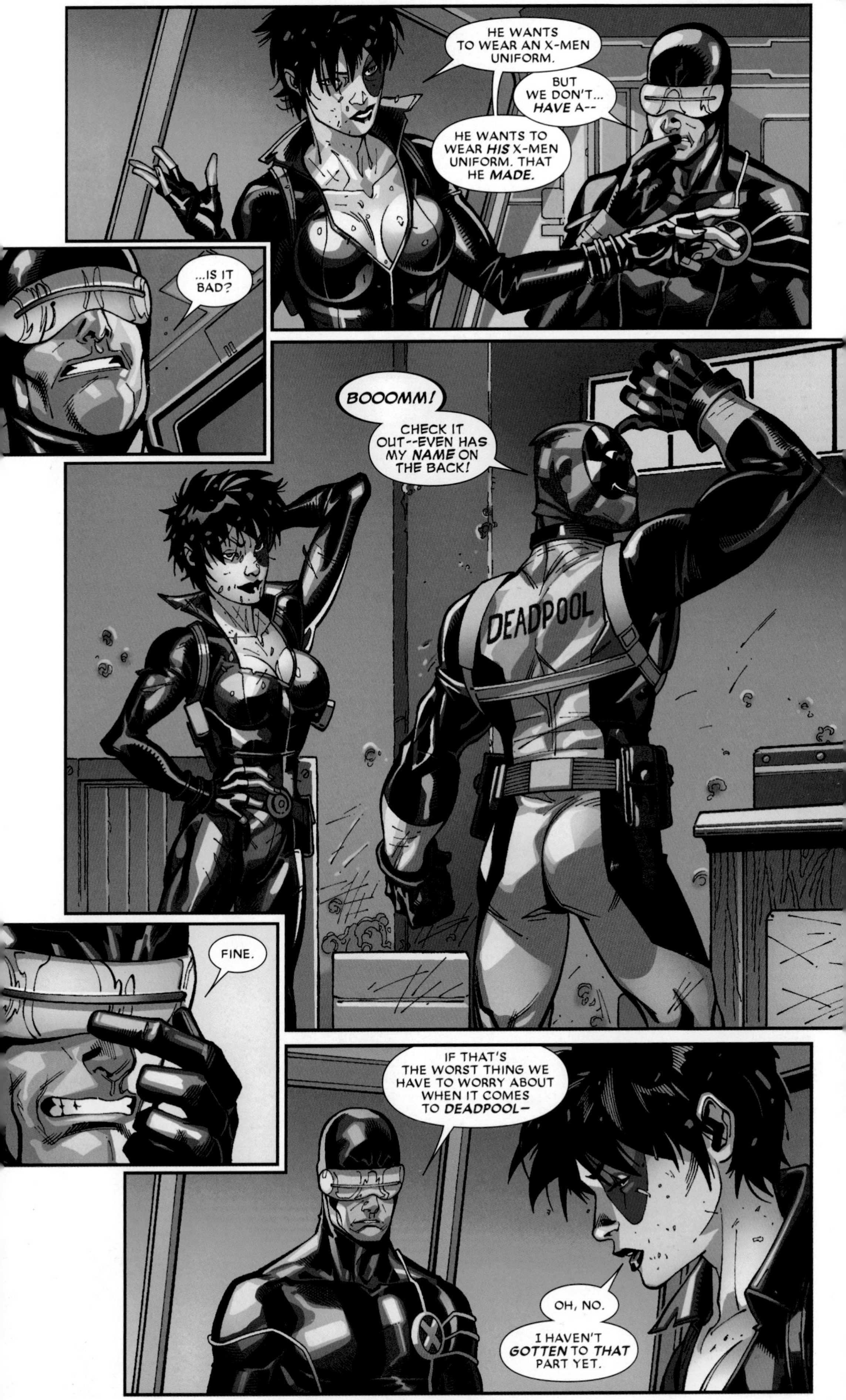
HE WANTS TO WEAR AN X-MEN UNIFORM.
BUT WE DON'T... HAVE A--
HE WANTS TO WEAR HIS X-MEN UNIFORM. THAT HE MADE.
...IS IT BAD?
BOOOMM!
CHECK IT OUT--EVEN HAS MY NAME ON THE BACK!
DEADPOOL
FINE.
IF THAT'S THE WORST THING WE HAVE TO WORRY ABOUT WHEN IT COMES TO DEADPOOL—
OH, NO.
I HAVEN'T GOTTEN TO THAT PART YET.

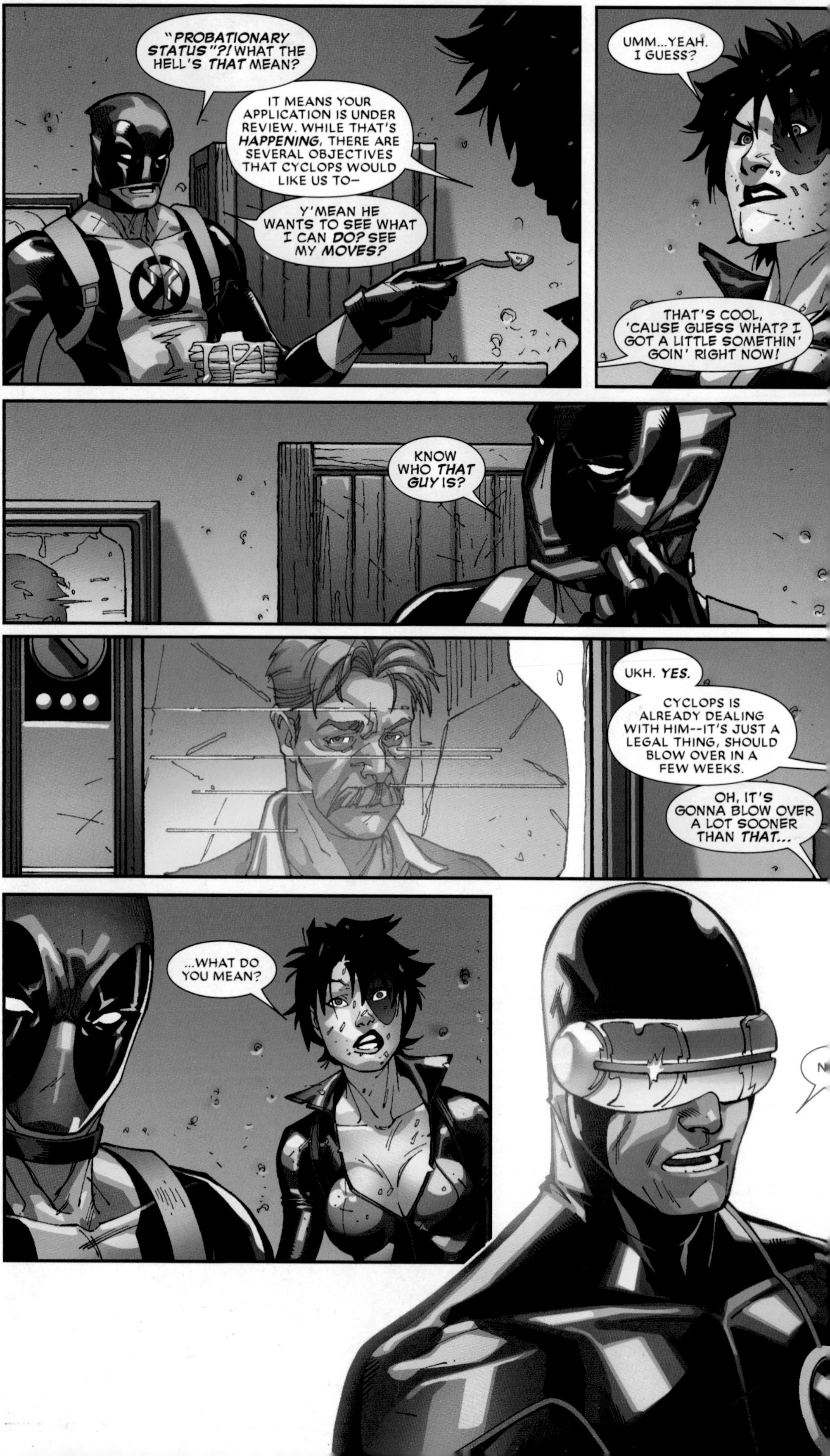
"PROBATIONARY STATUS"?! WHAT THE HELL'S THAT MEAN?
IT MEANS YOUR APPLICATION IS UNDER REVIEW. WHILE THAT'S HAPPENING, THERE ARE SEVERAL OBJECTIVES THAT CYCLOPS WOULD LIKE US TO–
Y'MEAN HE WANTS TO SEE WHAT I CAN DO? SEE MY MOVES?
UMM...YEAH. I GUESS?
THAT'S COOL, 'CAUSE GUESS WHAT? I GOT A LITTLE SOMETHIN' GOIN' RIGHT NOW!
KNOW WHO THAT GUY IS?
UKH. YES.
CYCLOPS IS ALREADY DEALING WITH HIM--IT'S JUST A LEGAL THING, SHOULD BLOW OVER IN A FEW WEEKS.
OH, IT'S GONNA BLOW OVER A LOT SOONER THAN THAT...
...WHAT DO YOU MEAN?

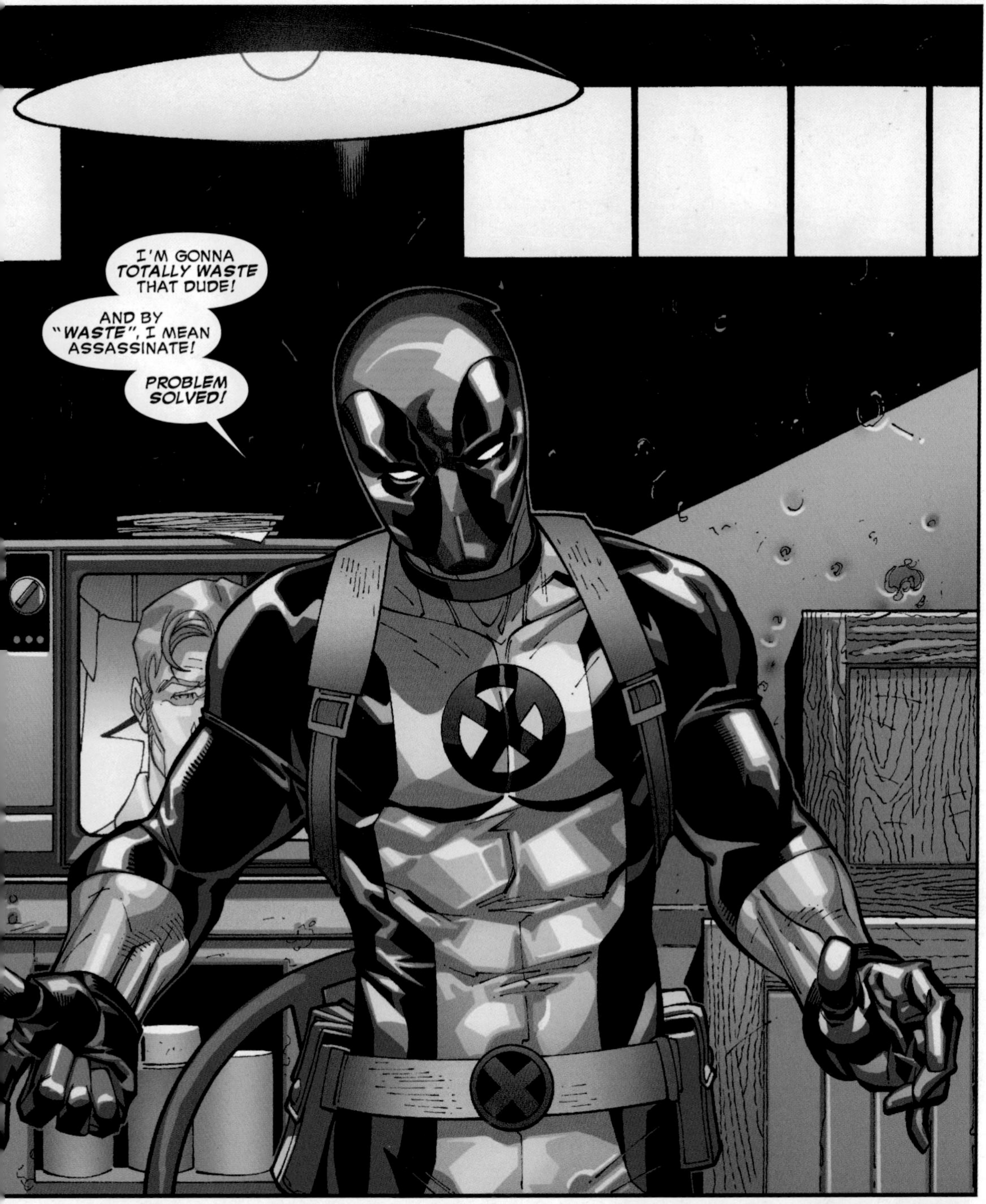
I'M GONNA TOTALLY WASTE THAT DUDE!
AND BY "WASTE", I MEAN ASSASSINATE!
PROBLEM SOLVED!
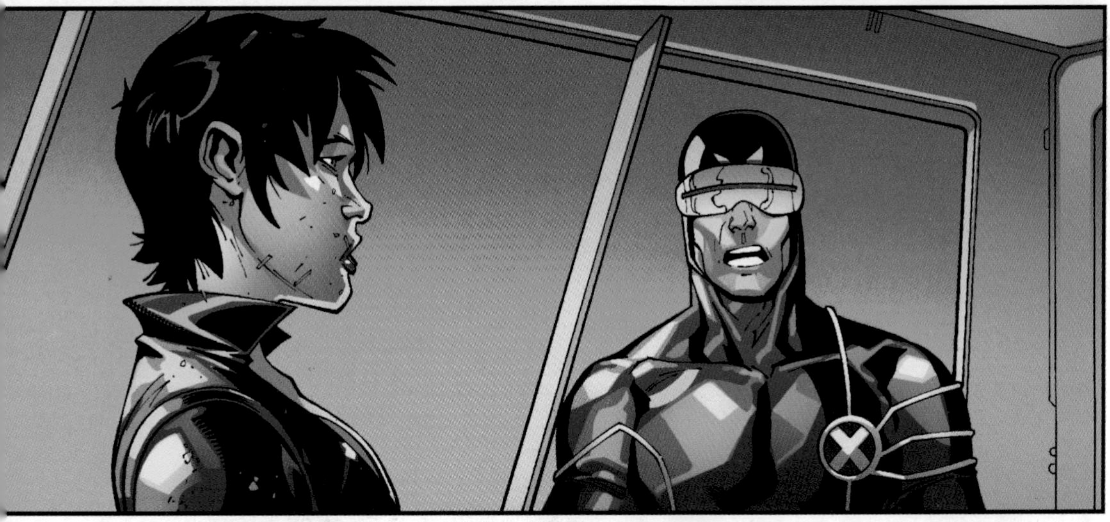

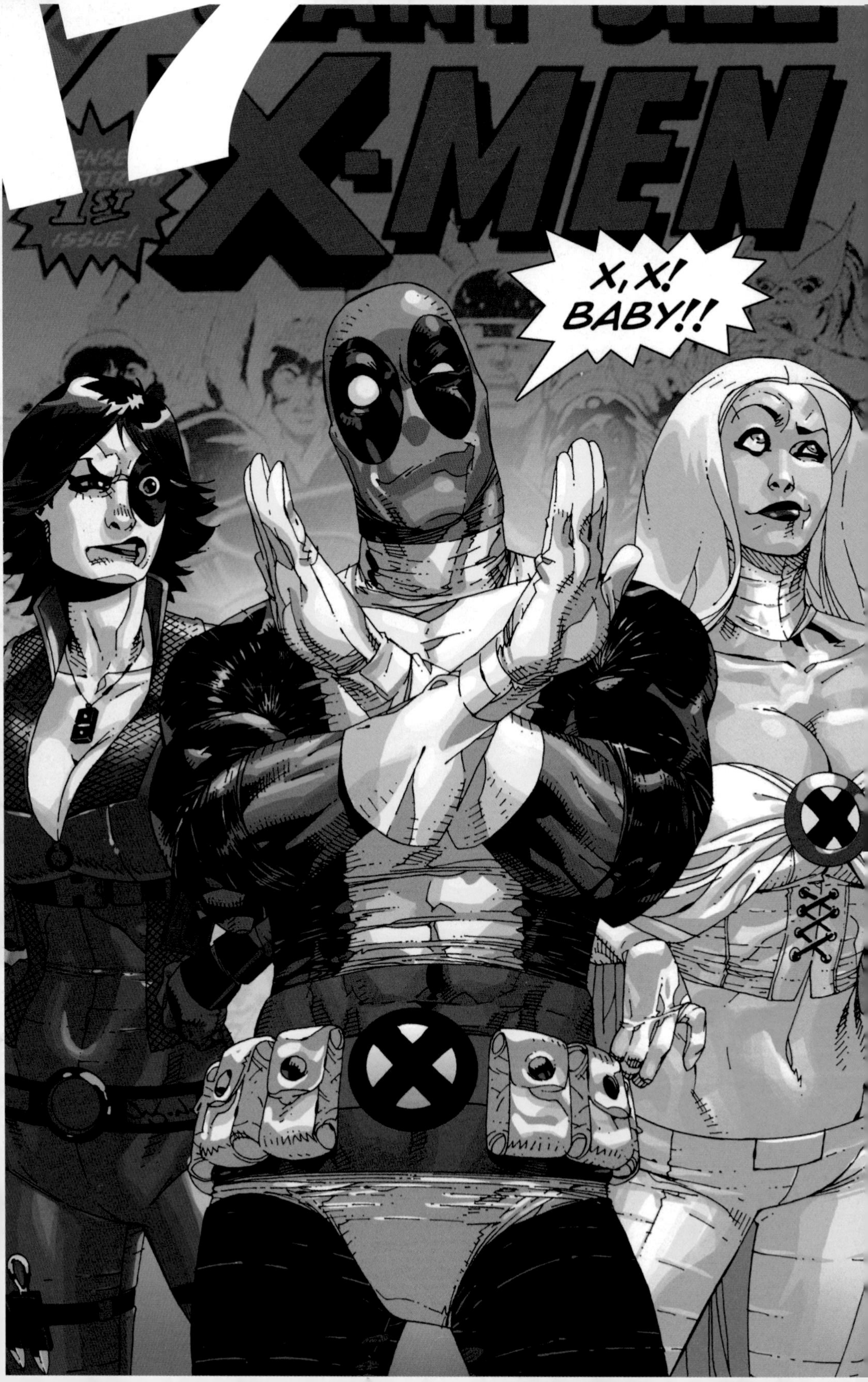
X-MEN
X,X! BABY!!

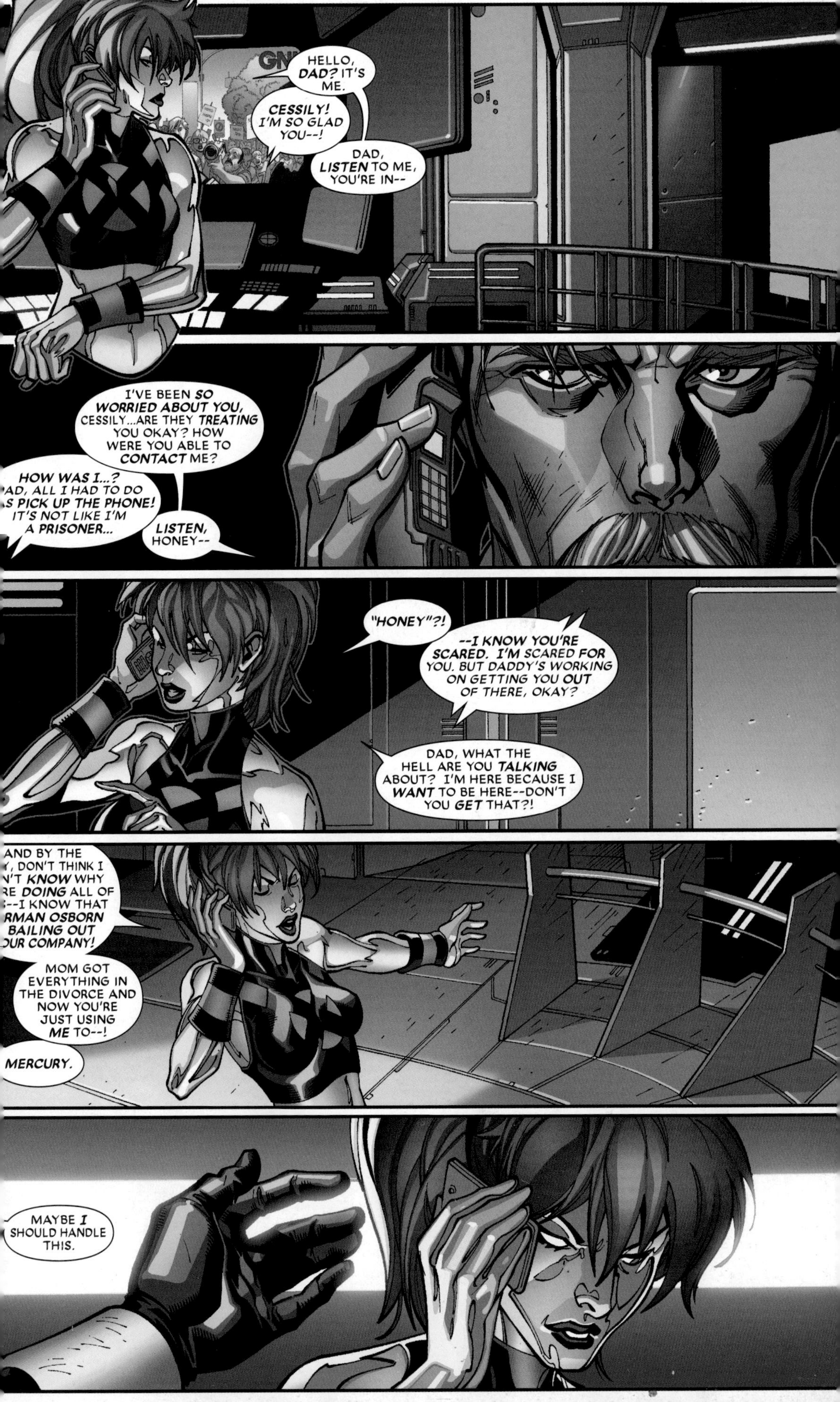
HELLO, DAD? IT'S ME.
CESSILY! I'M SO GLAD YOU--!
DAD, LISTEN TO ME, YOU'RE IN--
I'VE BEEN SO WORRIED ABOUT YOU, CESSILY...ARE THEY TREATING YOU OKAY? HOW WERE YOU ABLE TO CONTACT ME?
HOW WAS I...? AD, ALL I HAD TO DO S PICK UP THE PHONE! IT'S NOT LIKE I'M A PRISONER...
LISTEN, HONEY--
"HONEY"?!
--I KNOW YOU'RE SCARED. I'M SCARED FOR YOU. BUT DADDY'S WORKING ON GETTING YOU OUT OF THERE, OKAY?
DAD, WHAT THE HELL ARE YOU TALKING ABOUT? I'M HERE BECAUSE I WANT TO BE HERE--DON'T YOU GET THAT?!
AND BY THE , DON'T THINK I N'T KNOW WHY RE DOING ALL OF --I KNOW THAT RMAN OSBORN BAILING OUT UR COMPANY!
MOM GOT EVERYTHING IN THE DIVORCE AND NOW YOU'RE JUST USING ME TO--!
MERCURY.
MAYBE I SHOULD HANDLE THIS.

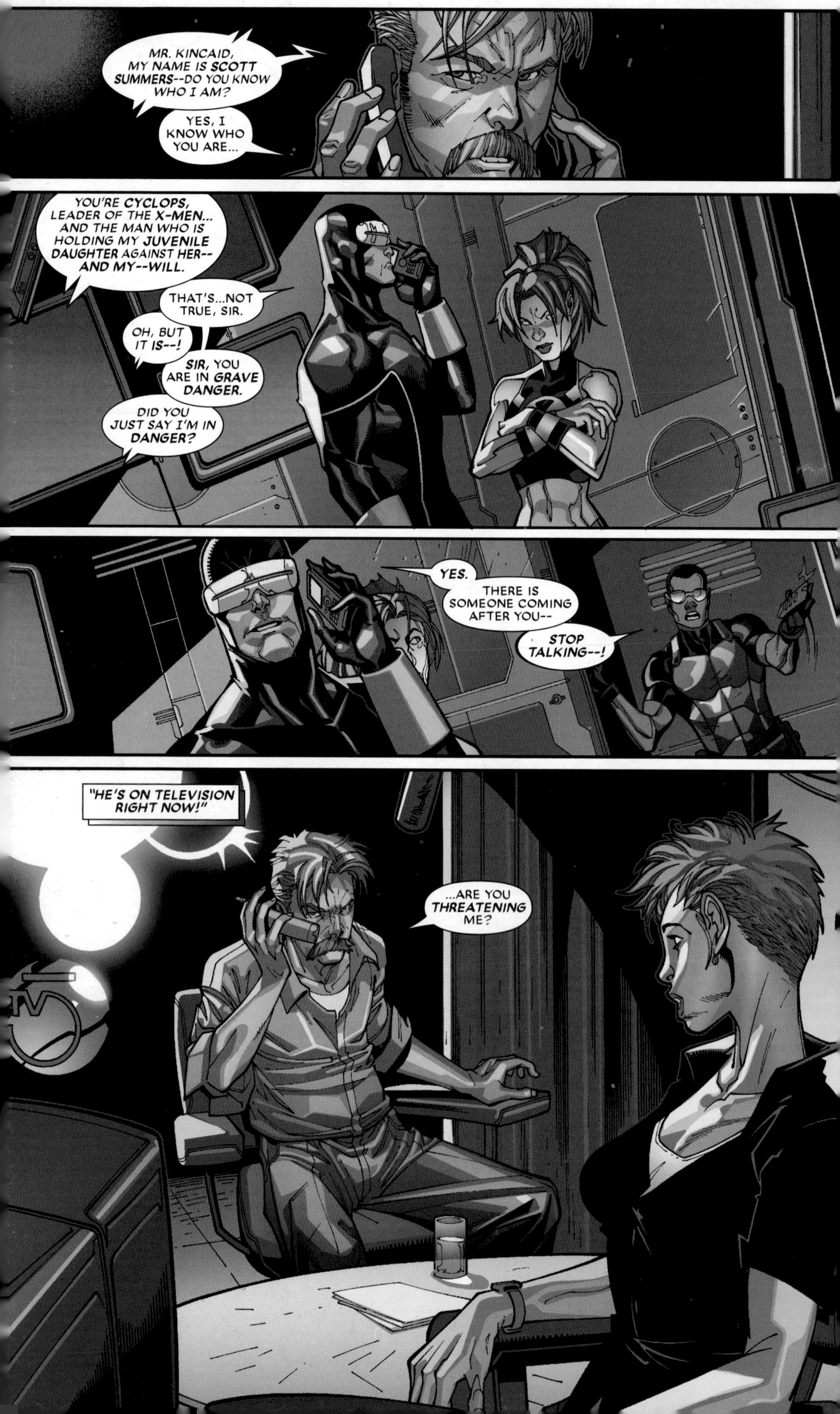

MR. KINCAID, MY NAME IS SCOTT SUMMERS--DO YOU KNOW WHO I AM?
YES, I KNOW WHO YOU ARE...
YOU'RE CYCLOPS, LEADER OF THE X-MEN... AND THE MAN WHO IS HOLDING MY JUVENILE DAUGHTER AGAINST HER--AND MY--WILL.
THAT'S...NOT TRUE, SIR.
OH, BUT IT IS--!
SIR, YOU ARE IN GRAVE DANGER.
DID YOU JUST SAY I'M IN DANGER?
YES. THERE IS SOMEONE COMING AFTER YOU--
STOP TALKING--!
"HE'S ON TELEVISION RIGHT NOW!"
...ARE YOU THREATENING ME?

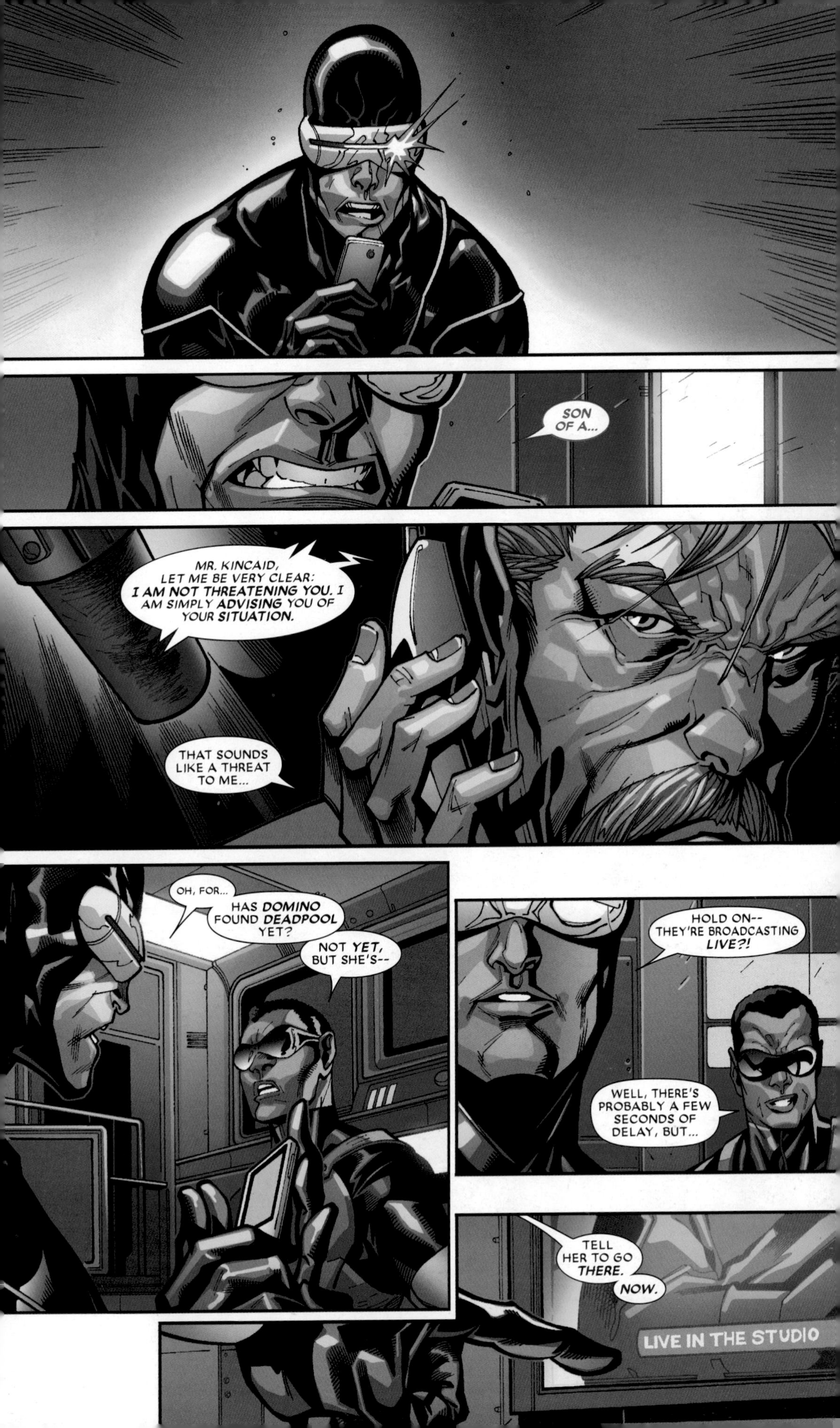
SON OF A...
MR. KINCAID, LET ME BE VERY CLEAR: I AM NOT THREATENING YOU. I AM SIMPLY ADVISING YOU OF YOUR SITUATION.
THAT SOUNDS LIKE A THREAT TO ME...
OH, FOR...
HAS DOMINO FOUND DEADPOOL YET?
NOT YET, BUT SHE'S--
HOLD ON-- THEY'RE BROADCASTING LIVE?!
WELL, THERE'S PROBABLY A FEW SECONDS OF DELAY, BUT...
TELL HER TO GO THERE.
NOW.
LIVE IN THE STUDIO

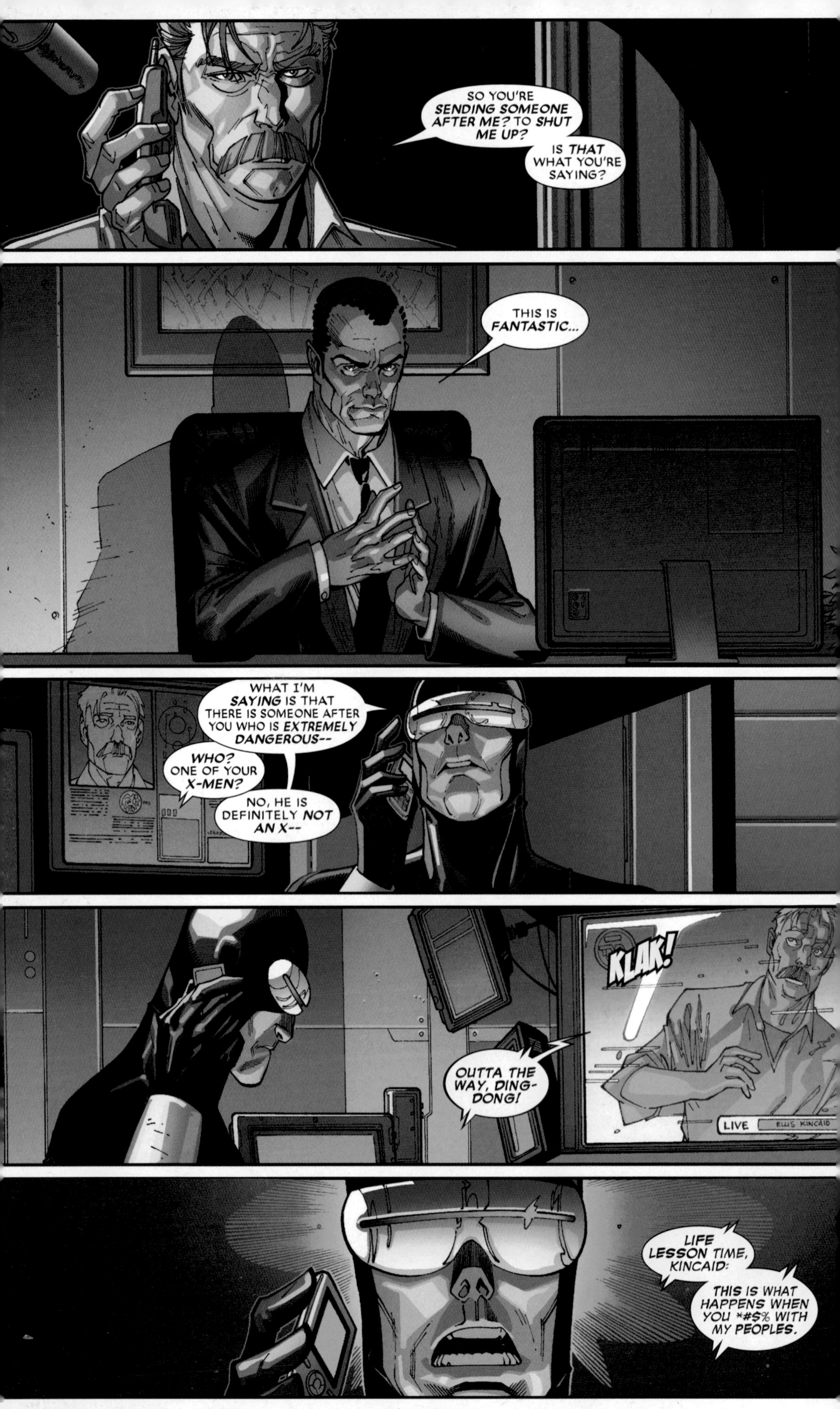
SO YOU'RE SENDING SOMEONE AFTER ME? TO SHUT ME UP?
IS THAT WHAT YOU'RE SAYING?
THIS IS FANTASTIC...
WHAT I'M SAYING IS THAT THERE IS SOMEONE AFTER YOU WHO IS EXTREMELY DANGEROUS--
WHO? ONE OF YOUR X-MEN?
NO, HE IS DEFINITELY NOT AN X--
KLAK!
OUTTA THE WAY, DING-DONG!
LIVE
ELLIS KINCAID
LIFE LESSON TIME, KINCAID:
THIS IS WHAT HAPPENS WHEN YOU *#$% WITH MY PEOPLES.

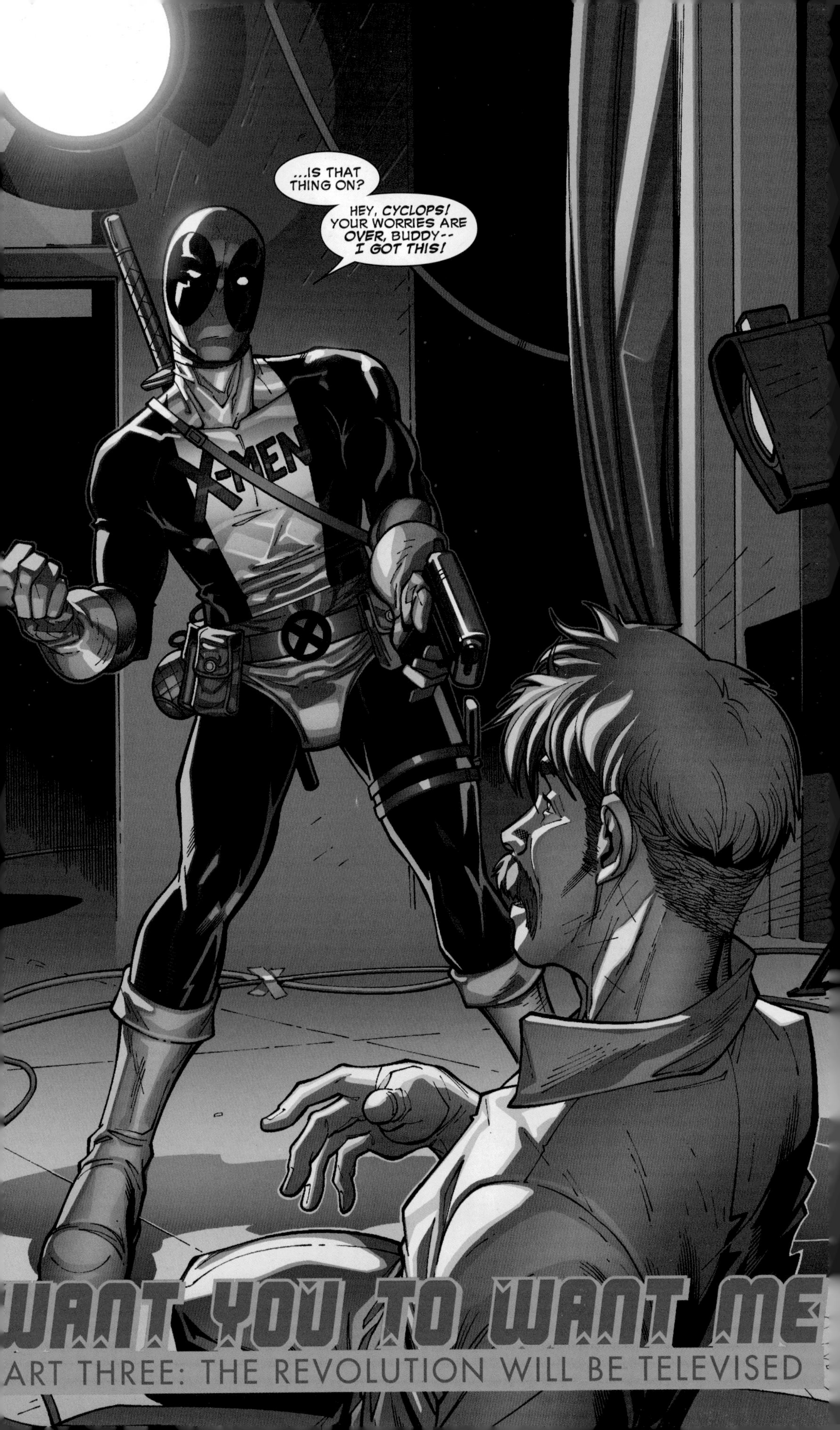
...IS THAT THING ON?
HEY, CYCLOPS! YOUR WORRIES ARE OVER, BUDDY-- I GOT THIS!
X-MEN
WANT YOU TO WANT ME
ART THREE: THE REVOLUTION WILL BE TELEVISED

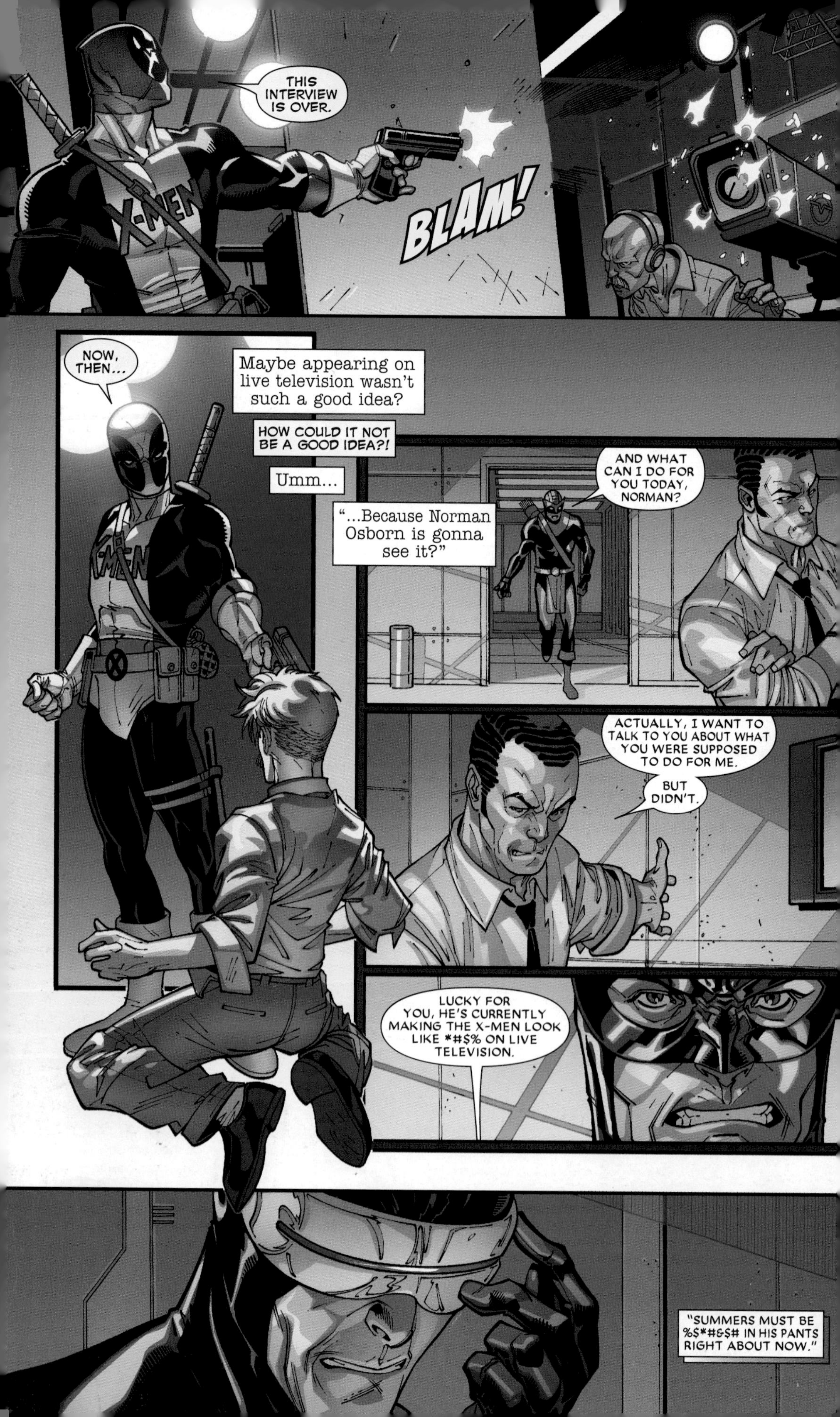
THIS INTERVIEW IS OVER.
BLAM!
NOW, THEN...
Maybe appearing on live television wasn't such a good idea?
HOW COULD IT NOT BE A GOOD IDEA?!
Umm...
"...Because Norman Osborn is gonna see it?"
AND WHAT CAN I DO FOR YOU TODAY, NORMAN?
ACTUALLY, I WANT TO TALK TO YOU ABOUT WHAT YOU WERE SUPPOSED TO DO FOR ME.
BUT DIDN'T.
LUCKY FOR YOU, HE'S CURRENTLY MAKING THE X-MEN LOOK LIKE *#$% ON LIVE TELEVISION.
"SUMMERS MUST BE %$*#&$# IN HIS PANTS RIGHT ABOUT NOW."

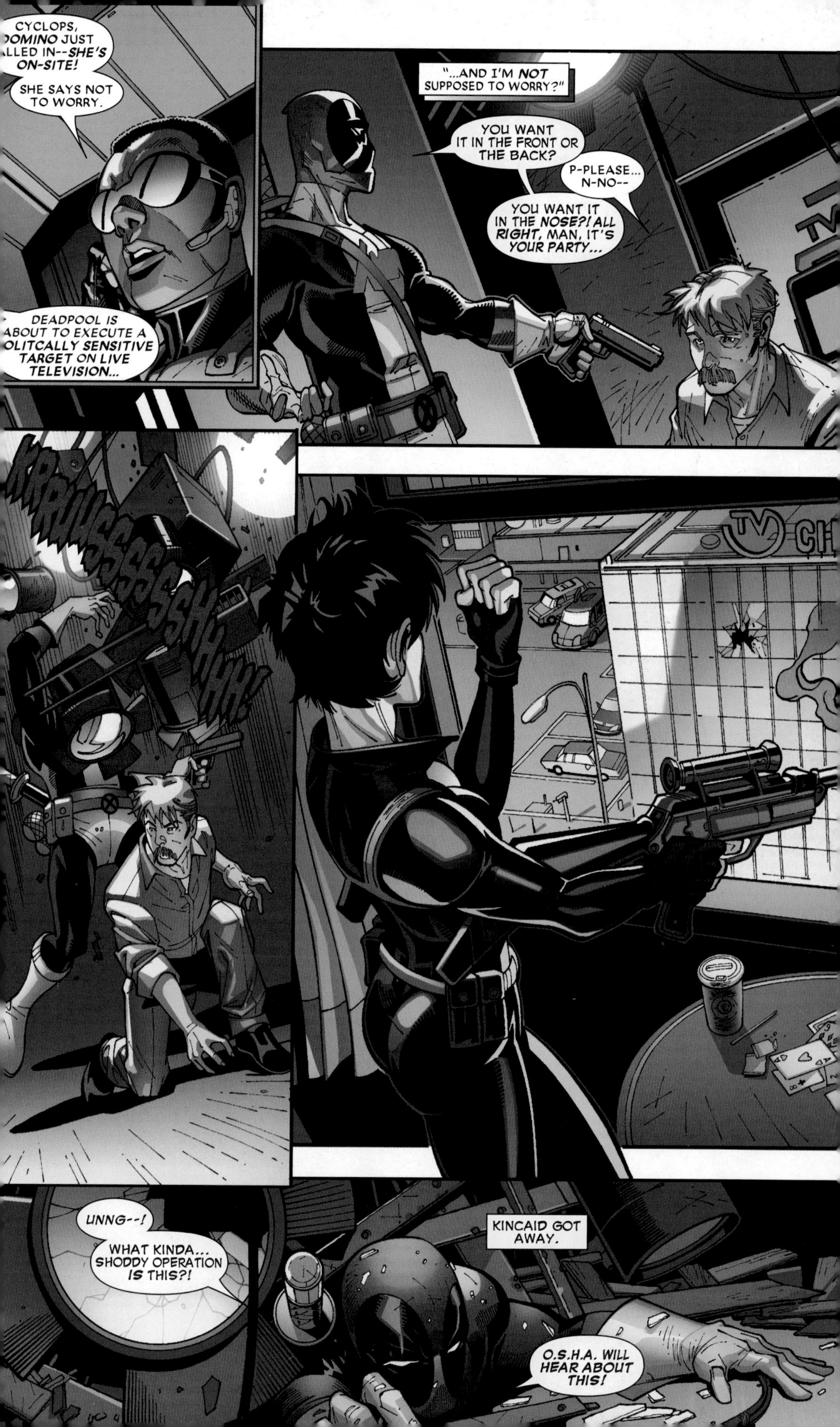
CYCLOPS, DOMINO JUST CALLED IN--SHE'S ON-SITE!
SHE SAYS NOT TO WORRY.
DEADPOOL IS ABOUT TO EXECUTE A POLITCALLY SENSITIVE TARGET ON LIVE TELEVISION...
"...AND I'M NOT SUPPOSED TO WORRY?"
YOU WANT IT IN THE FRONT OR THE BACK?
P-PLEASE... N-NO--
YOU WANT IT IN THE NOSE?! ALL RIGHT, MAN, IT'S YOUR PARTY...
KRRUSSSSSHHH!
UNNG--!
WHAT KINDA... SHODDY OPERATION IS THIS?!
KINCAID GOT AWAY.
O.S.H.A. WILL HEAR ABOUT THIS!

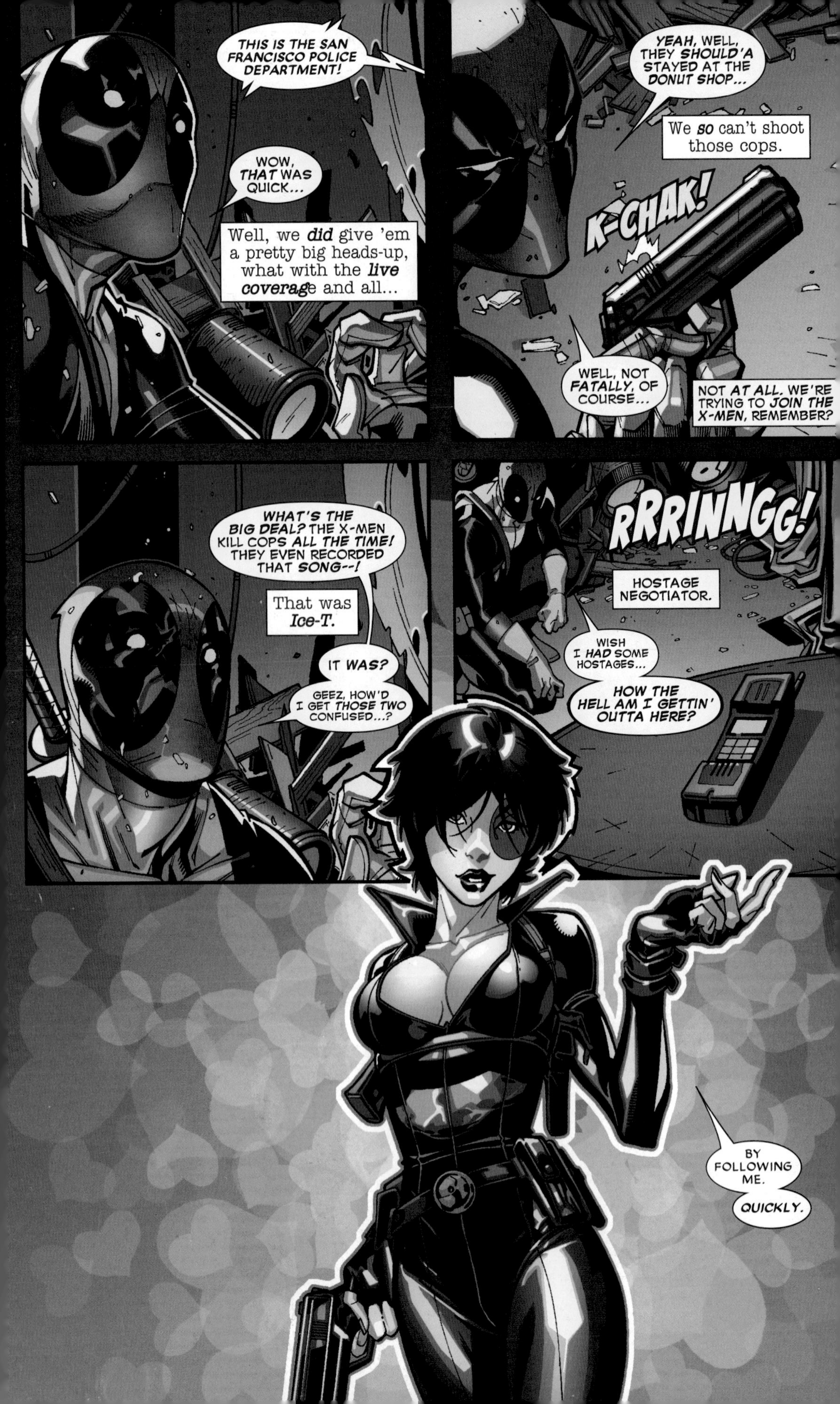

THIS IS THE SAN FRANCISCO POLICE DEPARTMENT!
WOW, THAT WAS QUICK...
Well, we did give 'em a pretty big heads-up, what with the live coverage and all...
YEAH, WELL, THEY SHOULD'A STAYED AT THE DONUT SHOP...
We so can't shoot those cops.
K-CHAK!
WELL, NOT FATALLY, OF COURSE...
NOT AT ALL. WE'RE TRYING TO JOIN THE X-MEN, REMEMBER?
WHAT'S THE BIG DEAL? THE X-MEN KILL COPS ALL THE TIME! THEY EVEN RECORDED THAT SONG--!
That was Ice-T.
IT WAS?
GEEZ, HOW'D I GET THOSE TWO CONFUSED...?
RRRINNGG!
HOSTAGE NEGOTIATOR.
WISH I HAD SOME HOSTAGES...
HOW THE HELL AM I GETTIN' OUTTA HERE?
BY FOLLOWING ME.
QUICKLY.

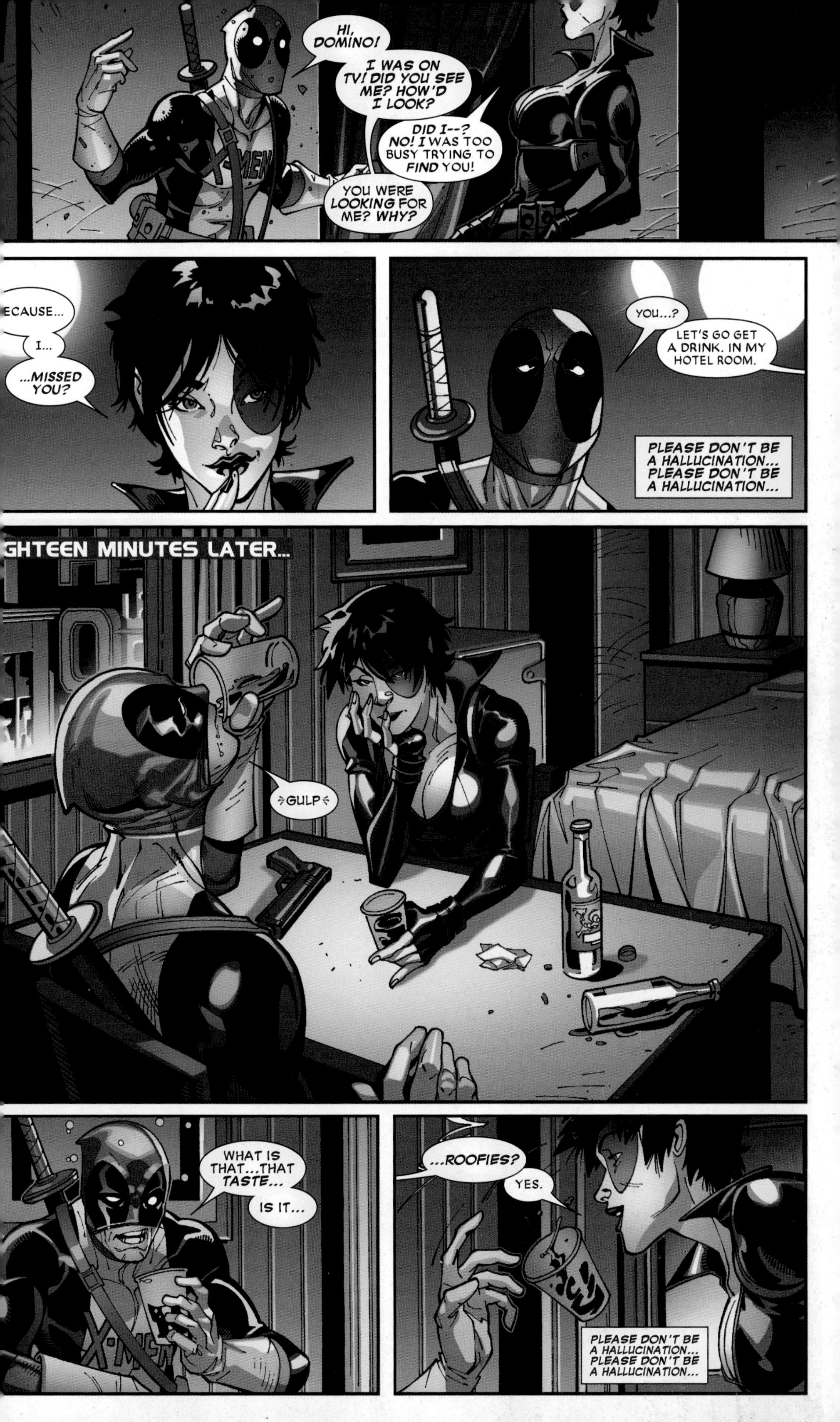
HI, DOMINO!
I WAS ON TV! DID YOU SEE ME? HOW'D I LOOK?
DID I--? NO! I WAS TOO BUSY TRYING TO FIND YOU!
YOU WERE LOOKING FOR ME? WHY?
ECAUSE...
I...
...MISSED YOU?
YOU...?
LET'S GO GET A DRINK. IN MY HOTEL ROOM.
PLEASE DON'T BE A HALLUCINATION... PLEASE DON'T BE A HALLUCINATION...
GHTEEN MINUTES LATER...
GULP
WHAT IS THAT...THAT TASTE...
IS IT...
...ROOFIES?
YES.
PLEASE DON'T BE A HALLUCINATION... PLEASE DON'T BE A HALLUCINATION...

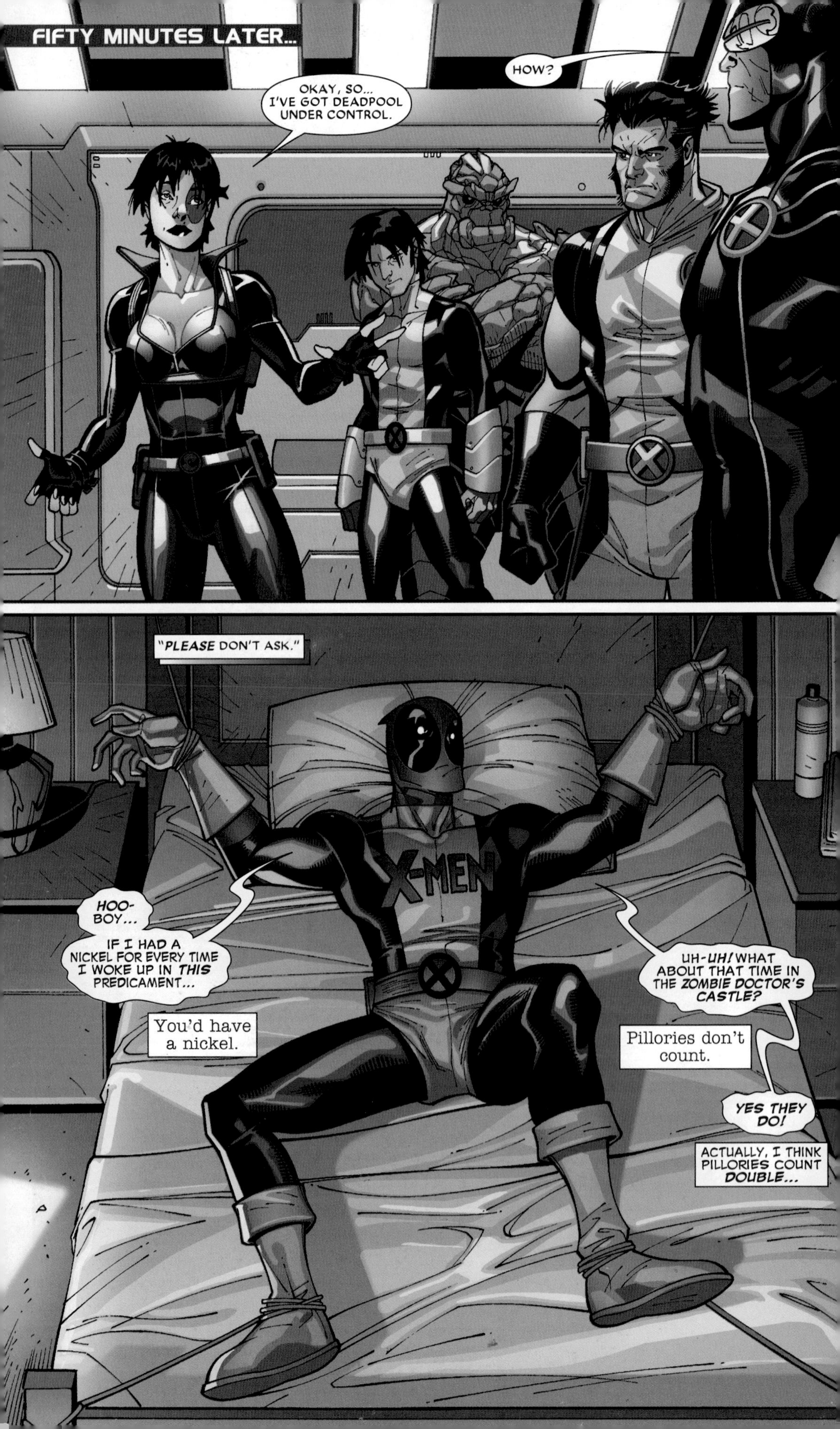
FIFTY MINUTES LATER...
OKAY, SO... I'VE GOT DEADPOOL UNDER CONTROL.
HOW?
"PLEASE DON'T ASK."
HOO-BOY...
IF I HAD A NICKEL FOR EVERY TIME I WOKE UP IN THIS PREDICAMENT...
You'd have a nickel.
UH-UH! WHAT ABOUT THAT TIME IN THE ZOMBIE DOCTOR'S CASTLE?
Pillories don't count.
YES THEY DO!
ACTUALLY, I THINK PILLORIES COUNT DOUBLE...

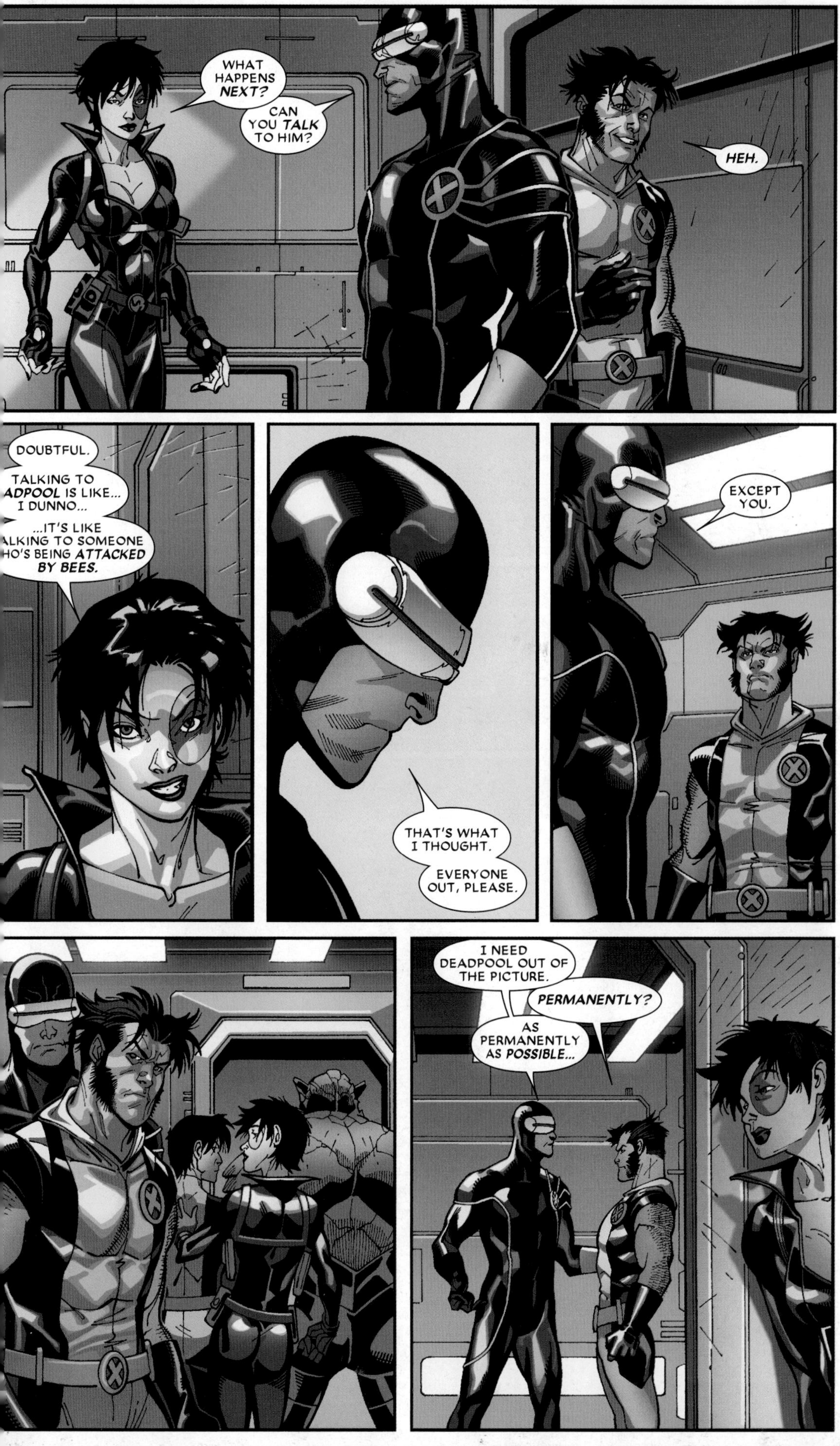
WHAT HAPPENS NEXT?
CAN YOU TALK TO HIM?
HEH.
DOUBTFUL.
TALKING TO ADPOOL IS LIKE... I DUNNO...
...IT'S LIKE ALKING TO SOMEONE HO'S BEING ATTACKED BY BEES.
THAT'S WHAT I THOUGHT.
EVERYONE OUT, PLEASE.
EXCEPT YOU.
I NEED DEADPOOL OUT OF THE PICTURE.
PERMANENTLY?
AS PERMANENTLY AS POSSIBLE...

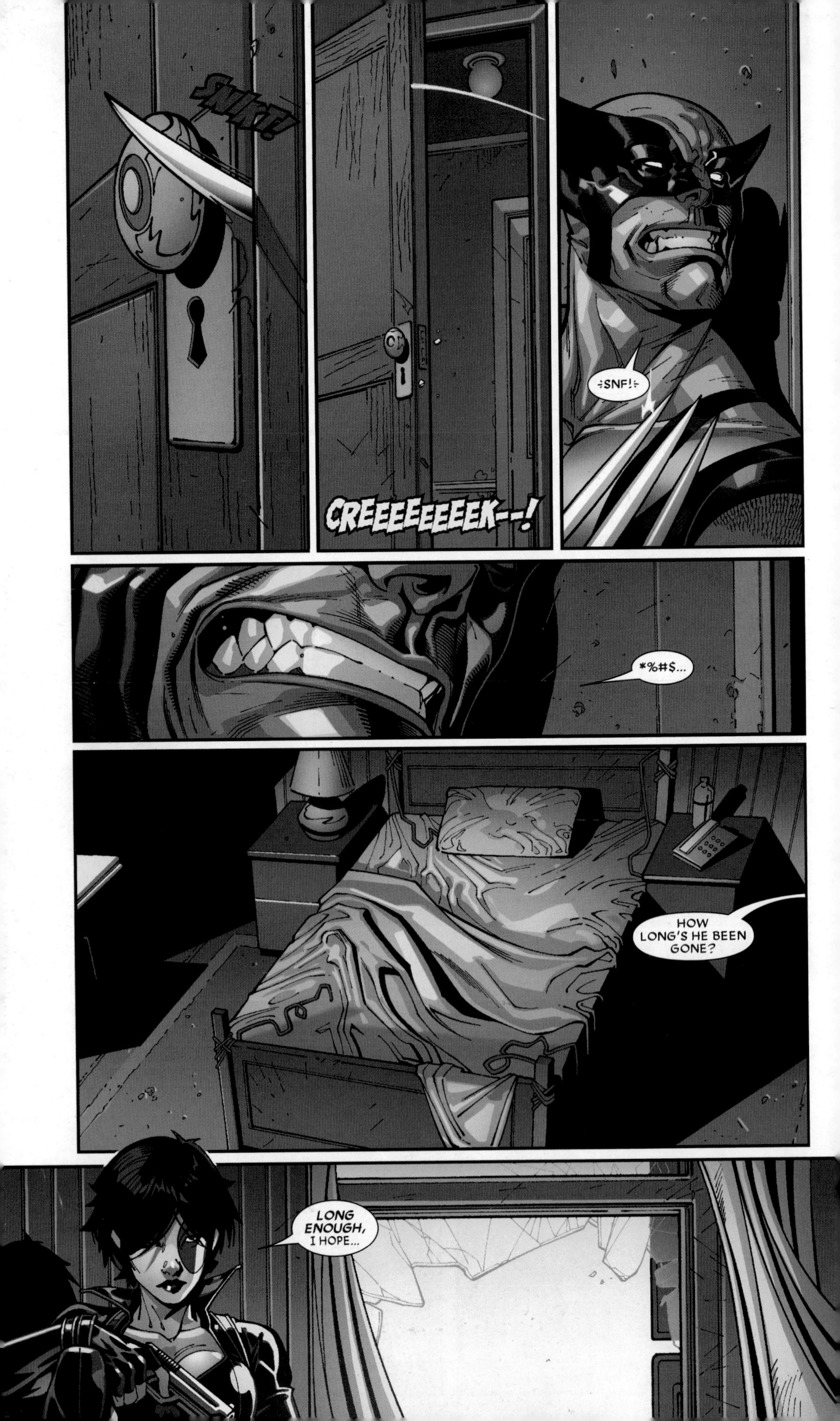
SNIKT!
CREEEEEEEEK--!
SNF!
*%#$...
HOW LONG'S HE BEEN GONE?
LONG ENOUGH, I HOPE...

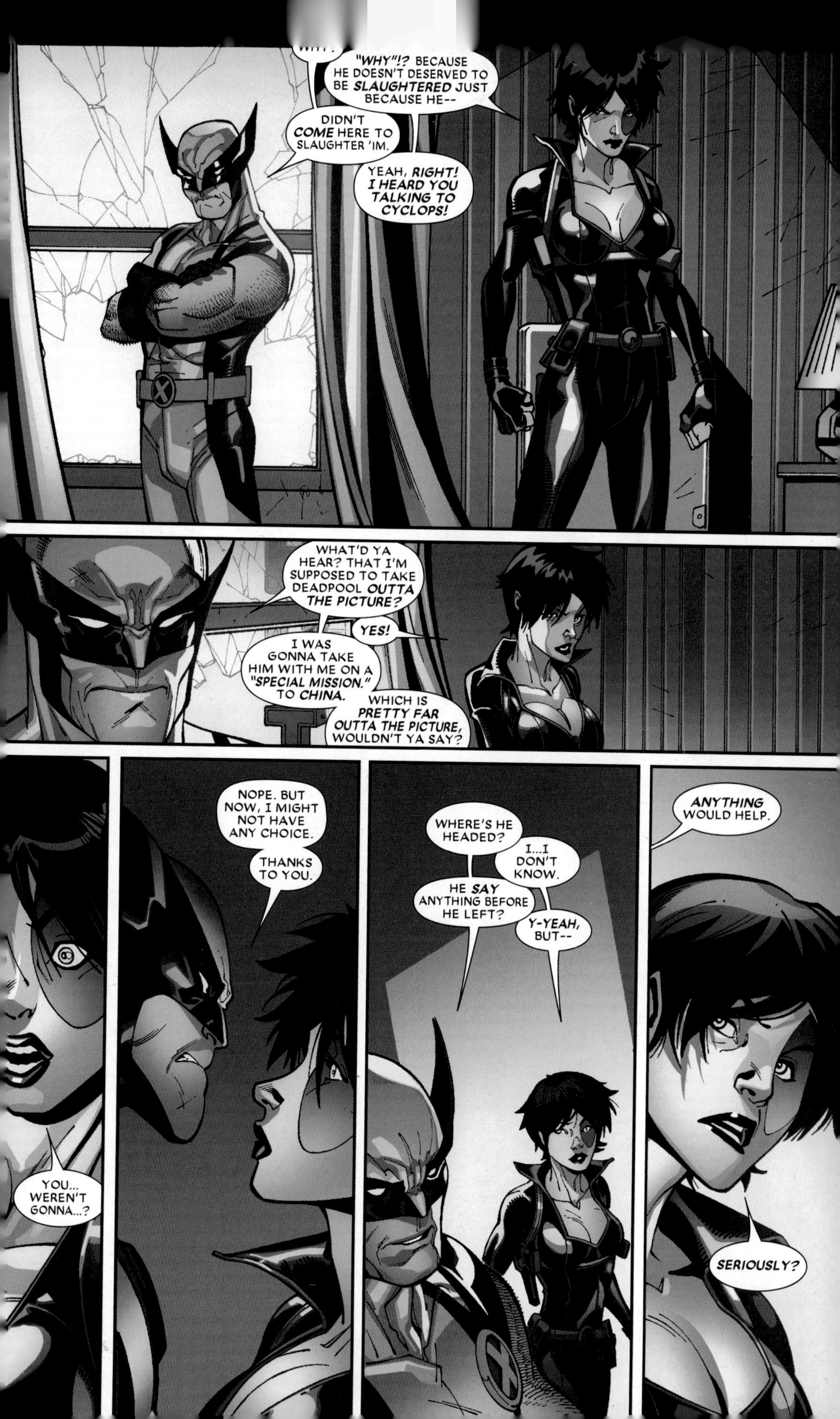
"WHY"!? BECAUSE HE DOESN'T DESERVED TO BE SLAUGHTERED JUST BECAUSE HE--
DIDN'T COME HERE TO SLAUGHTER 'IM.
YEAH, RIGHT! I HEARD YOU TALKING TO CYCLOPS!
WHAT'D YA HEAR? THAT I'M SUPPOSED TO TAKE DEADPOOL OUTTA THE PICTURE?
YES!
I WAS GONNA TAKE HIM WITH ME ON A "SPECIAL MISSION." TO CHINA.
WHICH IS PRETTY FAR OUTTA THE PICTURE, WOULDN'T YA SAY?
YOU... WEREN'T GONNA...?
NOPE. BUT NOW, I MIGHT NOT HAVE ANY CHOICE.
THANKS TO YOU.
WHERE'S HE HEADED?
I...I DON'T KNOW.
HE SAY ANYTHING BEFORE HE LEFT?
Y-YEAH, BUT--
ANYTHING WOULD HELP.
SERIOUSLY?

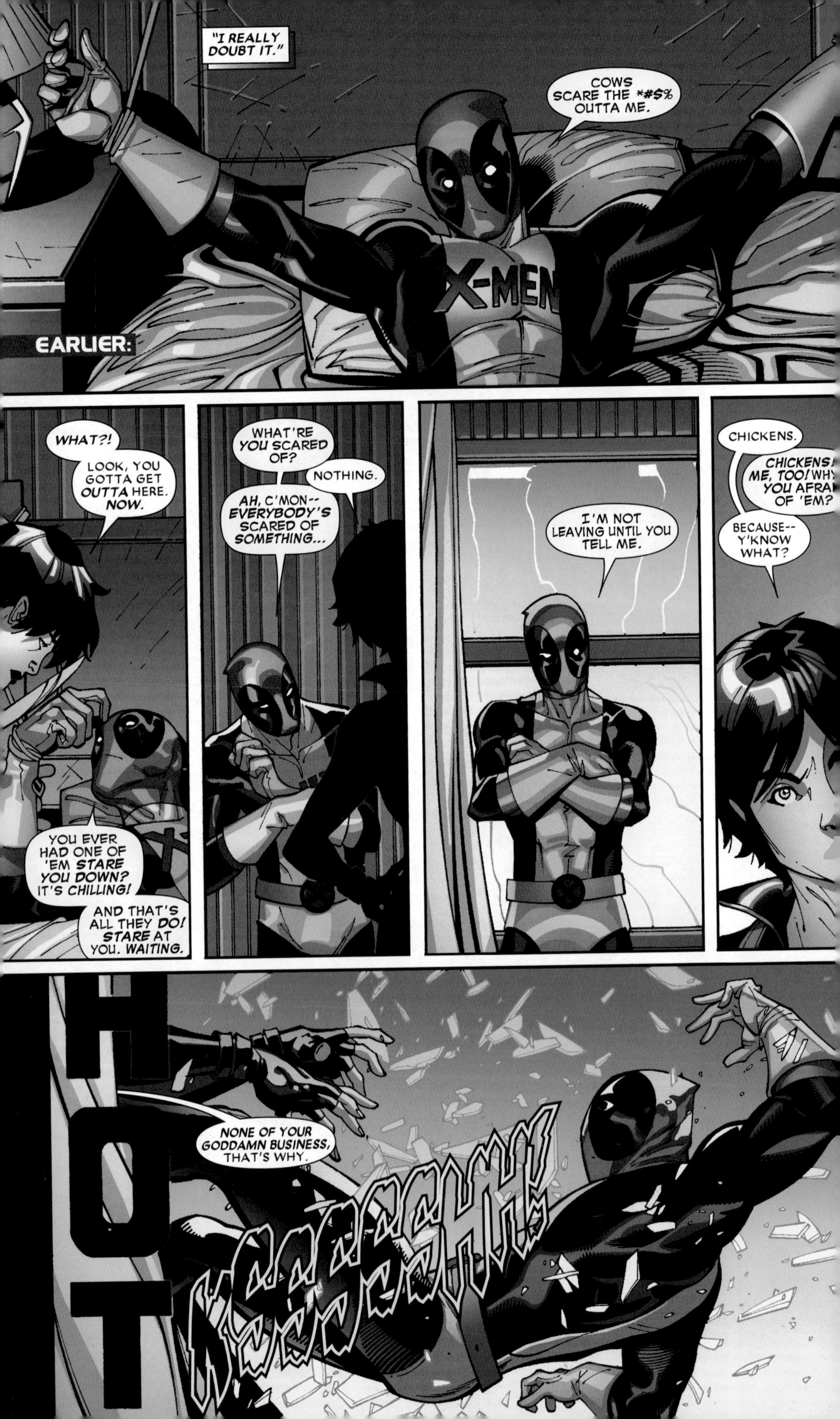
"I REALLY DOUBT IT."
COWS SCARE THE *#$% OUTTA ME.
EARLIER:
WHAT?!
LOOK, YOU GOTTA GET OUTTA HERE. NOW.
YOU EVER HAD ONE OF 'EM STARE YOU DOWN? IT'S CHILLING!
AND THAT'S ALL THEY DO! STARE AT YOU. WAITING.
WHAT'RE YOU SCARED OF?
NOTHING.
AH, C'MON-- EVERYBODY'S SCARED OF SOMETHING...
I'M NOT LEAVING UNTIL YOU TELL ME.
CHICKENS.
CHICKENS! ME, TOO! WHY YOU AFRA OF 'EM?
BECAUSE-- Y'KNOW WHAT?
NONE OF YOUR GODDAMN BUSINESS, THAT'S WHY.
HOT

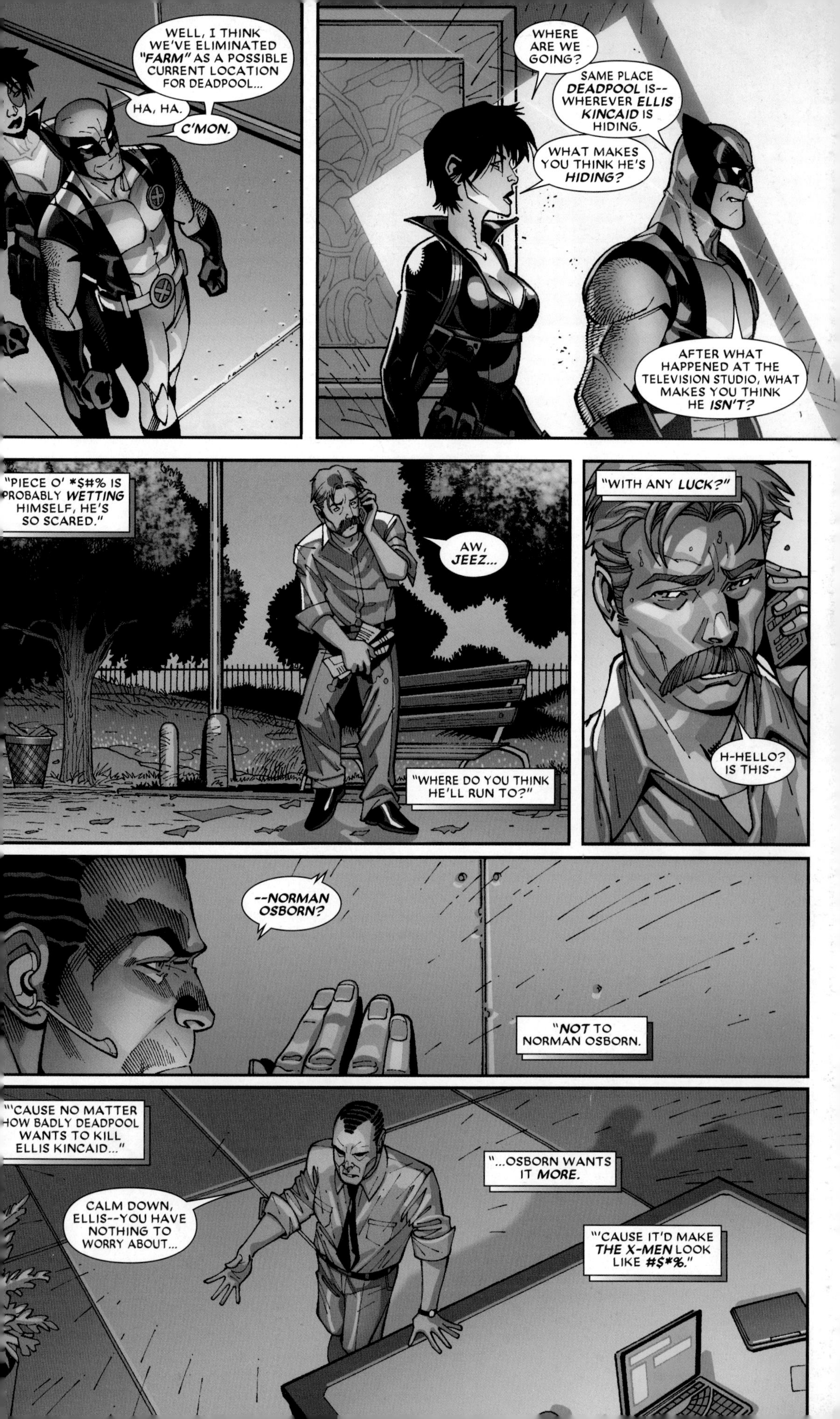
WELL, I THINK WE'VE ELIMINATED "FARM" AS A POSSIBLE CURRENT LOCATION FOR DEADPOOL...
HA, HA.
C'MON.
WHERE ARE WE GOING?
SAME PLACE DEADPOOL IS-- WHEREVER ELLIS KINCAID IS HIDING.
WHAT MAKES YOU THINK HE'S HIDING?
AFTER WHAT HAPPENED AT THE TELEVISION STUDIO, WHAT MAKES YOU THINK HE ISN'T?
"PIECE O' *$#% IS PROBABLY WETTING HIMSELF, HE'S SO SCARED."
AW, JEEZ...
"WHERE DO YOU THINK HE'LL RUN TO?"
"WITH ANY LUCK?"
H-HELLO? IS THIS--
--NORMAN OSBORN?
"NOT TO NORMAN OSBORN.
"'CAUSE NO MATTER HOW BADLY DEADPOOL WANTS TO KILL ELLIS KINCAID..."
"...OSBORN WANTS IT MORE.
CALM DOWN, ELLIS--YOU HAVE NOTHING TO WORRY ABOUT...
"'CAUSE IT'D MAKE THE X-MEN LOOK LIKE #$*%."

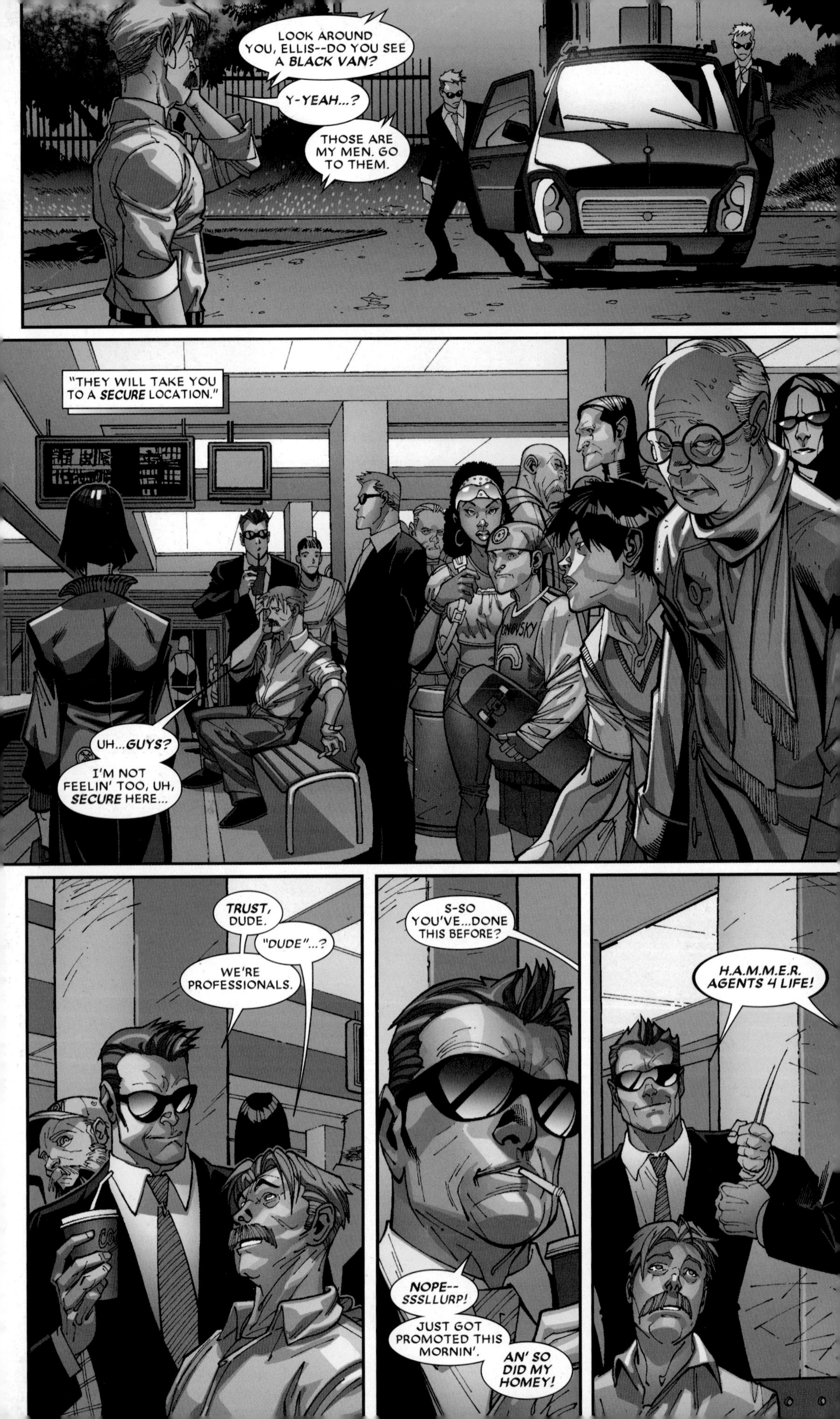
LOOK AROUND YOU, ELLIS--DO YOU SEE A BLACK VAN?
Y-YEAH...?
THOSE ARE MY MEN. GO TO THEM.
"THEY WILL TAKE YOU TO A SECURE LOCATION."
UH...GUYS?
I'M NOT FEELIN' TOO, UH, SECURE HERE...
TRUST, DUDE.
"DUDE"...?
WE'RE PROFESSIONALS.
S-SO YOU'VE...DONE THIS BEFORE?
NOPE-- SSSLLURP!
JUST GOT PROMOTED THIS MORNIN'.
AN' SO DID MY HOMEY!
H.A.M.M.E.R. AGENTS 4 LIFE!

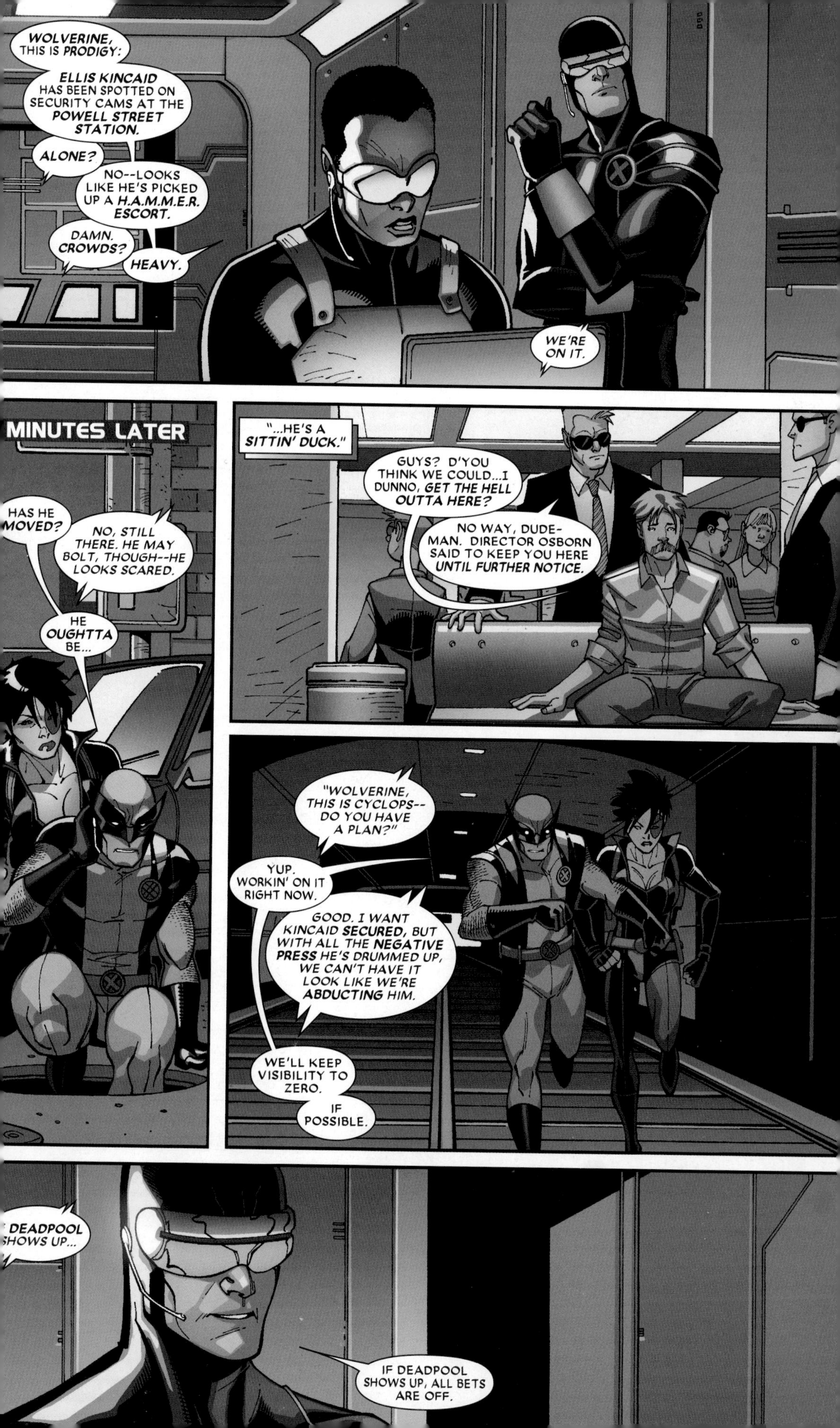
WOLVERINE, THIS IS PRODIGY:
ELLIS KINCAID HAS BEEN SPOTTED ON SECURITY CAMS AT THE POWELL STREET STATION.
ALONE?
NO--LOOKS LIKE HE'S PICKED UP A H.A.M.M.E.R. ESCORT.
DAMN. CROWDS?
HEAVY.
WE'RE ON IT.
MINUTES LATER
HAS HE MOVED?
NO, STILL THERE. HE MAY BOLT, THOUGH--HE LOOKS SCARED.
HE OUGHTTA BE...
"...HE'S A SITTIN' DUCK."
GUYS? D'YOU THINK WE COULD...I DUNNO, GET THE HELL OUTTA HERE?
NO WAY, DUDE-MAN. DIRECTOR OSBORN SAID TO KEEP YOU HERE UNTIL FURTHER NOTICE.
"WOLVERINE, THIS IS CYCLOPS--DO YOU HAVE A PLAN?"
YUP. WORKIN' ON IT RIGHT NOW.
GOOD. I WANT KINCAID SECURED, BUT WITH ALL THE NEGATIVE PRESS HE'S DRUMMED UP, WE CAN'T HAVE IT LOOK LIKE WE'RE ABDUCTING HIM.
WE'LL KEEP VISIBILITY TO ZERO.
IF POSSIBLE.
DEADPOOL SHOWS UP...
IF DEADPOOL SHOWS UP, ALL BETS ARE OFF.

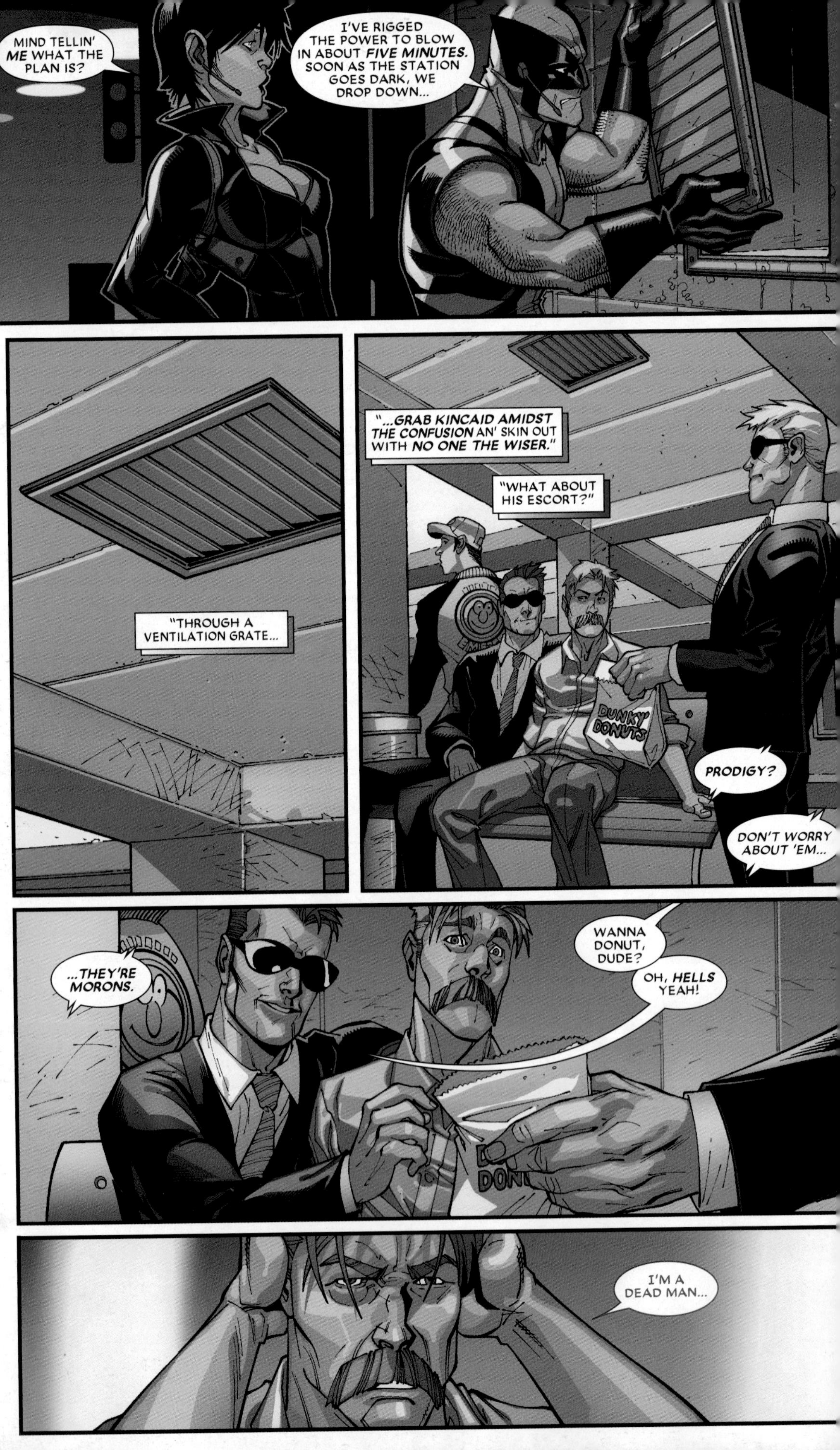

MIND TELLIN' ME WHAT THE PLAN IS?
I'VE RIGGED THE POWER TO BLOW IN ABOUT FIVE MINUTES. SOON AS THE STATION GOES DARK, WE DROP DOWN...
"THROUGH A VENTILATION GRATE...
"...GRAB KINCAID AMIDST THE CONFUSION AN' SKIN OUT WITH NO ONE THE WISER."
"WHAT ABOUT HIS ESCORT?"
DUNKY' DONUTS
PRODIGY?
DON'T WORRY ABOUT 'EM...
...THEY'RE MORONS.
WANNA DONUT, DUDE?
OH, HELLS YEAH!
I'M A DEAD MAN...

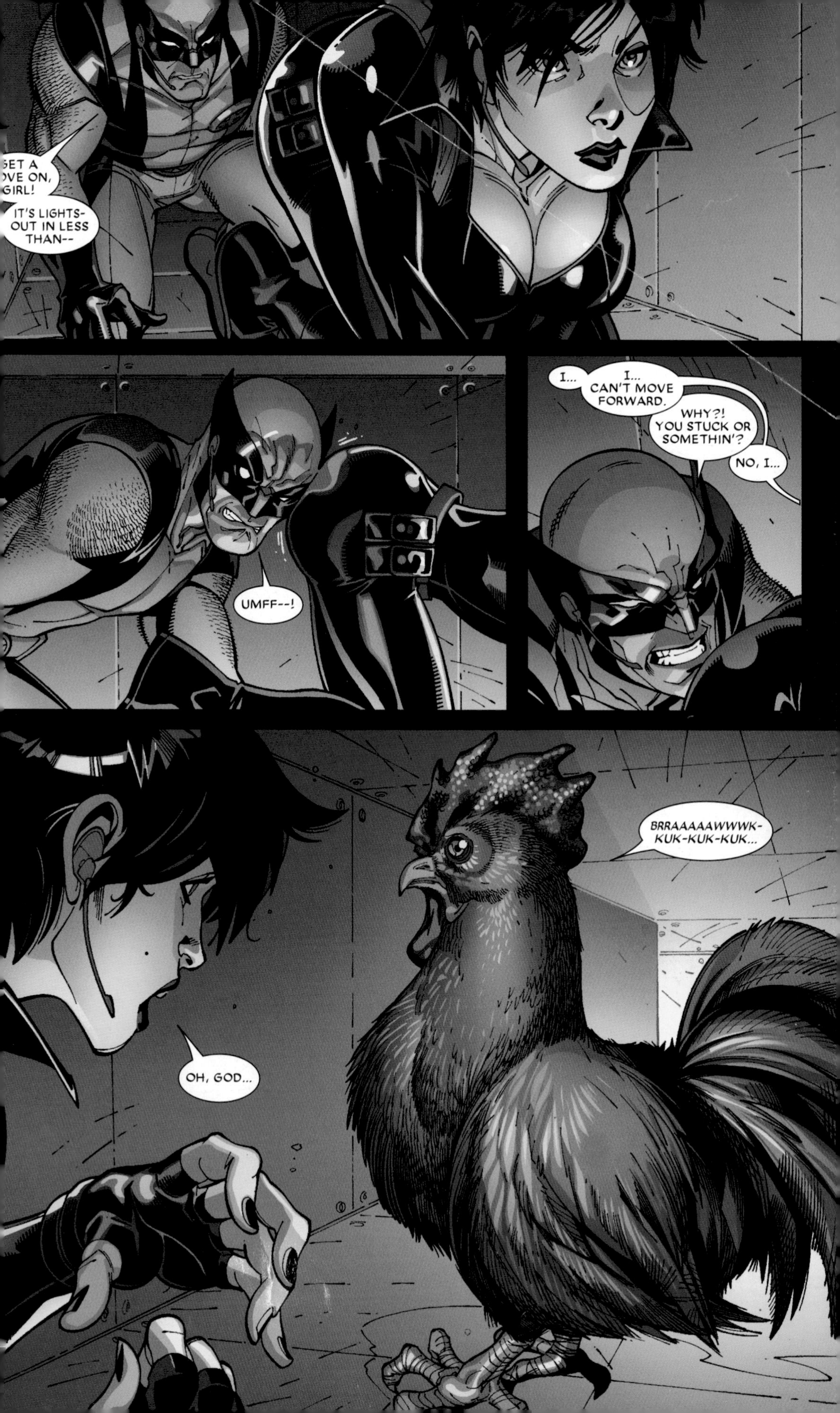

GET A
OVE ON,
GIRL!
IT'S LIGHTS-
OUT IN LESS
THAN--
UMFF--!
I...
I...
CAN'T MOVE
FORWARD.
WHY?!
YOU STUCK OR
SOMETHIN'?
NO, I...
BRRAAAAAWWWK-
KUK-KUK-KUK...
OH, GOD...

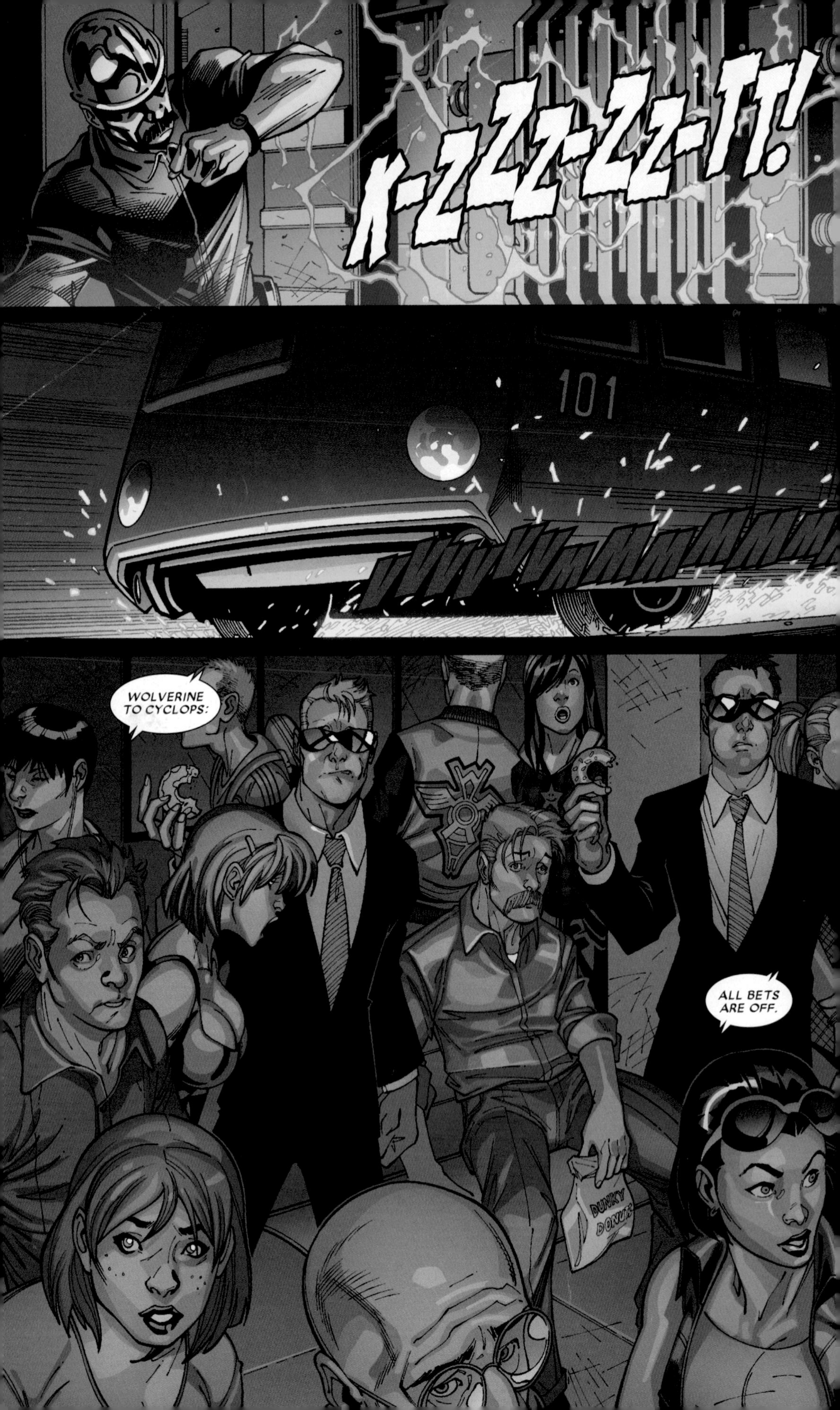
K-ZZZ-ZZ-TT!
101
WOLVERINE TO CYCLOPS:
ALL BETS ARE OFF.
DUNKY DONUTS

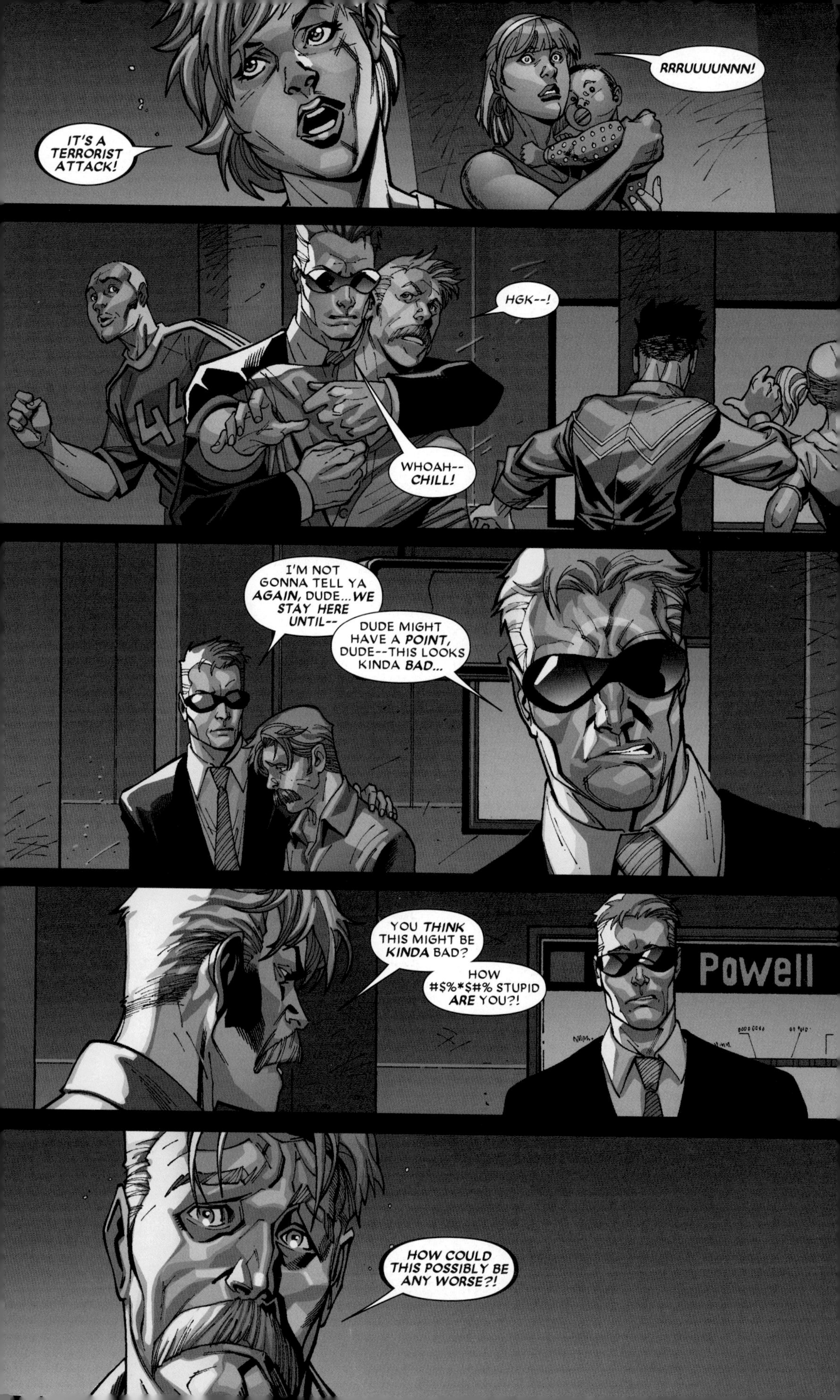
IT'S A TERRORIST ATTACK!
RRRUUUUNNN!
HGK--!
WHOAH-- CHILL!
I'M NOT GONNA TELL YA AGAIN, DUDE...WE STAY HERE UNTIL--
DUDE MIGHT HAVE A POINT, DUDE--THIS LOOKS KINDA BAD...
YOU THINK THIS MIGHT BE KINDA BAD?
HOW #$%*$#% STUPID ARE YOU?!
Powell
HOW COULD THIS POSSIBLY BE ANY WORSE?!

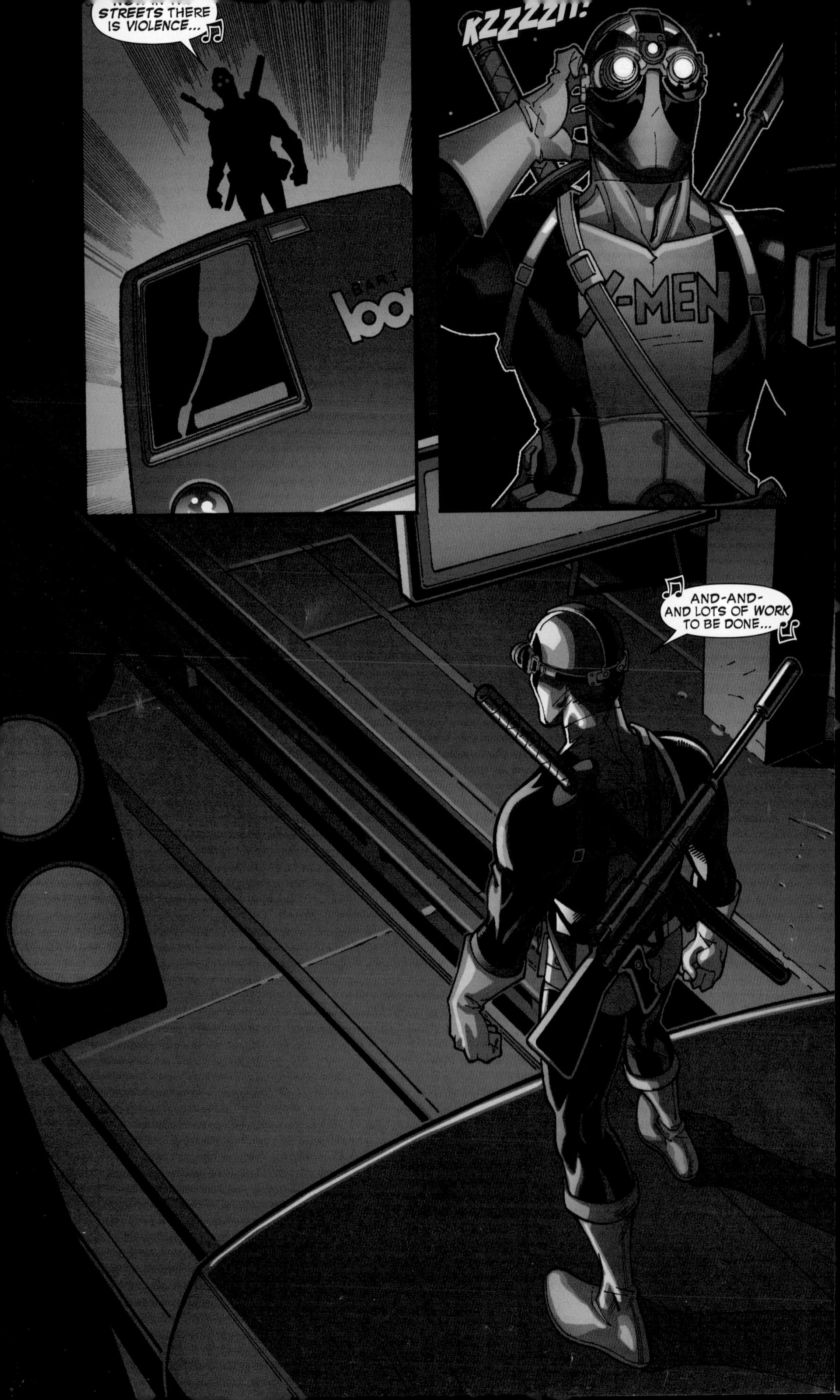

STREETS THERE IS VIOLENCE...
KZZZZ
AND-AND-AND LOTS OF WORK TO BE DONE...

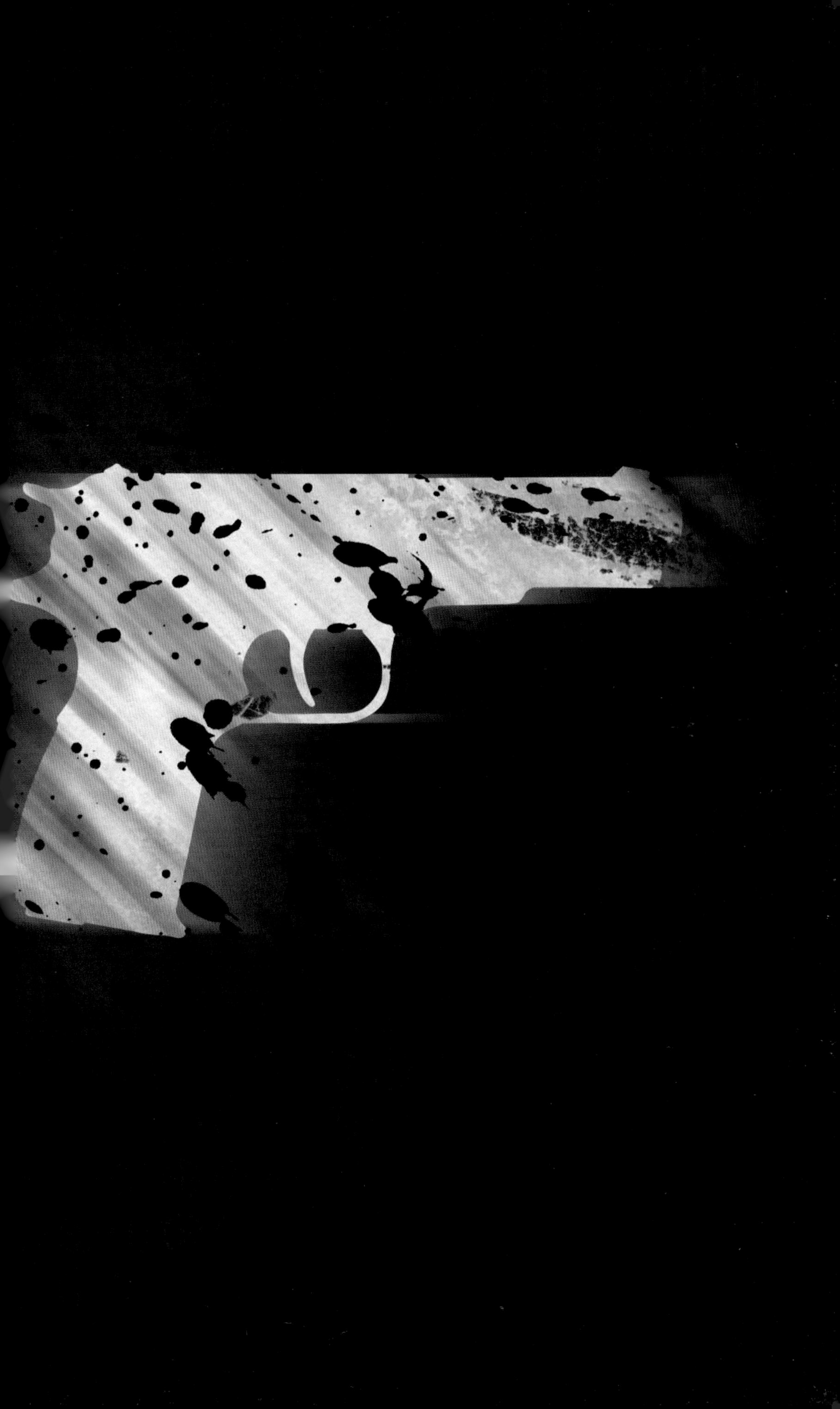

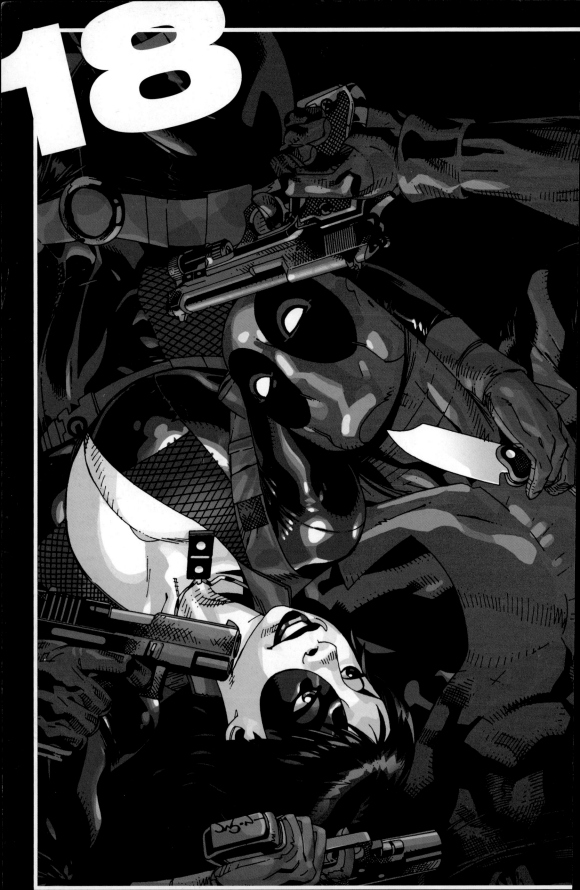

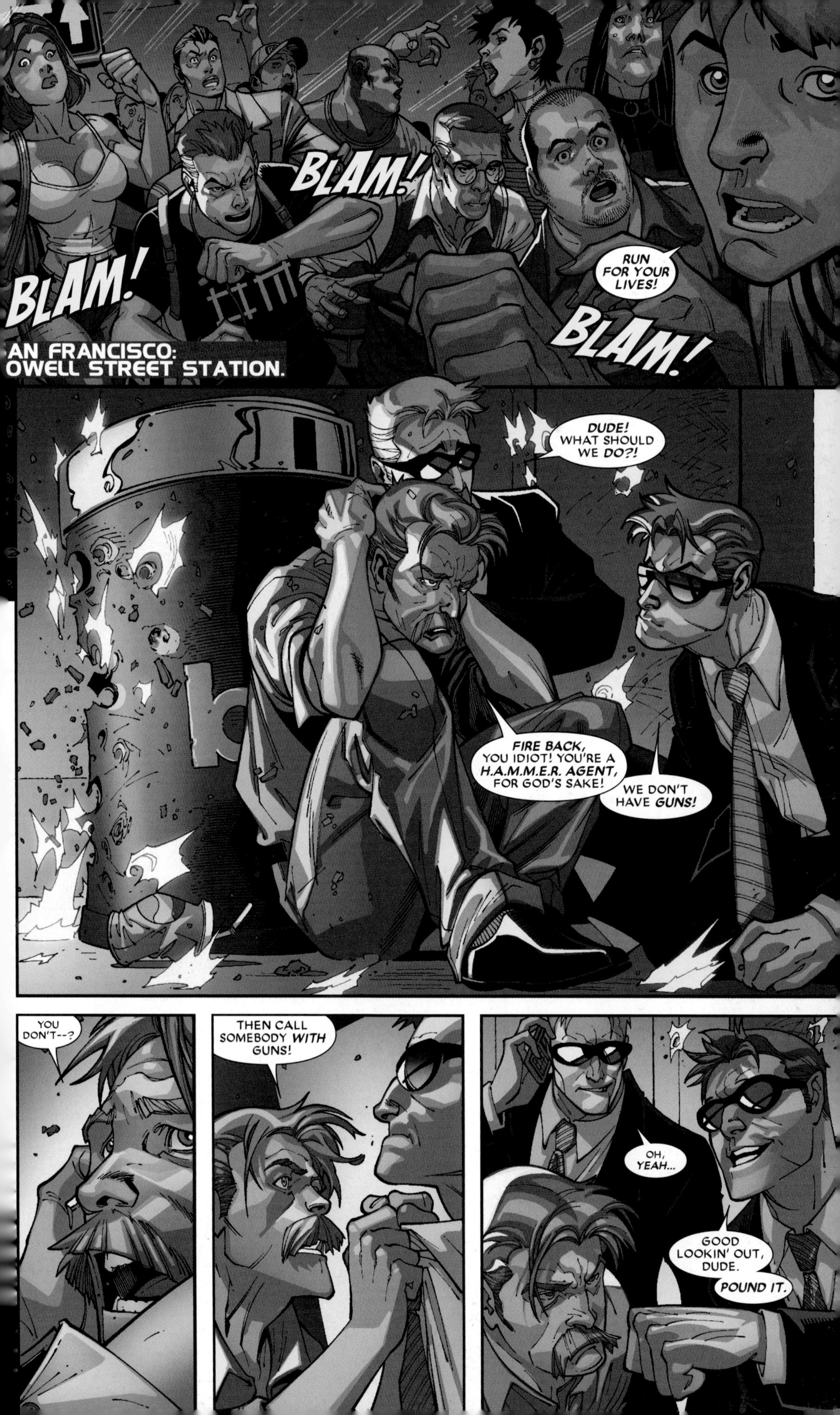
BLAM!
BLAM!
RUN FOR YOUR LIVES!
BLAM!
AN FRANCISCO: OWELL STREET STATION.
DUDE! WHAT SHOULD WE DO?!
FIRE BACK, YOU IDIOT! YOU'RE A H.A.M.M.E.R. AGENT, FOR GOD'S SAKE!
WE DON'T HAVE GUNS!
YOU DON'T--?
THEN CALL SOMEBODY WITH GUNS!
OH, YEAH...
GOOD LOOKIN' OUT, DUDE.
POUND IT.

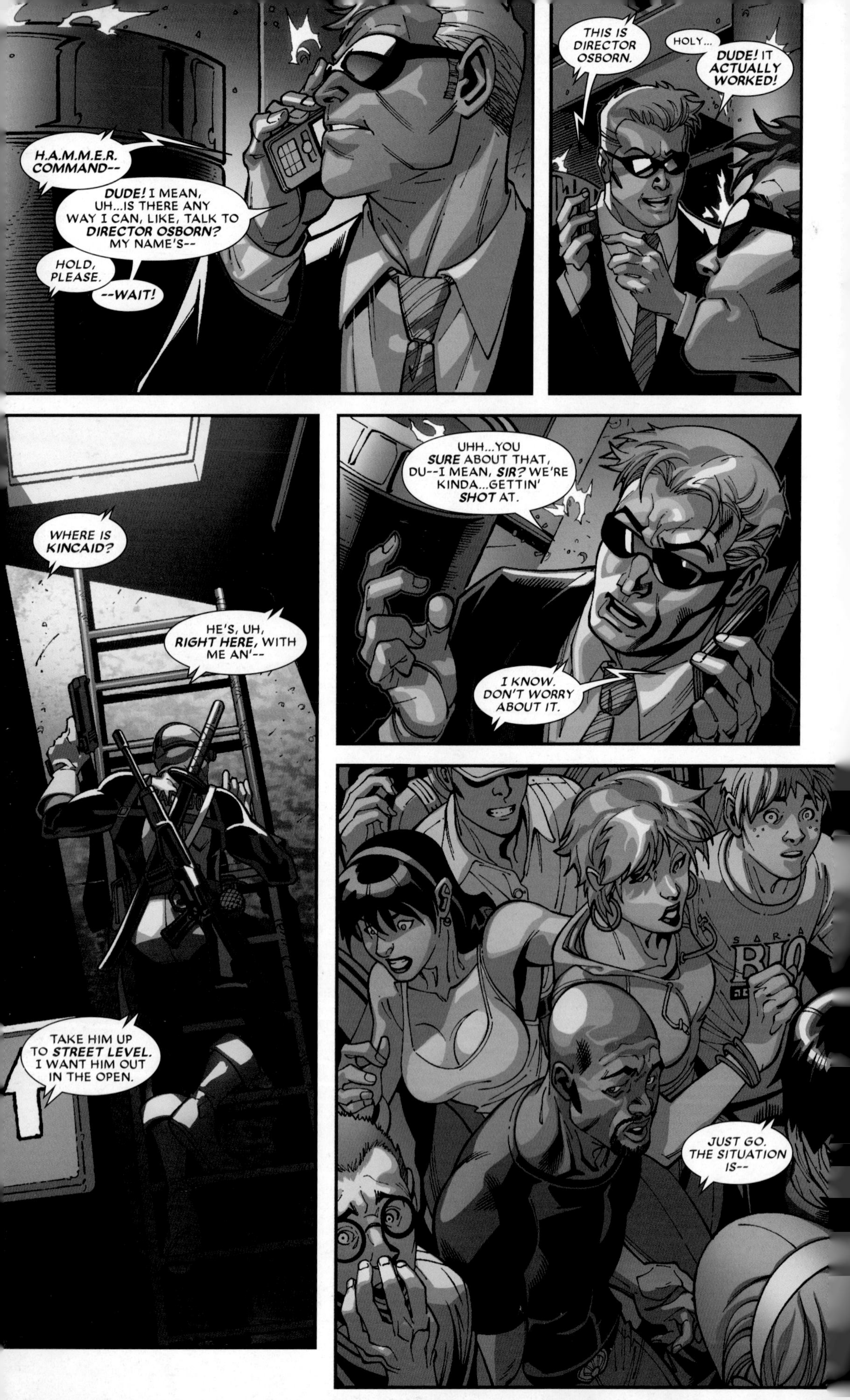
H.A.M.M.E.R. COMMAND--
DUDE! I MEAN, UH...IS THERE ANY WAY I CAN, LIKE, TALK TO DIRECTOR OSBORN? MY NAME'S--
HOLD, PLEASE.
--WAIT!
THIS IS DIRECTOR OSBORN.
HOLY... DUDE! IT ACTUALLY WORKED!
WHERE IS KINCAID?
HE'S, UH, RIGHT HERE, WITH ME AN'--
UHH...YOU SURE ABOUT THAT, DU--I MEAN, SIR? WE'RE KINDA...GETTIN' SHOT AT.
I KNOW. DON'T WORRY ABOUT IT.
TAKE HIM UP TO STREET LEVEL. I WANT HIM OUT IN THE OPEN.
JUST GO. THE SITUATION IS--

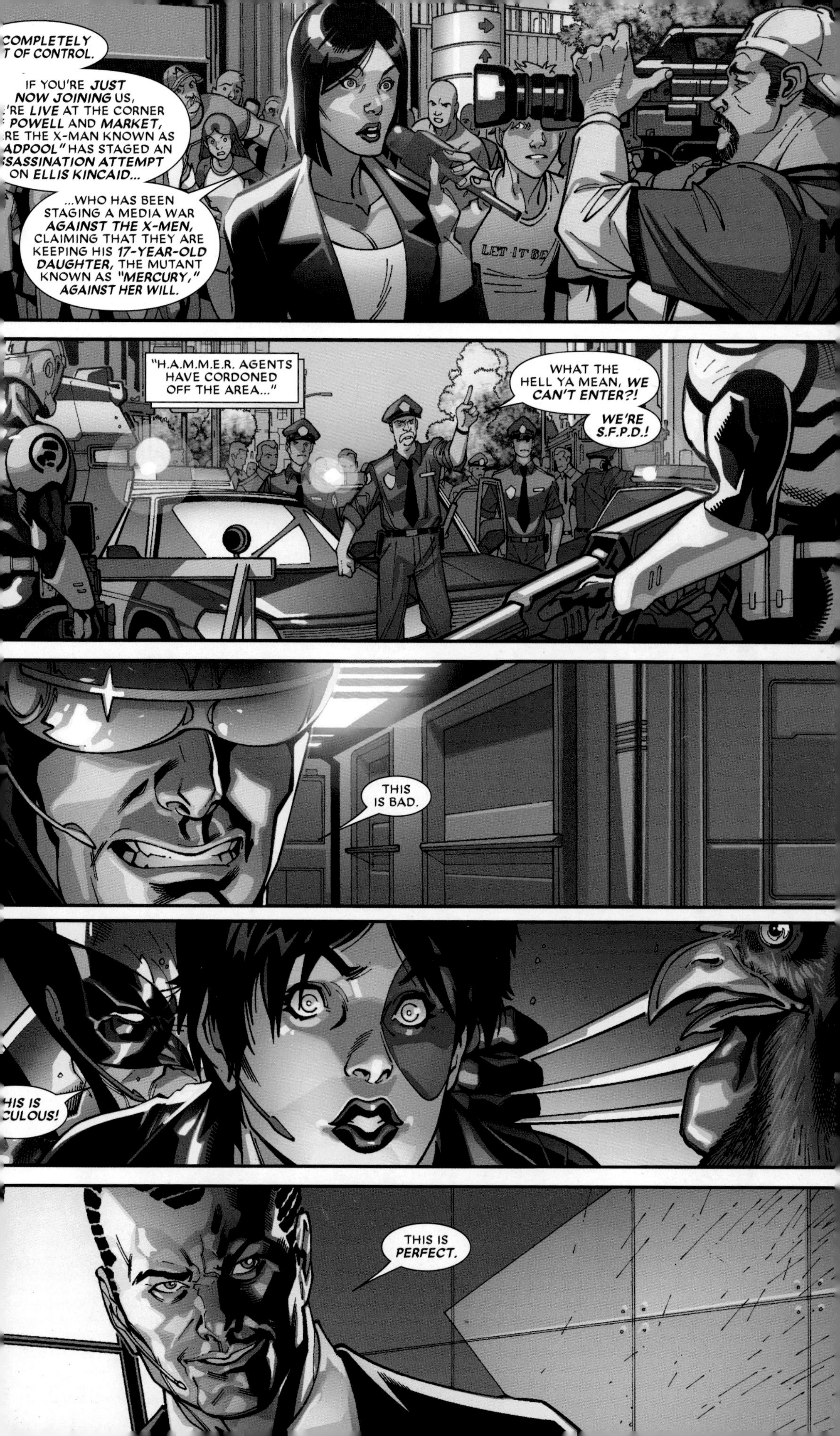
COMPLETELY
T OF CONTROL.
IF YOU'RE JUST NOW JOINING US, 'RE LIVE AT THE CORNER POWELL AND MARKET, RE THE X-MAN KNOWN AS ADPOOL" HAS STAGED AN SASSINATION ATTEMPT ON ELLIS KINCAID...
...WHO HAS BEEN STAGING A MEDIA WAR AGAINST THE X-MEN, CLAIMING THAT THEY ARE KEEPING HIS 17-YEAR-OLD DAUGHTER, THE MUTANT KNOWN AS "MERCURY," AGAINST HER WILL.
LET IT BE
"H.A.M.M.E.R. AGENTS HAVE CORDONED OFF THE AREA..."
WHAT THE HELL YA MEAN, WE CAN'T ENTER?!
WE'RE S.F.P.D.!
THIS IS BAD.
HIS IS
CULOUS!
THIS IS PERFECT.

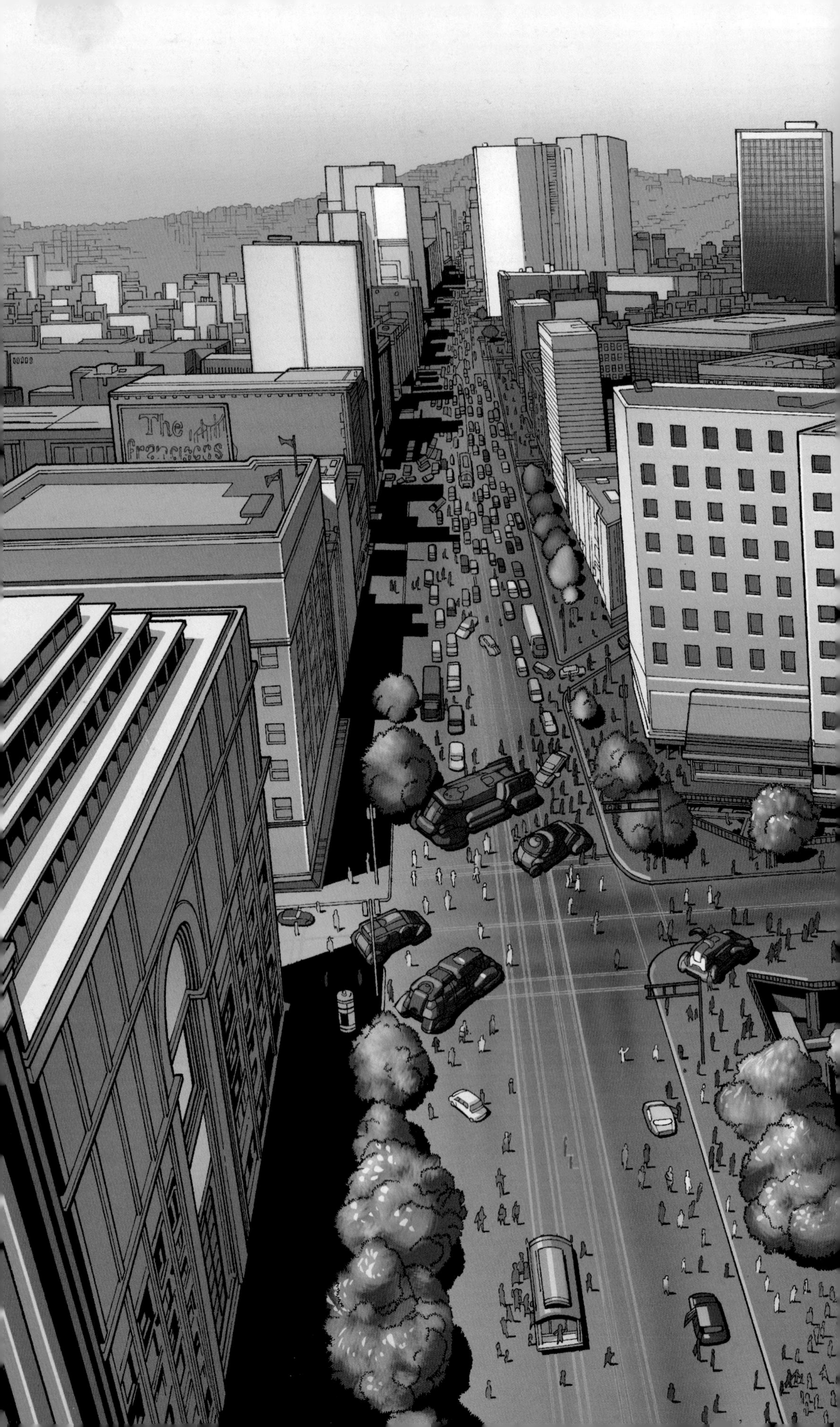
The

WANT YOU TO WANT ME
CONCLUSION
YOU HAVE THE RIGHT NOT TO BE KILLED
THIS IS... A PUBLIC...SERVICE... ANNOUNCEMENT!
WITH GUITARS!
X-MEN

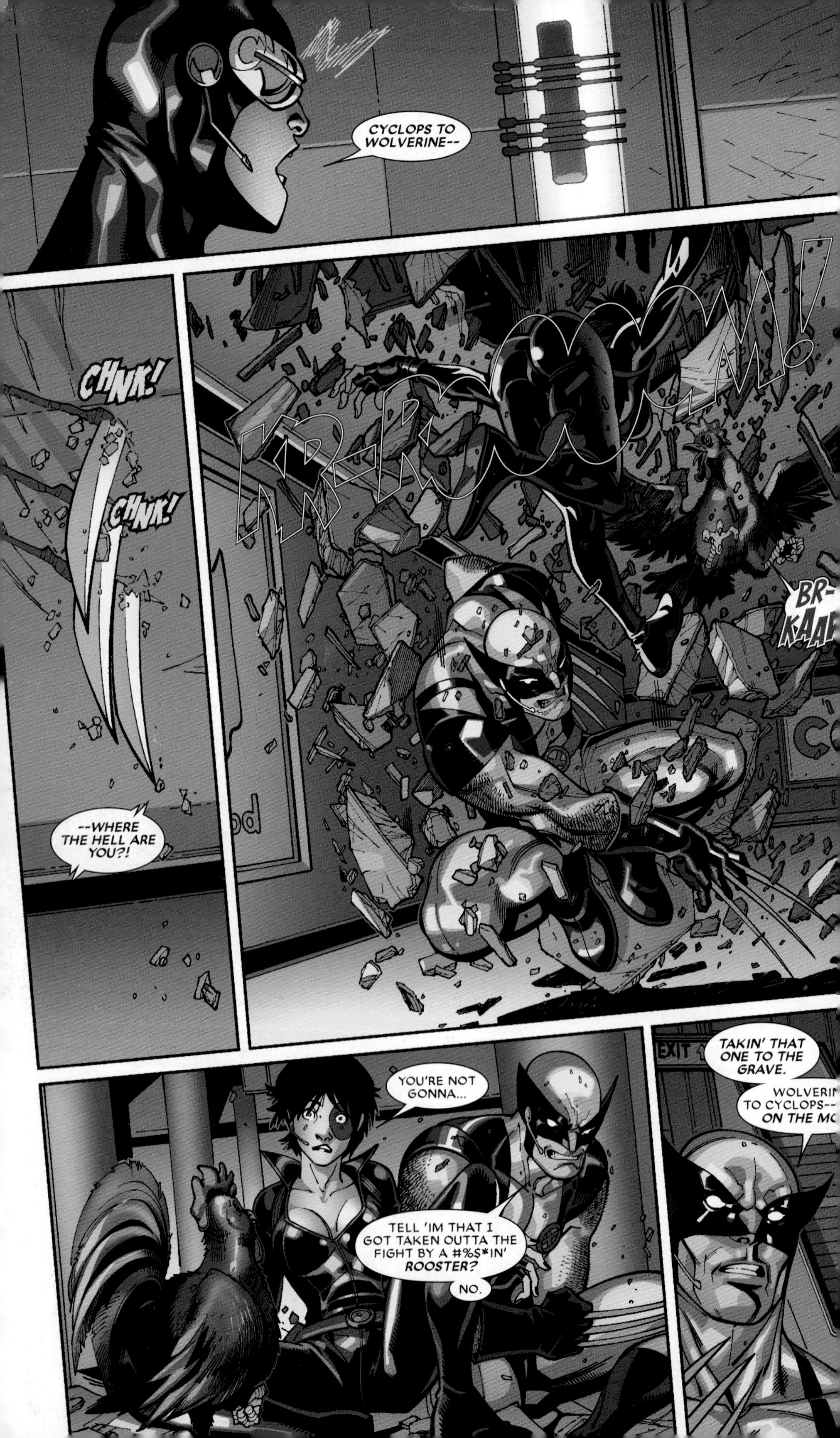
CYCLOPS TO WOLVERINE--
CHNK!
CHNK!
--WHERE THE HELL ARE YOU?!
BR-KAA
YOU'RE NOT GONNA...
TELL 'IM THAT I GOT TAKEN OUTTA THE FIGHT BY A #%$*IN' ROOSTER?
NO.
EXIT
TAKIN' THAT ONE TO THE GRAVE.
WOLVERIN TO CYCLOPS-- ON THE M

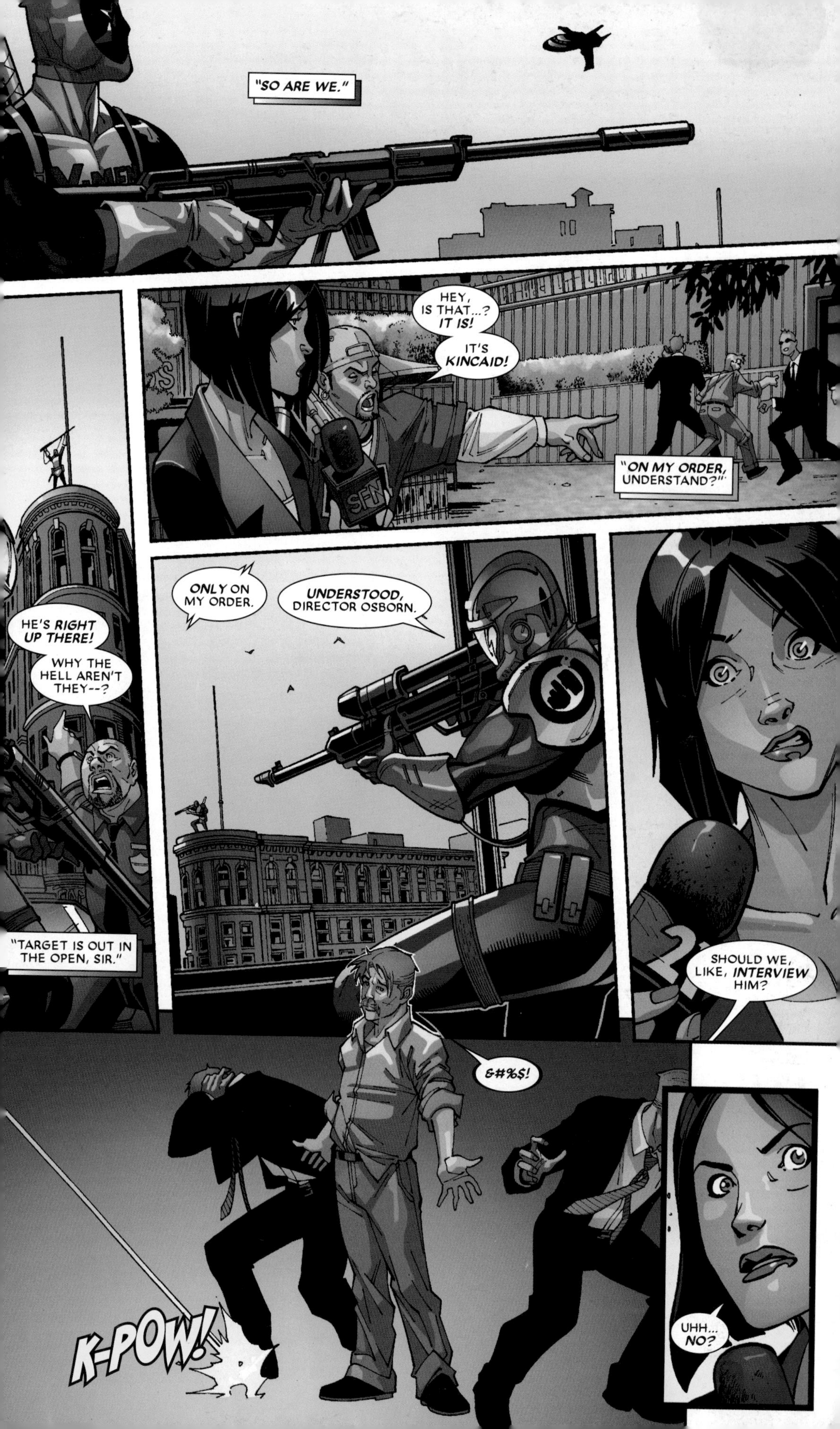
"SO ARE WE."
HEY, IS THAT...? IT IS!
IT'S KINCAID!
"ON MY ORDER, UNDERSTAND?"
HE'S RIGHT UP THERE!
WHY THE HELL AREN'T THEY--?
"TARGET IS OUT IN THE OPEN, SIR."
ONLY ON MY ORDER.
UNDERSTOOD, DIRECTOR OSBORN.
SHOULD WE, LIKE, INTERVIEW HIM?
&#%$!
K-POW!
UHH... NO?

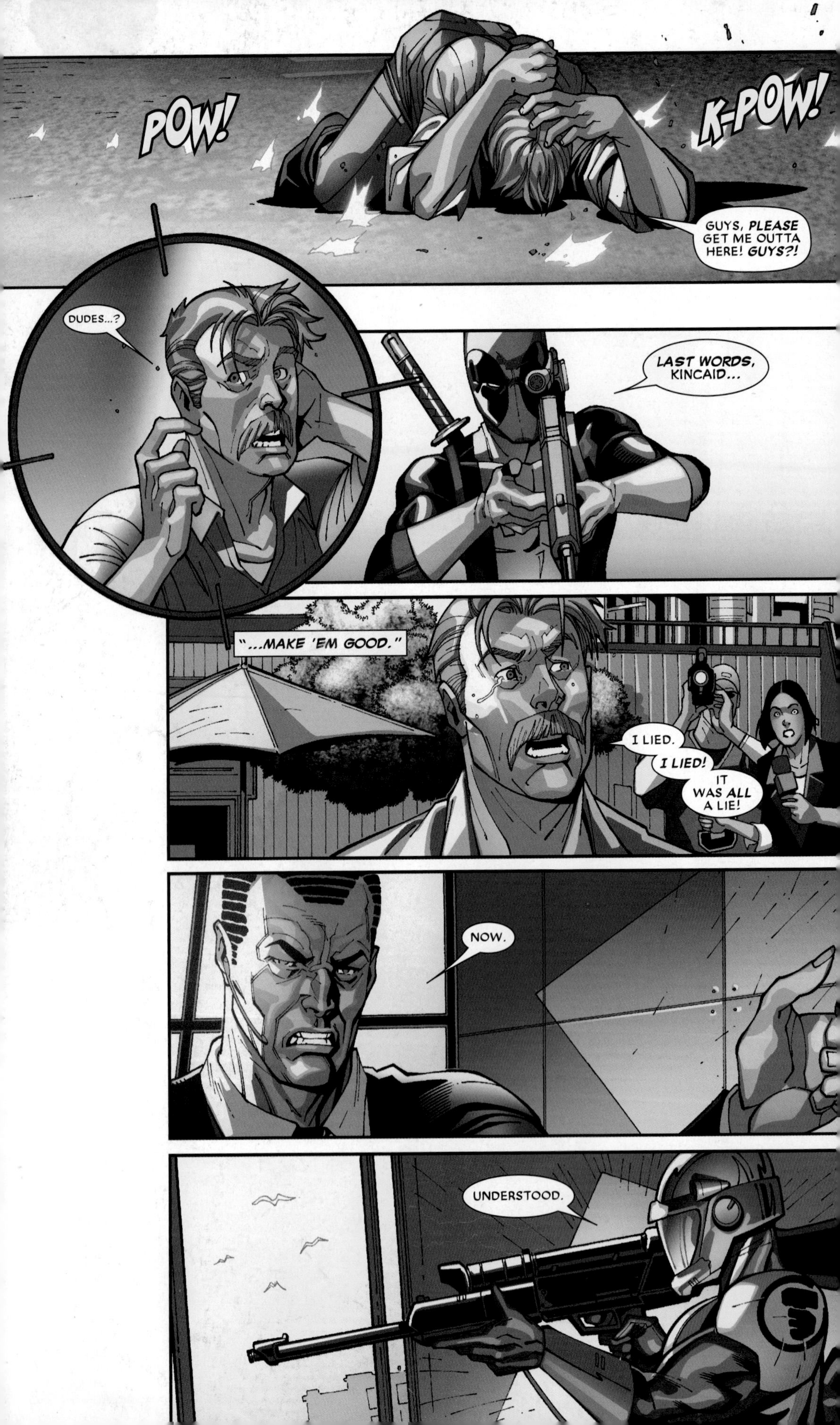
POW!
K-POW!
GUYS, PLEASE GET ME OUTTA HERE! GUYS?!
DUDES...?
LAST WORDS, KINCAID...
"...MAKE 'EM GOOD."
I LIED.
I LIED!
IT WAS ALL A LIE!
NOW.
UNDERSTOOD.

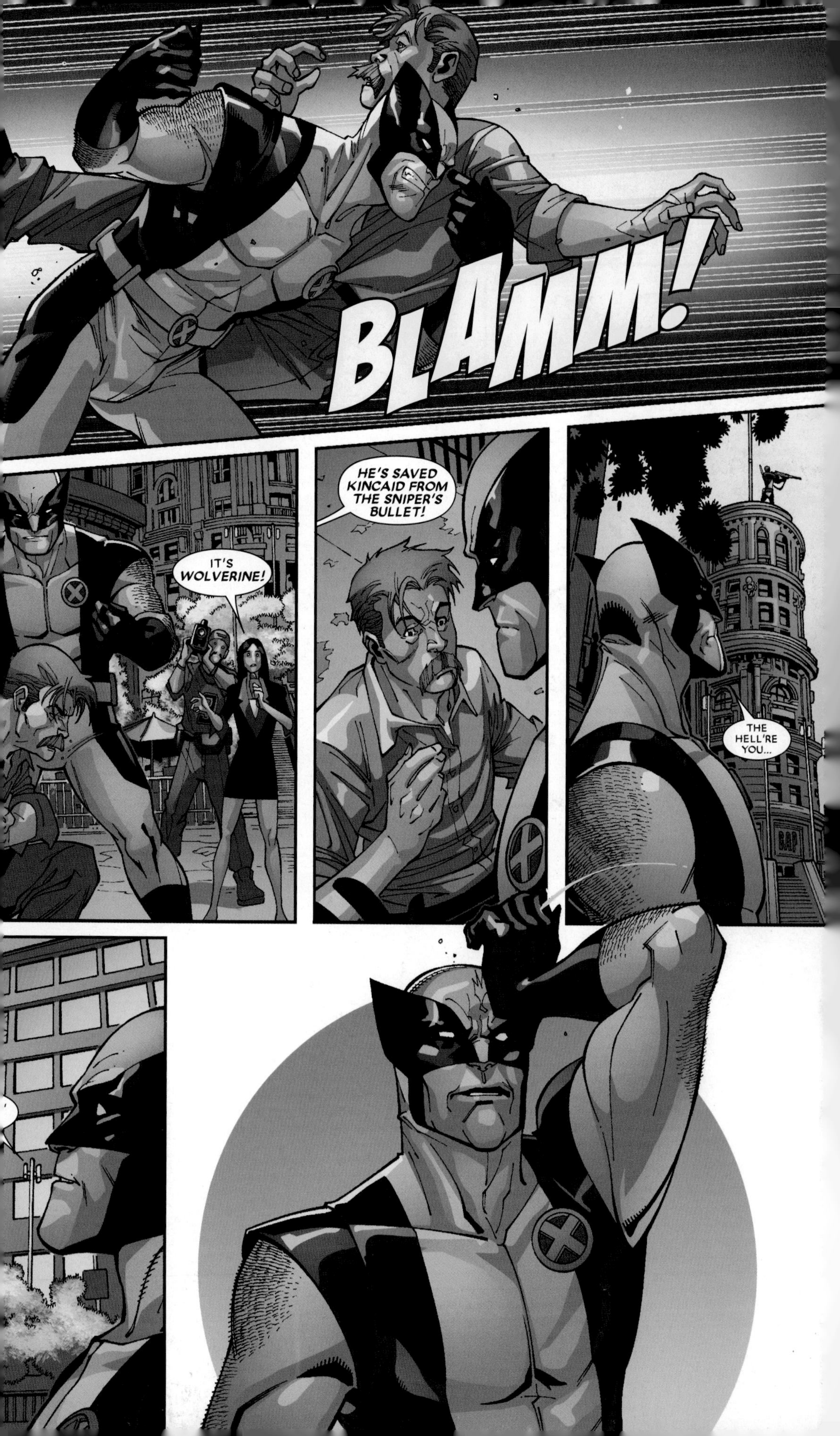
BLAMM!
IT'S WOLVERINE!
HE'S SAVED KINCAID FROM THE SNIPER'S BULLET!
THE HELL'RE YOU...

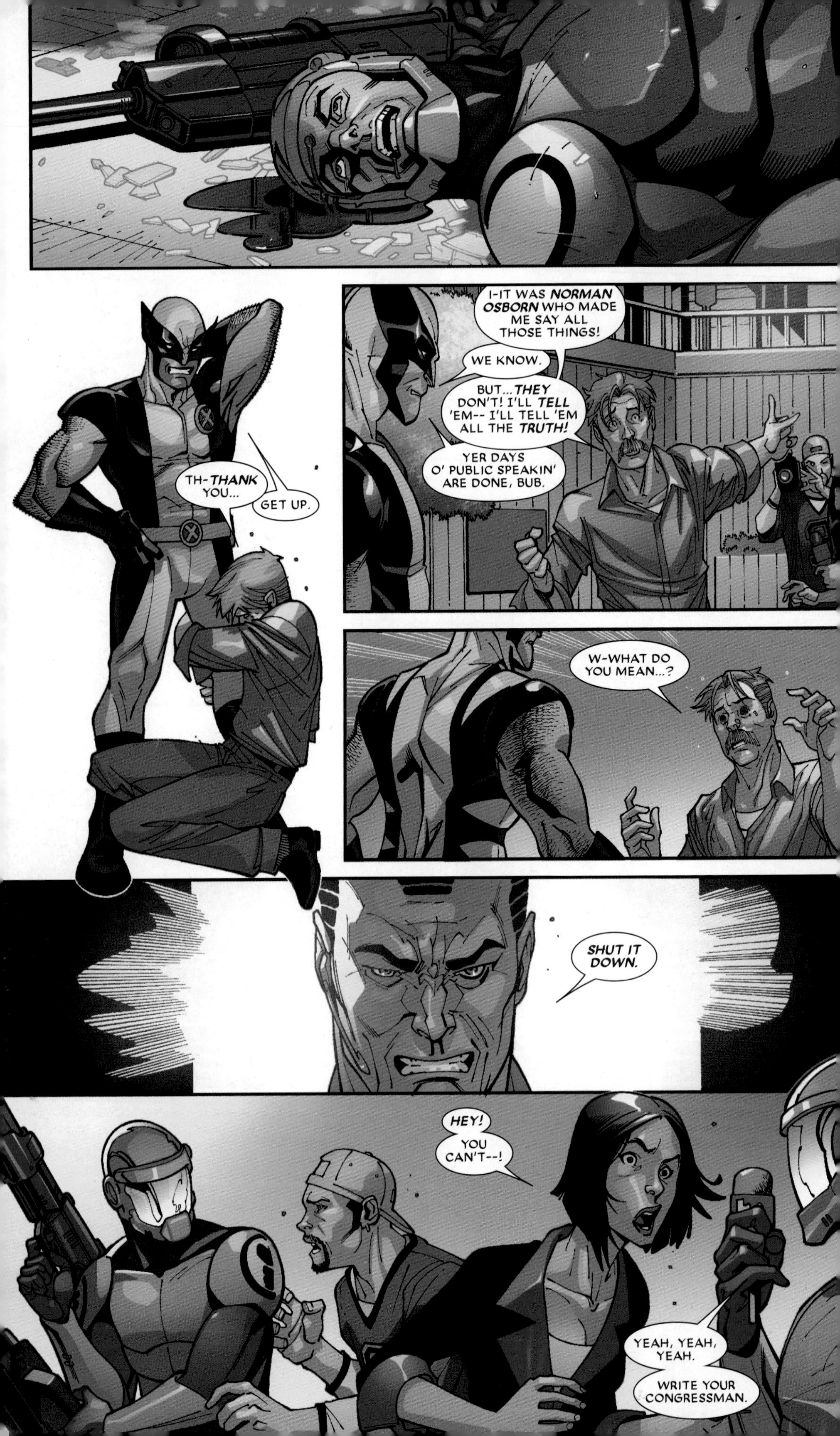
TH-THANK YOU...
GET UP.
I-IT WAS NORMAN OSBORN WHO MADE ME SAY ALL THOSE THINGS!
WE KNOW.
BUT... THEY DON'T! I'LL TELL 'EM-- I'LL TELL 'EM ALL THE TRUTH!
YER DAYS O' PUBLIC SPEAKIN' ARE DONE, BUB.
W-WHAT DO YOU MEAN...?
SHUT IT DOWN.
HEY!
YOU CAN'T--!
YEAH, YEAH, YEAH.
WRITE YOUR CONGRESSMAN.

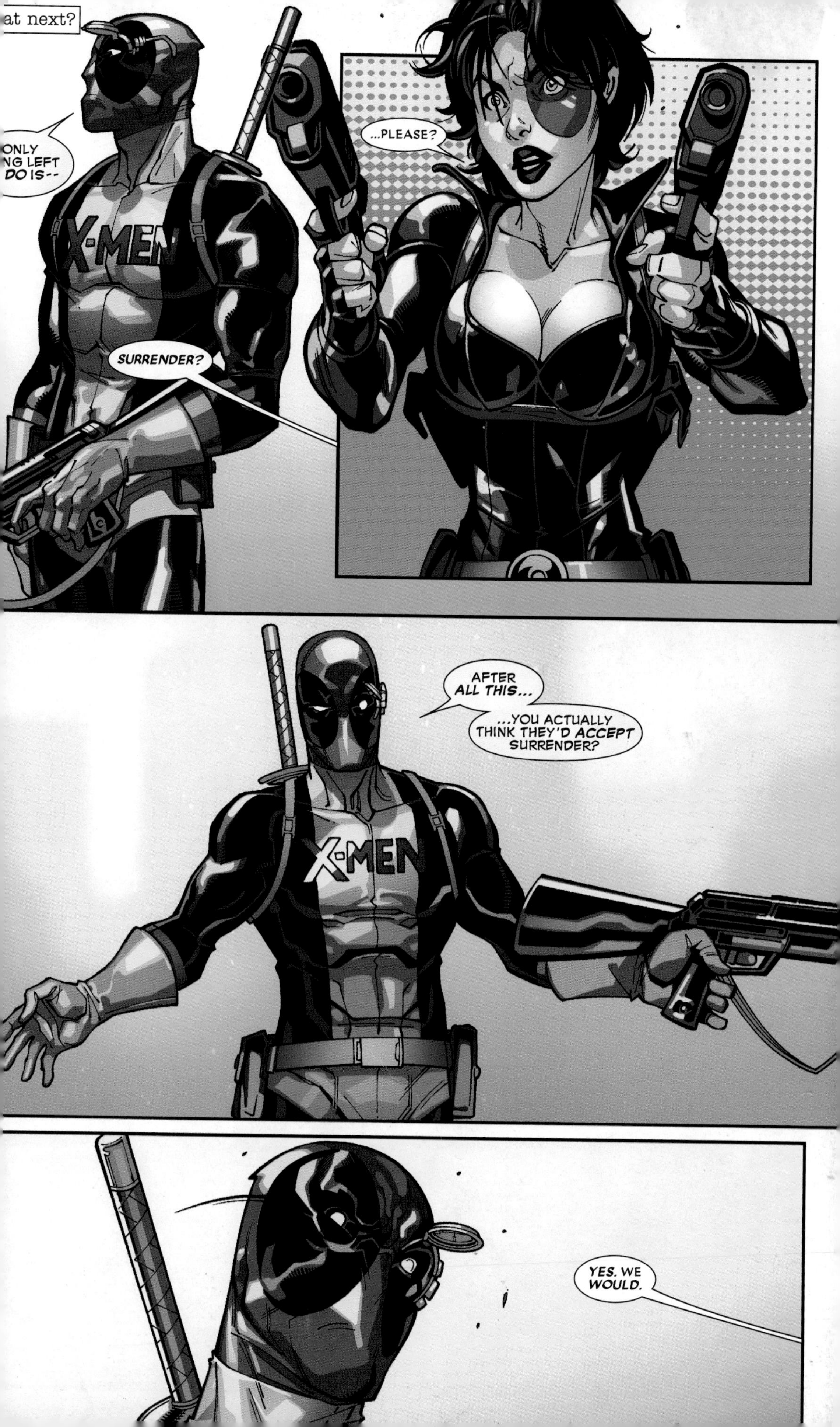
at next?
ONLY
NG LEFT
DO IS--
...PLEASE?
SURRENDER?
AFTER
ALL THIS...
...YOU ACTUALLY
THINK THEY'D ACCEPT
SURRENDER?
YES. WE
WOULD.

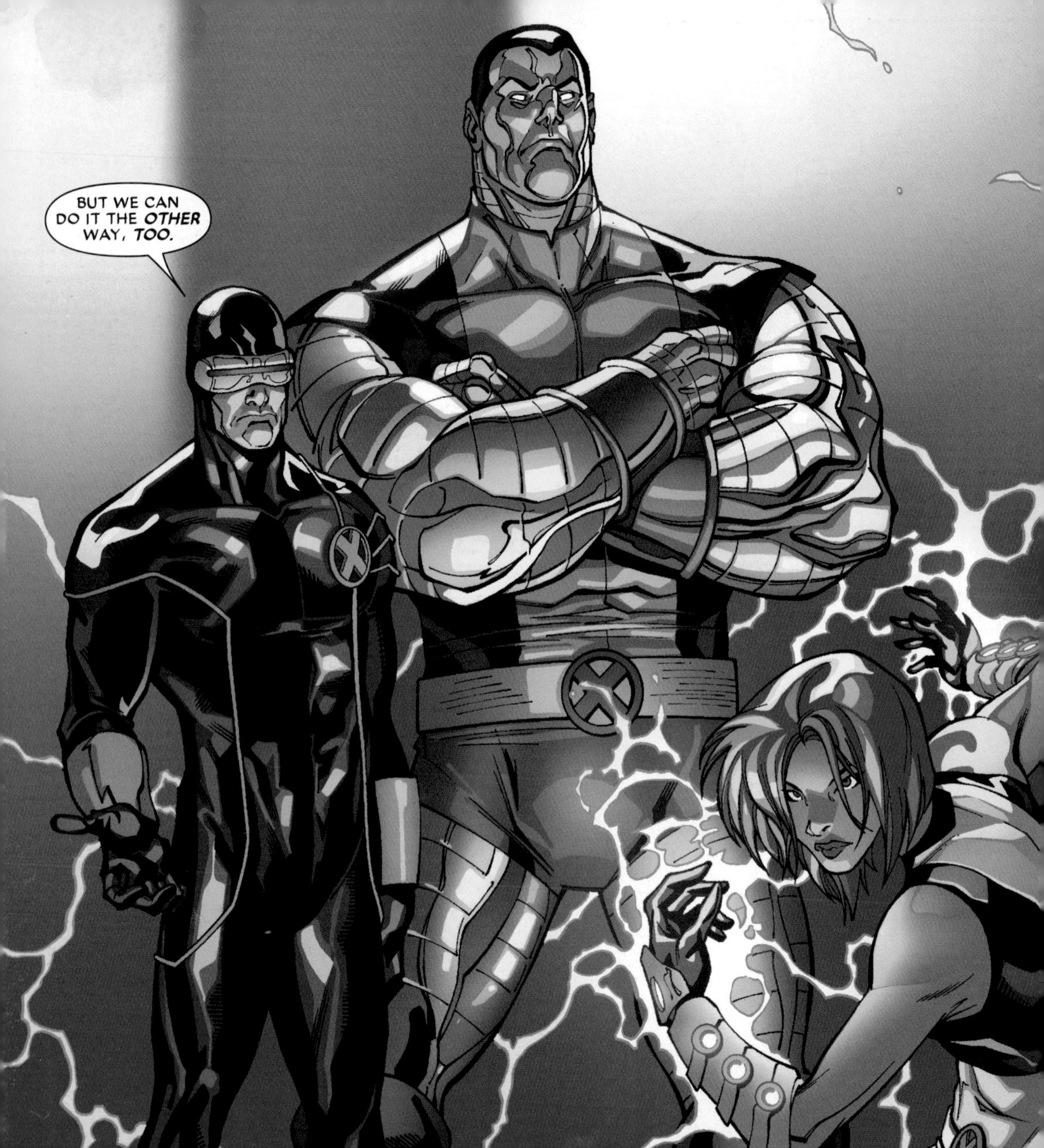
BUT WE CAN DO IT THE OTHER WAY, TOO.

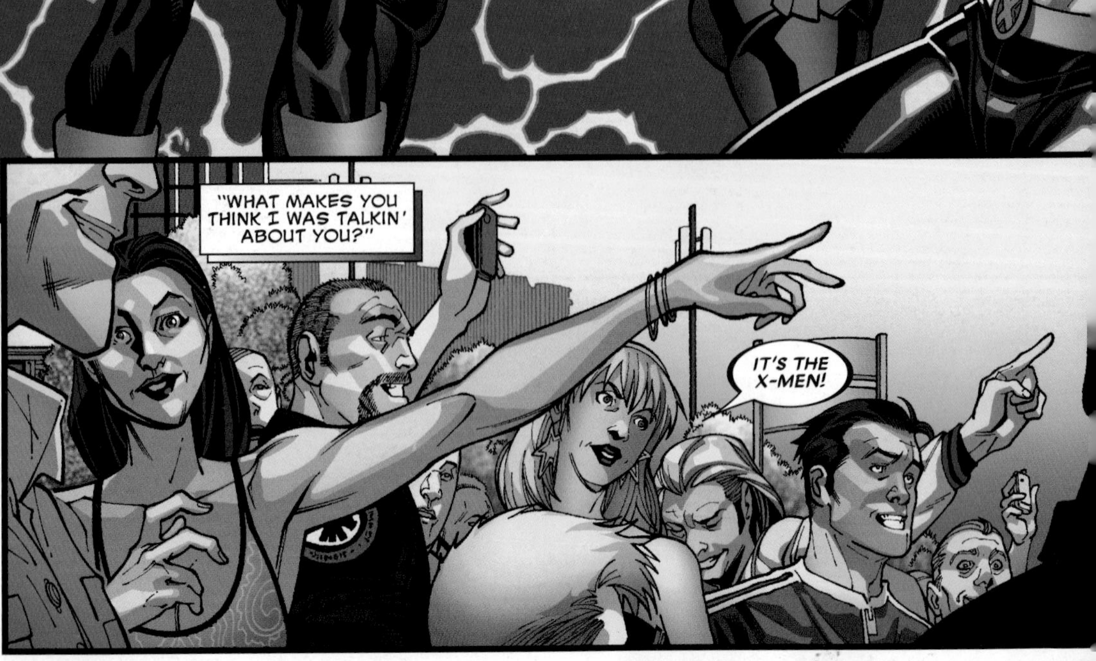
"WHAT MAKES YOU THINK I WAS TALKIN' ABOUT YOU?"
IT'S THE X-MEN!

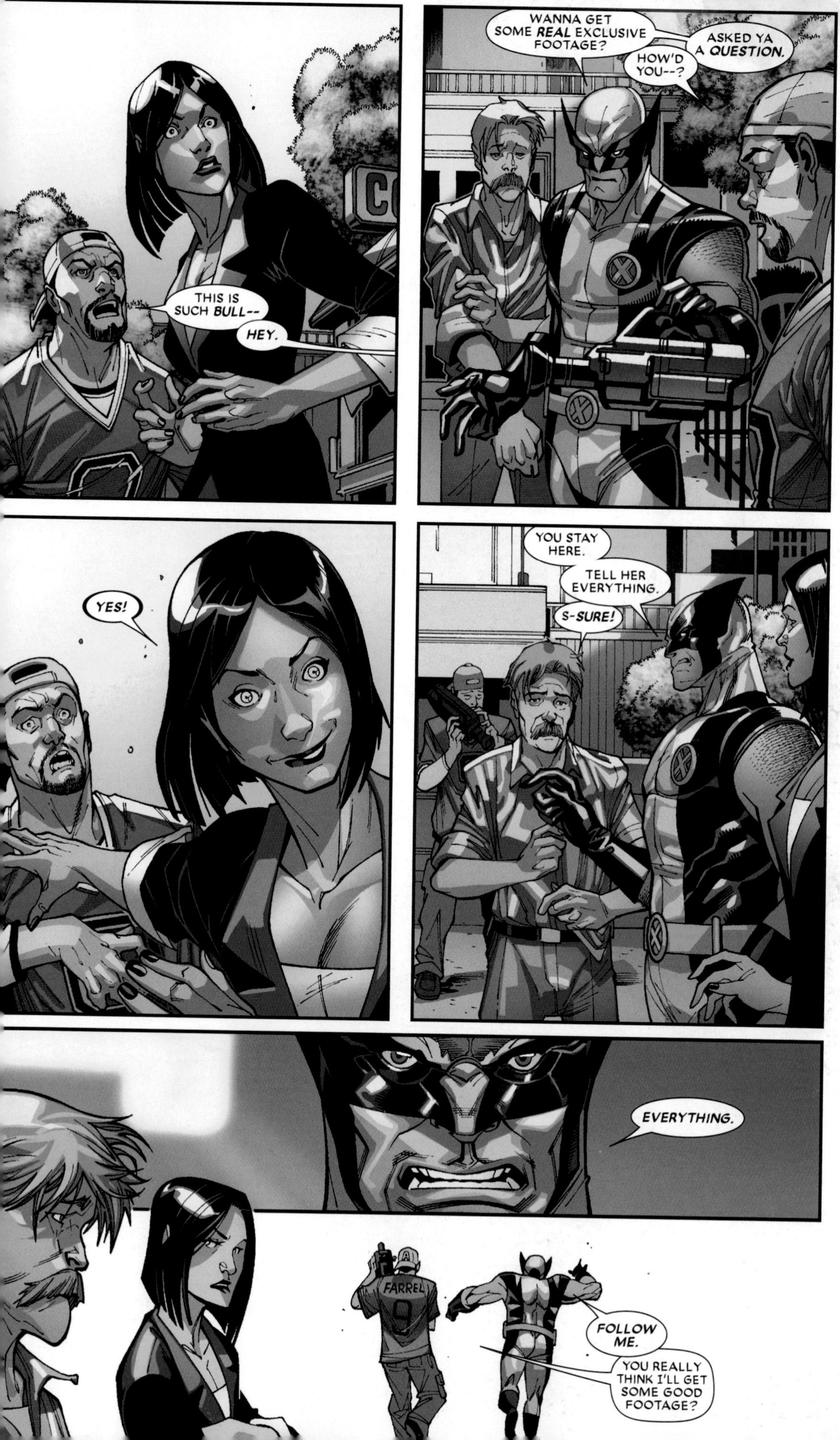
THIS IS SUCH BULL--
HEY.
WANNA GET SOME REAL EXCLUSIVE FOOTAGE?
ASKED YA A QUESTION.
HOW'D YOU--?
YES!
YOU STAY HERE.
TELL HER EVERYTHING.
S-SURE!
EVERYTHING.
FARREL
FOLLOW ME.
YOU REALLY THINK I'LL GET SOME GOOD FOOTAGE?

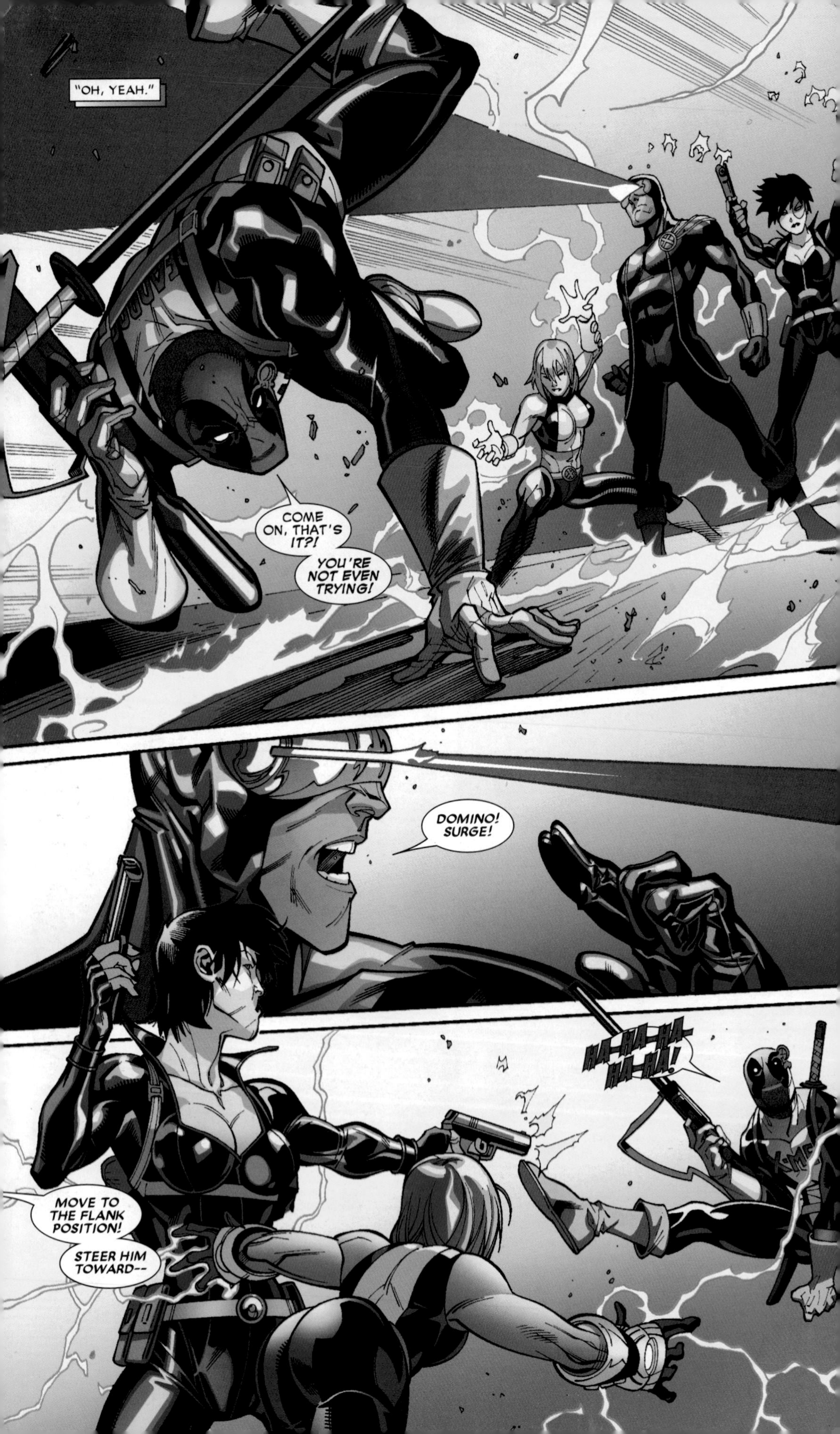
"OH, YEAH."
COME ON, THAT'S IT?!
YOU'RE NOT EVEN TRYING!
DOMINO! SURGE!
HA-HA-HA-HA-HA!
MOVE TO THE FLANK POSITION!
STEER HIM TOWARD--

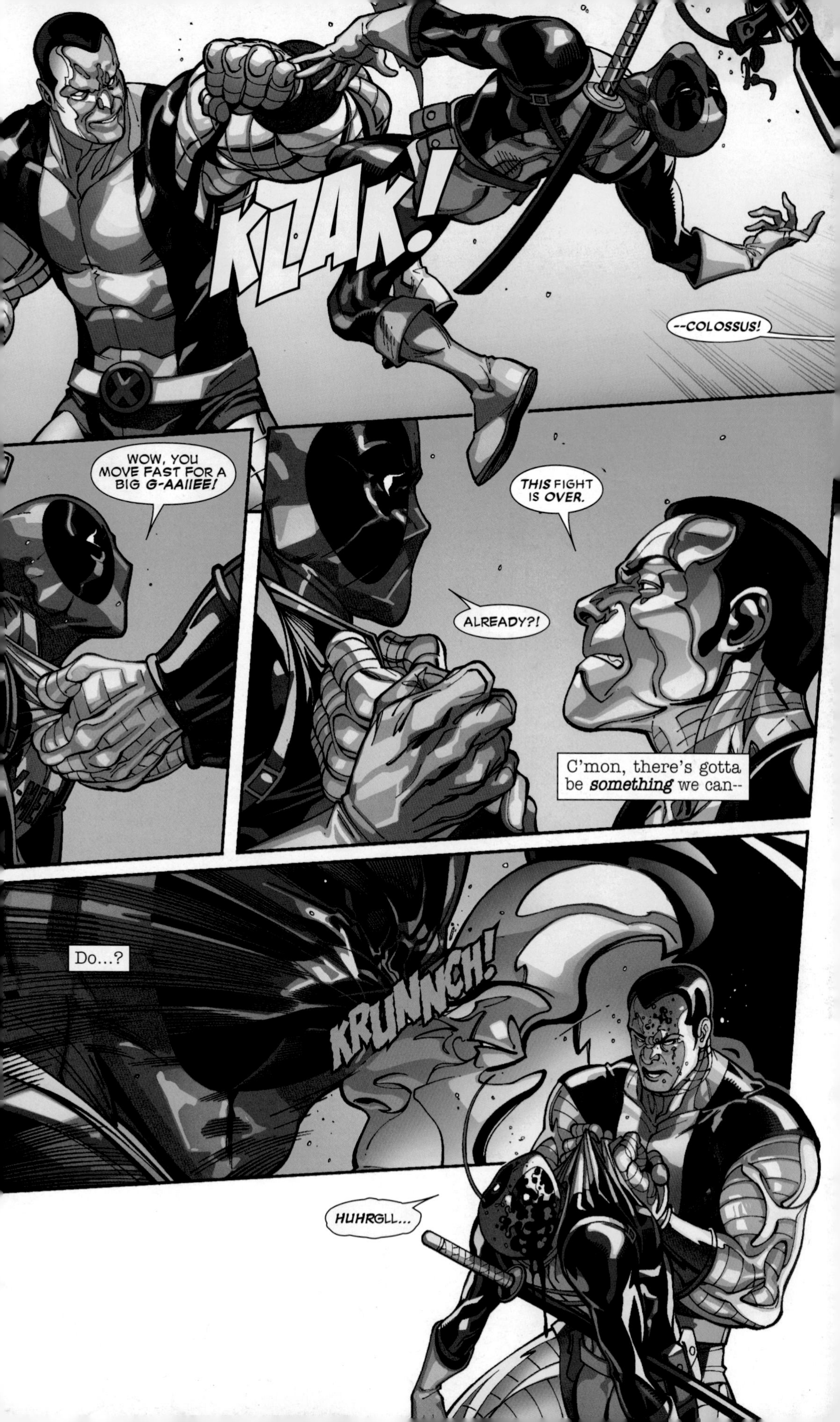

KLAK!
--COLOSSUS!
WOW, YOU MOVE FAST FOR A BIG G-AAIIEE!
THIS FIGHT IS OVER.
ALREADY?!
C'mon, there's gotta be something we can--
Do...?
KRUNNCH!
HUHRGLL...

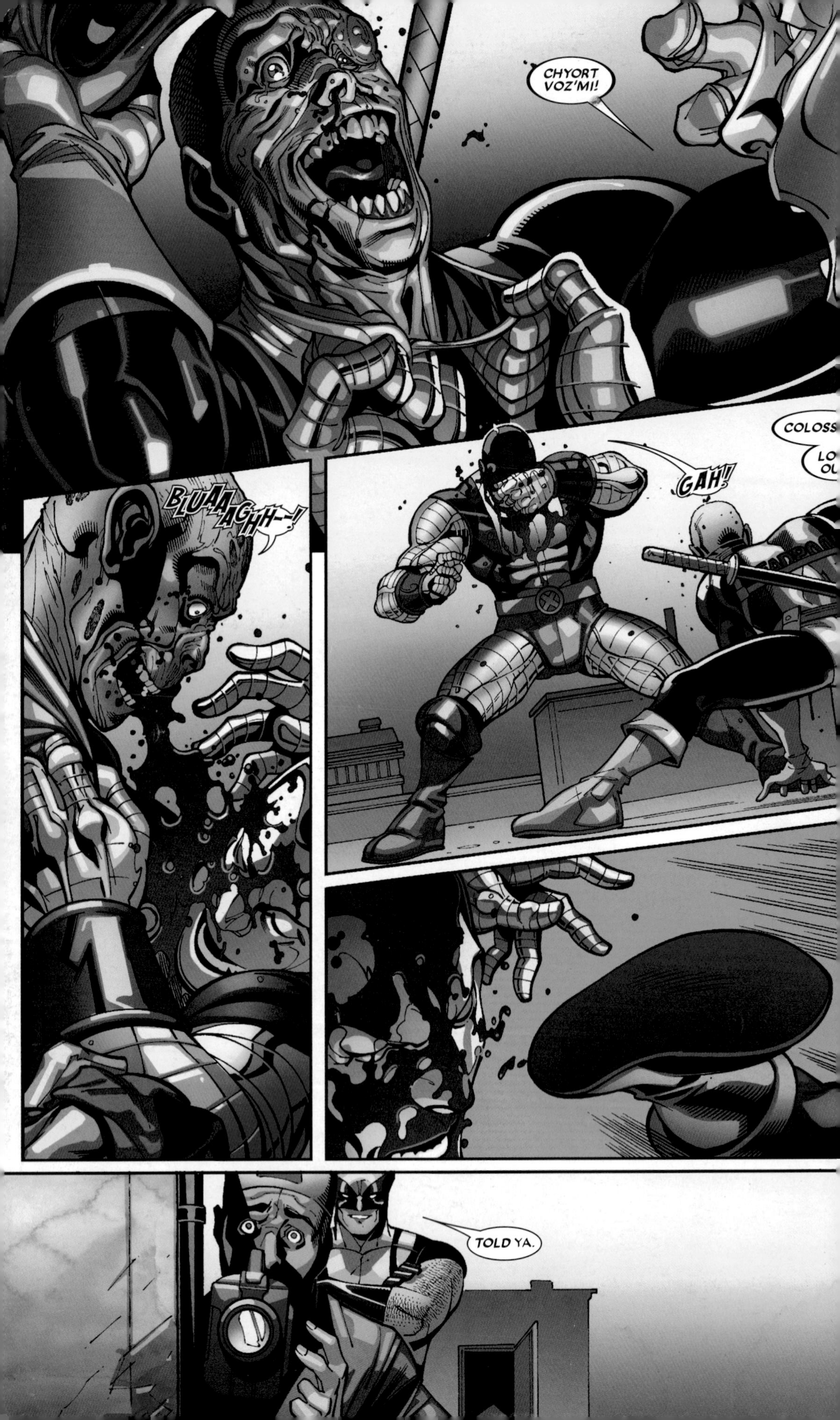
CHYORT VOZ'MI!
COLOSS
BLUAAAGHH--!
GAH!
TOLD YA.

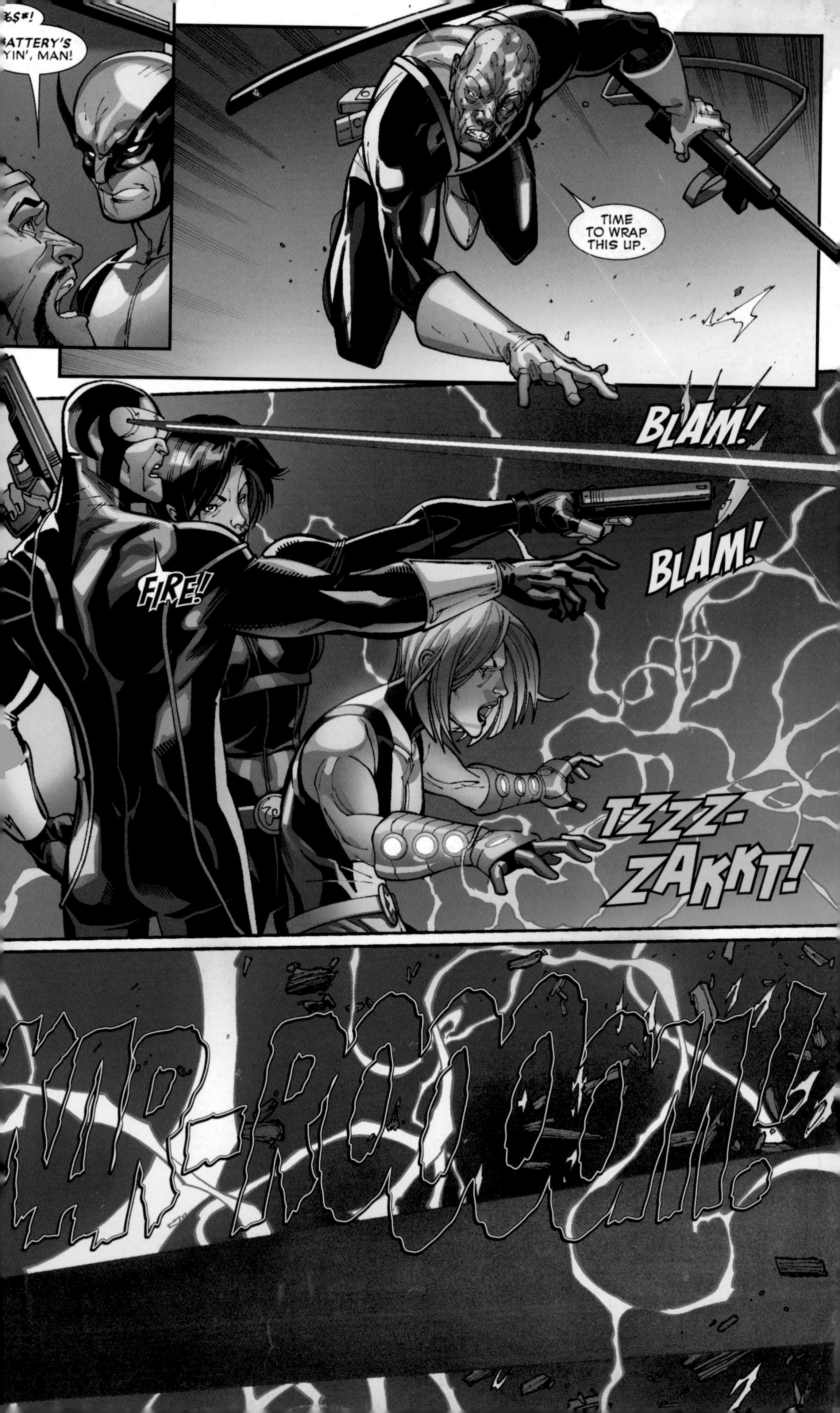
%$*!
ATTERY'S YIN', MAN!
TIME TO WRAP THIS UP.
BLAM!
FIRE!
BLAM!
TZZZ-ZAKKT!

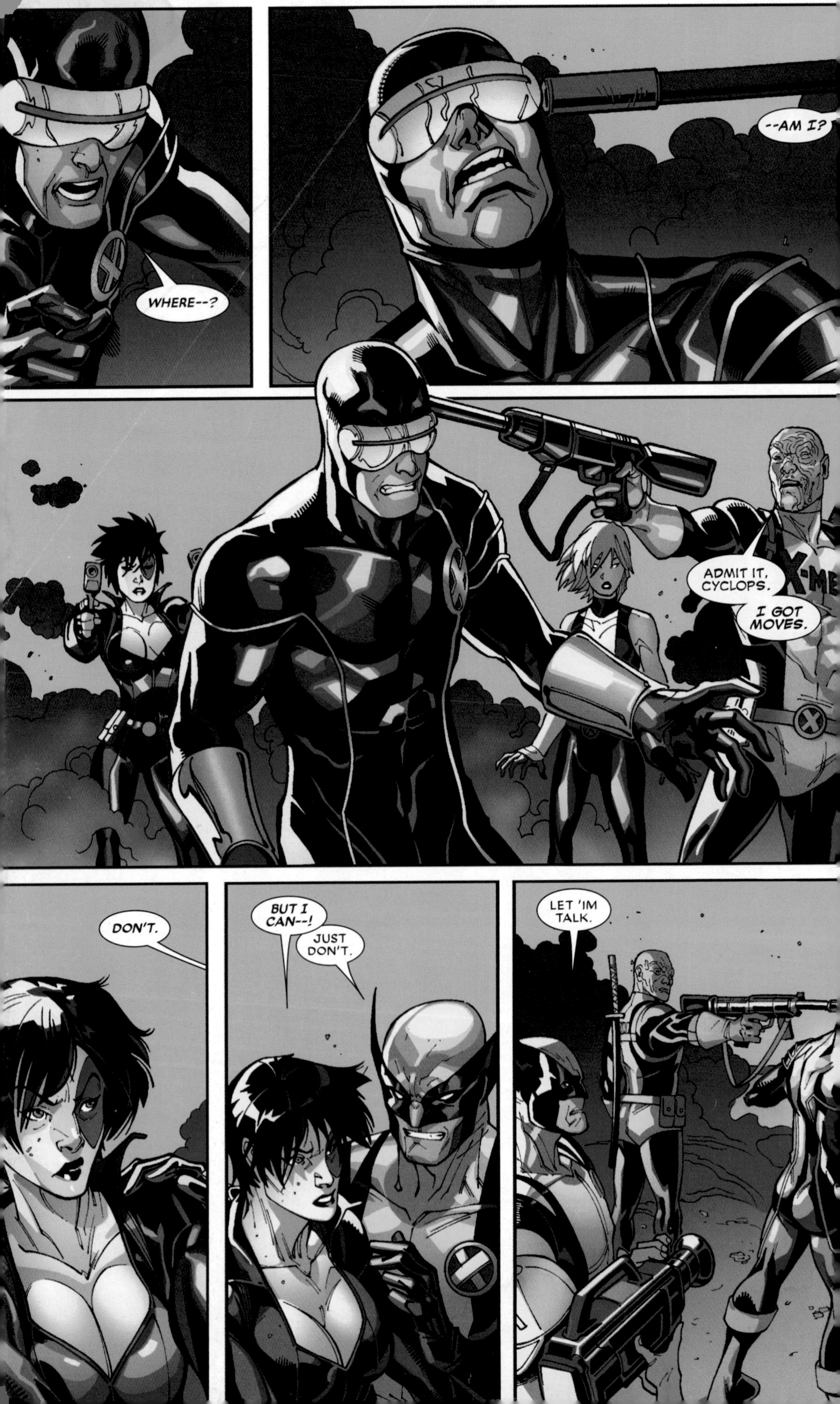
WHERE--?
--AM I?
ADMIT IT, CYCLOPS.
I GOT MOVES.
DON'T.
BUT I CAN--!
JUST DON'T.
LET 'IM TALK.

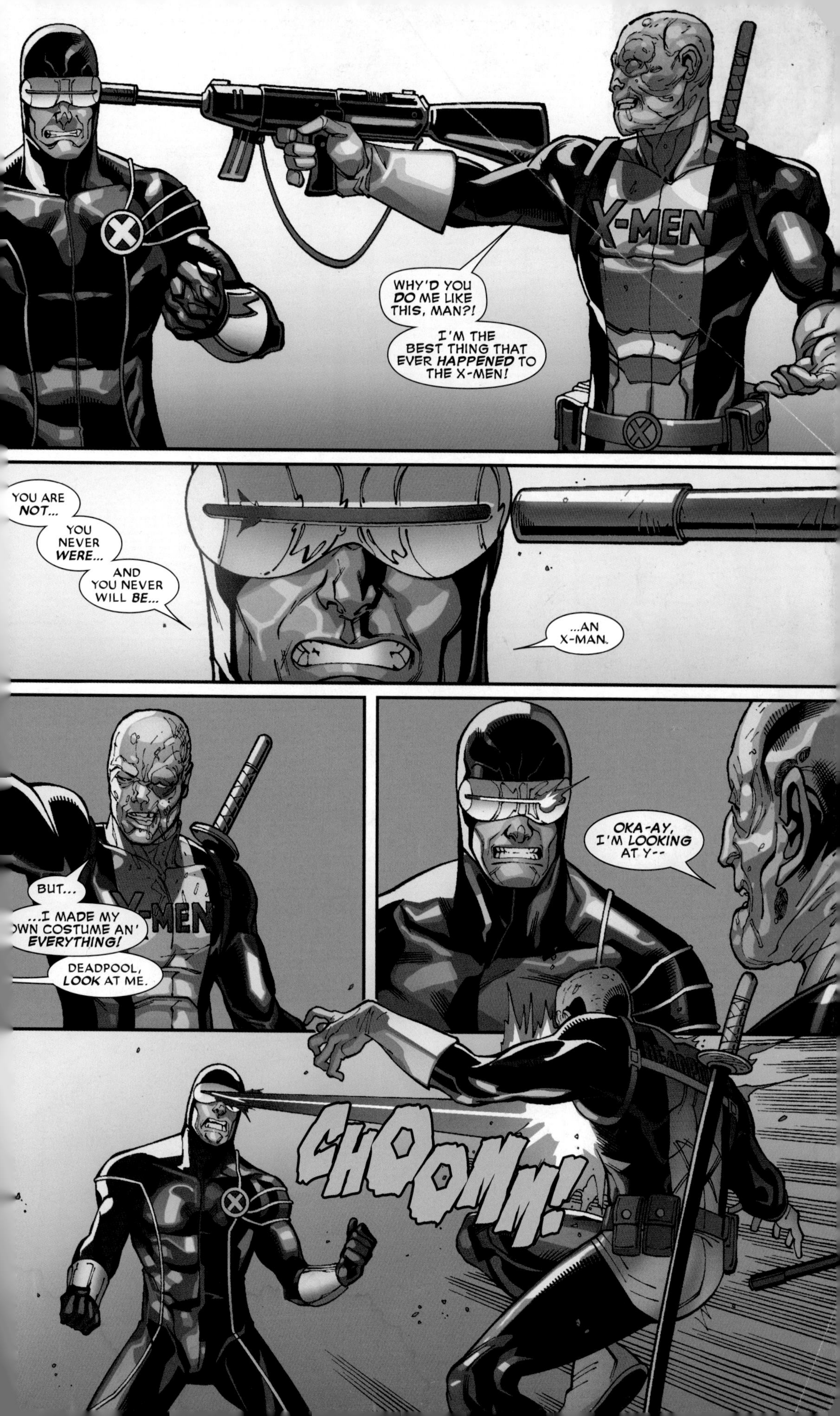
WHY'D YOU DO ME LIKE THIS, MAN?!
I'M THE BEST THING THAT EVER HAPPENED TO THE X-MEN!
YOU ARE NOT...
YOU NEVER WERE...
AND YOU NEVER WILL BE...
...AN X-MAN.
BUT...
...I MADE MY OWN COSTUME AN' EVERYTHING!
DEADPOOL, LOOK AT ME.
OKA-AY, I'M LOOKING AT Y--
CHOOMM!

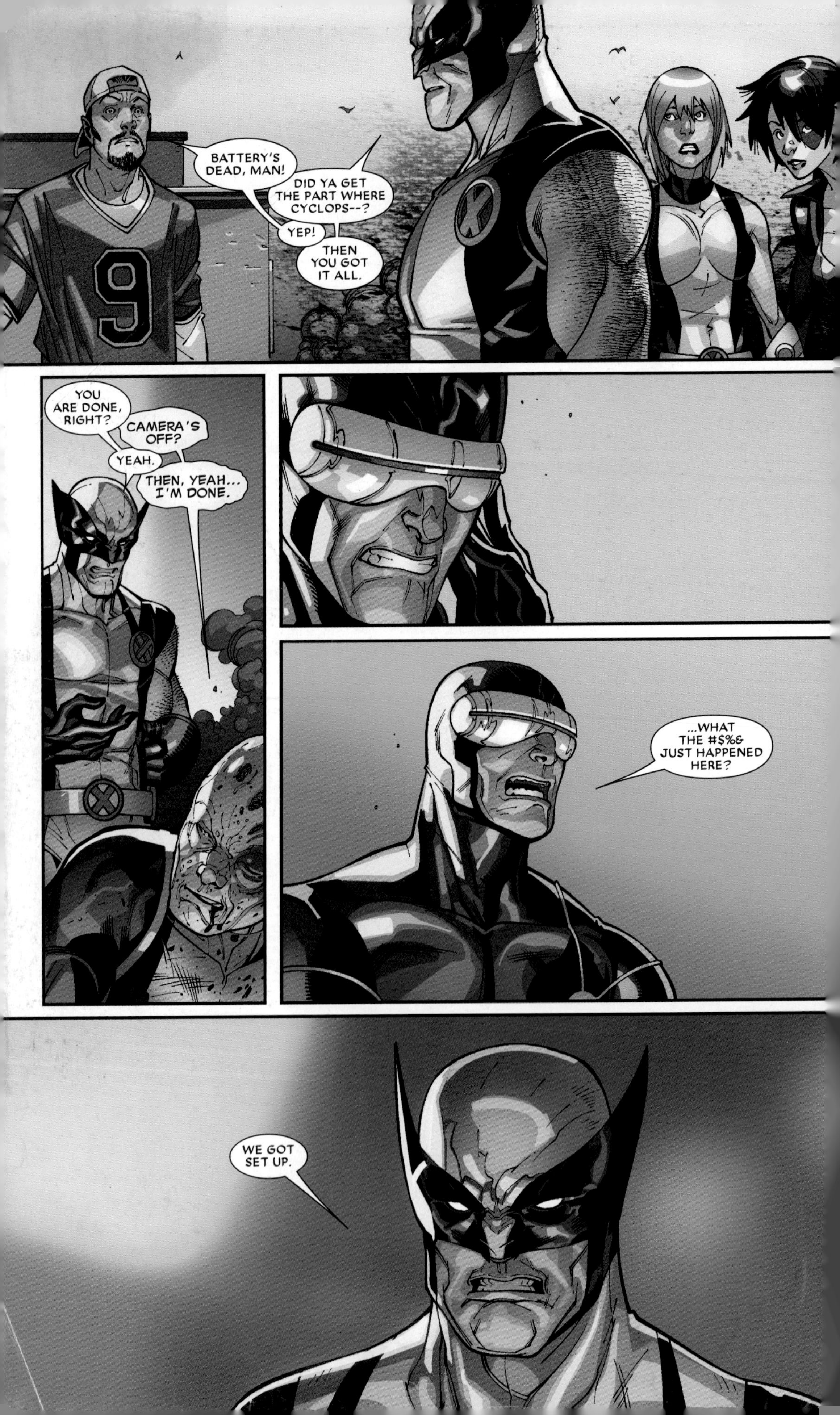

BATTERY'S DEAD, MAN!
DID YA GET THE PART WHERE CYCLOPS--?
YEP!
THEN YOU GOT IT ALL.
YOU ARE DONE, RIGHT?
CAMERA'S OFF?
YEAH.
THEN, YEAH... I'M DONE.
...WHAT THE #$%& JUST HAPPENED HERE?
WE GOT SET UP.

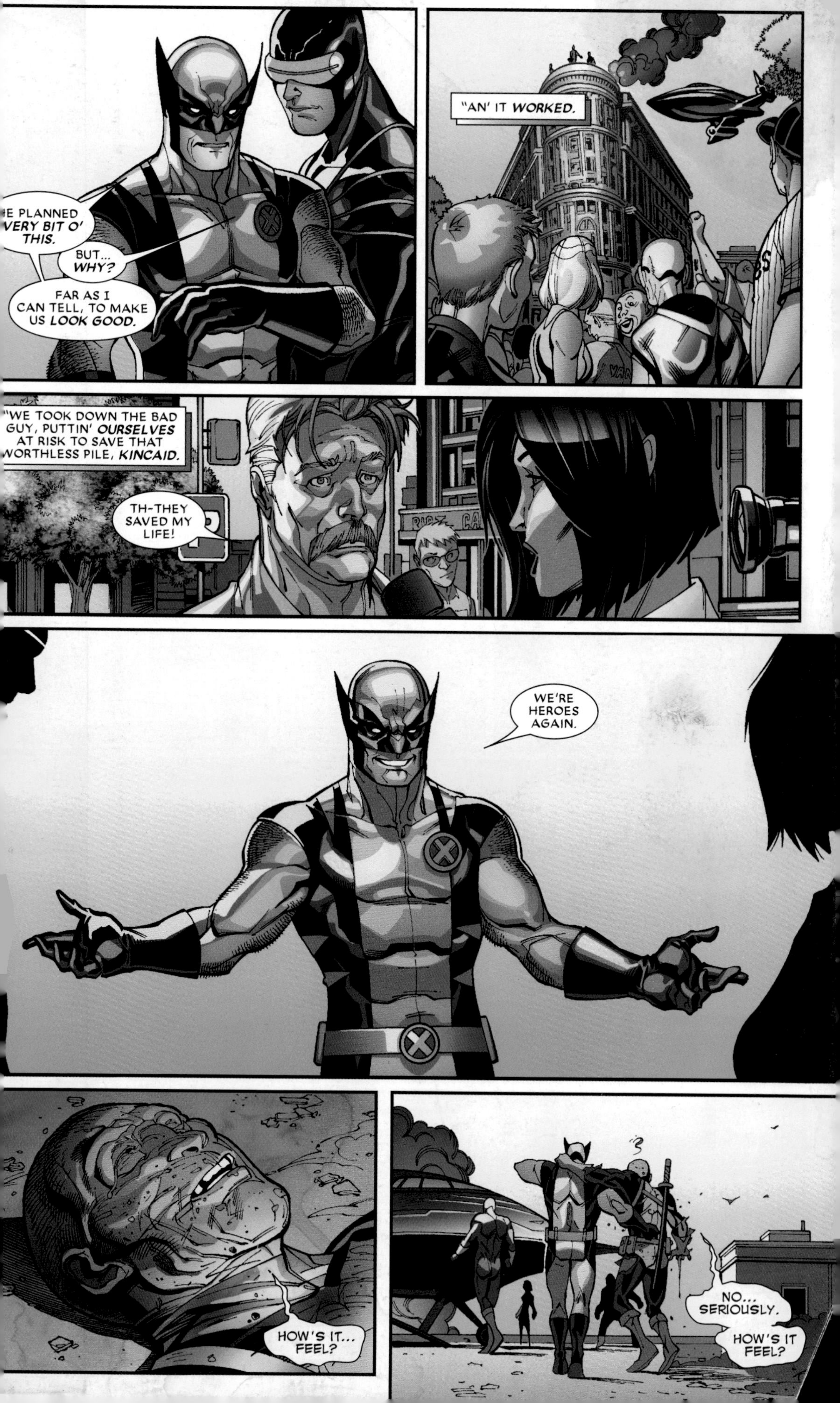

E PLANNED VERY BIT O' THIS.
BUT... WHY?
FAR AS I CAN TELL, TO MAKE US LOOK GOOD.
"AN' IT WORKED.
"WE TOOK DOWN THE BAD GUY, PUTTIN' OURSELVES AT RISK TO SAVE THAT WORTHLESS PILE, KINCAID.
TH-THEY SAVED MY LIFE!
WE'RE HEROES AGAIN.
HOW'S IT... FEEL?
NO... SERIOUSLY.
HOW'S IT FEEL?

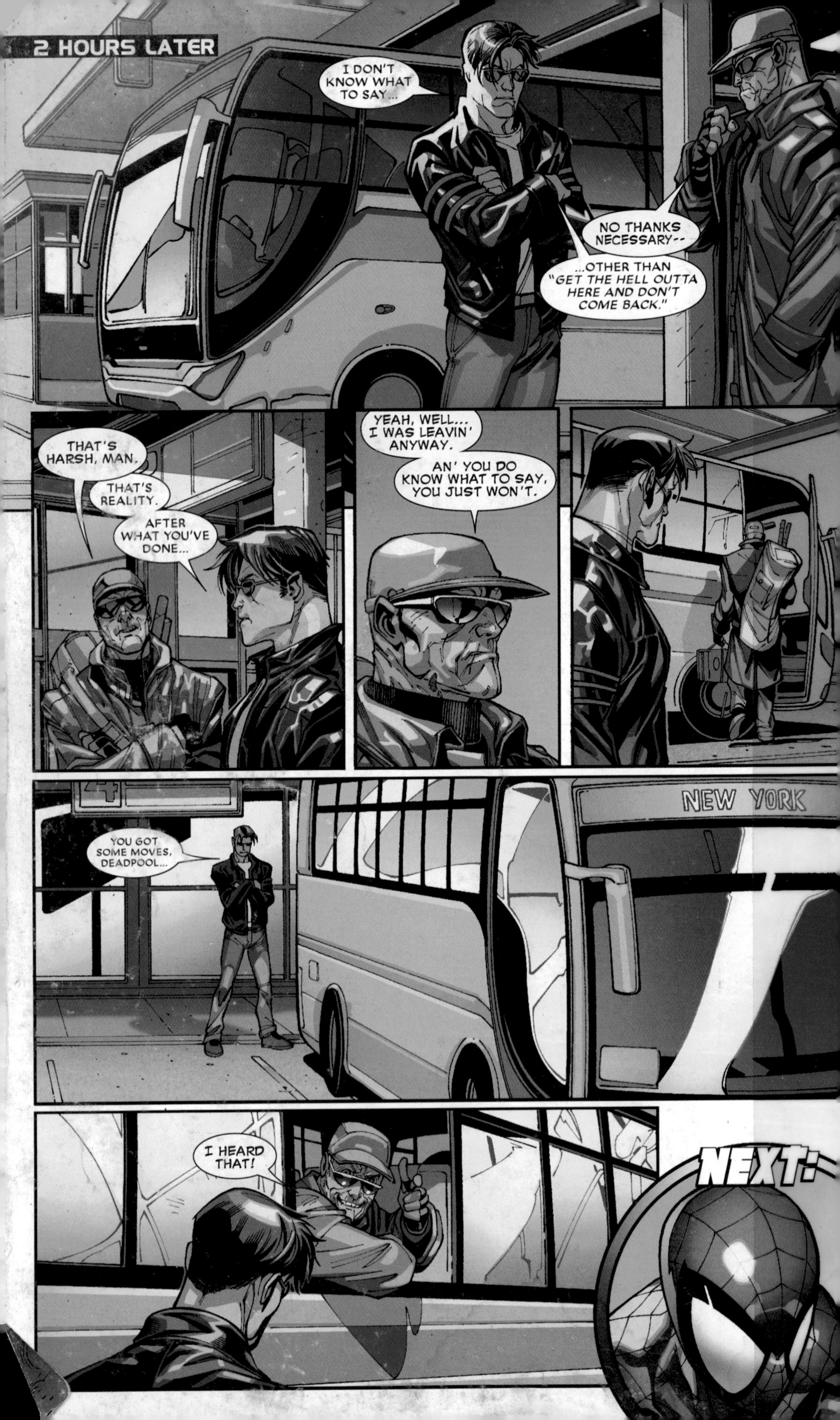
2 HOURS LATER
I DON'T KNOW WHAT TO SAY...
NO THANKS NECESSARY--
...OTHER THAN "GET THE HELL OUTTA HERE AND DON'T COME BACK."
THAT'S HARSH, MAN.
THAT'S REALITY.
AFTER WHAT YOU'VE DONE...
YEAH, WELL... I WAS LEAVIN' ANYWAY.
AN' YOU DO KNOW WHAT TO SAY, YOU JUST WON'T.
NEW YORK
YOU GOT SOME MOVES, DEADPOOL...
I HEARD THAT!
NEXT: